Safe and Secure:
Secure Your Home Network and
Protect Your Privacy Online

Arman Danesh, Felix Lau, and Ali Mehrassa

SAMS

A Division of Macmillan USA
201 West 103rd St., Indianapolis, Indiana, 46290 USA

Safe and Secure: Secure Your Home Network and Protect Your Privacy Online

Copyright © 2002 by Sams Publishing

International Standard Book Number: 0-672-32243-9

Library of Congress Catalog Card Number: 2001093491

Printed in the United States of America

First Printing: August 2001

04   03   02   01   4   3   2

Trademarks

Warning and Disclaimer

ASSOCIATE PUBLISHER
Jeff Koch

ACQUISITIONS EDITOR
William E. Brown

DEVELOPMENT EDITOR
Mark Renfrow

MANAGING EDITOR
Matt Purcell

PROJECT EDITOR
George E. Nedeff

PRODUCTION EDITOR
Rhonda Tinch-Mize
Seth Kerney

INDEXER
Kelly Castell

PROOFREADER
Rowena Rappaport

TECHNICAL EDITOR
Mark Hall

REVIEWER
Darragh Nagle

INTERIOR DESIGNER
Anne Jones

COVER DESIGNER
Aren Howell

PAGE LAYOUT
Susan Geiselman

Overview

Contents

About the Lead Author

Arman Danesh is the author of numerous books on computers, including *Special Edition Using Linux System Administration* from Que and *Mastering Linux* from Sybex. His professional experience includes almost three years as the senior network administrator at Landegg International University in Switzerland, where he had to maintain an educational network and ensure its security and integrity while being connected to the Internet. He currently maintains a network of mail and Web servers that are connected to the Internet using ADSL and need to be kept secure and manages Web sites for international organizations including The Baha'i World (www.bahai.org) and The Baha'i World News Service (www.bahaiworldnews.org). He is also a graduate student in computer science and his thesis research relates to security models for ad hoc networks.

About the Contributing Authors

Felix Lau is pursuing an advanced degree in computer science at Simon Fraser University. He graduated from the University of British Columbia in 1997 with a Bachelor of Computer Science degree, specializing in distributed systems and networking. His current research focuses in the area of groupware, collaborative technologies, and distributed computing. As an independent consultant, he has helped companies develop wireless ad hoc collaborative applications.

Ali Mehrassa is pursuing a bachelor of science degree in computer science at Simon Fraser University. His career in information technology began as a quality assurance analyst in the computer game industry.

About the Tech Editor

Mark Hall has been providing technical edits for more than 12 years now with more than 160 titles edited to date. Mark has coauthored three books and written many "How to" primers. Mark has a masters degree in Computer Science education, a Novell CNE since 1990, and more than 18 years experience as a private network consultant specializing in Network design and security.

About the Reviewer

Darragh Nagle studied computer science in high school, at the University of New Mexico, and at Arizona State University. His career in computer programming brought him into the field of Unix systems programming for Sun, Solbourne, and Cray systems. Darragh worked for Cray Research, and then for Cray Computer in Colorado Springs with the team that developed the Cray-3.

He went on to work for Northrop Grumman, where he participated with the CERT team as a manufacturer member, providing computer security vulnerability reports and security patches. Darragh went on to designing security applications, and currently works for a wireless networking company doing Unix internals and embedded device programming. He lives with his family in Florida, and composes music, flies airplanes, and enjoys nature and camping.

Dedication

To my kuchulu: May your life be safe and secure.
—Arman Danesh

To my parents, family, and Winnie for starting me on my journey
—Felix Lau

This book is dedicated to Sascha. Your support, strength, and love are an
inspiration to me each and every day.
—Ali Mehrassa

Acknowledgments

I need to start by thanking William Brown at Sams for taking a chance on this book in the face of skepticism. As well, thanks go to the entire staff at Sams Publishing; as always, a book like this is a team effort and without the contribution of editors, production staff, and numerous others in the Sams family, this book would still be an idea in our minds. My gratitude also goes out to the entire crew in the EDGE Lab at Simon Fraser University who tolerated the never-ending refrain of "we have to finish the book!"

As always, my wife, Tahirih, is owed my gratitude. She not only tolerated the long hours I had to commit to this project as she has always done when I take on a book project, but also she did this in the face of the stresses of pregnancy. Without her, none of my books would have been possible.

—Arman Danesh

This book was indeed a team effort. Being my first book, I would like to thank William Brown for his help and support during this learning process. I would also like to thank the entire staff at Sams Publishing for their efforts and time on the development, review, and production of the book. Acknowledgement goes out to Keith Shu, Kori Inkpen, and the entire EDGE Lab at Simon Fraser University for their support and understanding during the writing process. My interest in computers and technology in general is due in large part to my parents, family, and especially Ming Lau. Finally, I could not have undertaken this project without the help of my friends and coauthors, Arman Danesh and Ali Mehrassa.

—Felix Lau

I'd like to thank all of my friends and family for their kind words and for always reminding me that I can do anything. Special thanks go to my friends at Science Alive for their numerous pep talks, to Kelsey Hamer for sharing his knowledge with me, to my parents for always being there for me, and to Arman Danesh for always making me believe this was possible.

—Ali Mehrassa

Tell Us What You Think!

As the reader of this book, *you* are our most important critic and commentator. We value your opinion and want to know what we're doing right, what we could do better, what areas you'd like to see us publish in, and any other words of wisdom you're willing to pass our way.

As an Associate Publisher for Sams Publishing, I welcome your comments. You can fax, e-mail, or write me directly to let me know what you did or didn't like about this book—as well as what we can do to make our books stronger.

Please note that I cannot help you with technical problems related to the topic of this book, and that due to the high volume of mail I receive, I might not be able to reply to every message.

When you write, please be sure to include this book's title and author as well as your name and phone or fax number. I will carefully review your comments and share them with the author and editors who worked on the book.

Fax: 317-581-4770

E-mail: feedback@samspublishing.com

Mail: Jeff Koch
Associate Publisher
Sams Publishing
201 West 103rd Street
Indianapolis, IN 46290 USA

Introduction

The Internet is a daunting place. Every day the media is filled with stories about threats from the Internet. Large companies have their computer systems invaded by attackers, government Web sites are altered by pranksters, and people's credit card information is stolen.

This can only leave individual home Internet users concerned, asking themselves; "If Microsoft can't keep itself safe, how can I?"

This isn't unreasonable to ask yourself. Consider a few of the more recently publicized facts about computer security on the Internet:

- By some accounts, more than 4,000 denial-of-service attacks take place each week. These attacks attempt to bring Internet sites down by flooding them with false requests. But, many home computers of innocent Internet users are taken over by attackers to conduct these attacks. Can you be sure that your computer isn't being used to attack major Internet sites?

- A study released in March 2001 by the Computer Security Institute showed a marked increase in Internet intruders into corporate computer networks—up 25% from the previous year to 40% of companies. In addition, 94% of companies reported virus incidents, which is up 85% from the previous year.

- Computer worms, such as the famous Melissa and Anna Kournikova worms, run rampant on the Internet. The VBS Worm Generator, software that can be used to easily make worms like these famed worms which have shut down e-mail systems worldwide, has been downloaded from the Internet thousands of times: Almost anyone can build their own worms with this software.

- The CERT Coordination Center, a federally-funded research agency at Carnegie Mellon University that tracks security incidents on the Internet, reports a tenfold increase in the number of reported security breaches each year during the 1990s, jumping from about 250 in 1990 to more than 21,000 in 2000.

In addition to the security threats, home computer users face real privacy threats. Not only could you be unwittingly allowing companies and individuals on the Internet to track your movements and snoop on your private communications, but also those things you think you have the right to keep private might not be:

- Court cases have allowed companies to inspect employees' private home computers to look for evidence that the employees were involved in organizing illegal job action.

- Companies that provide employees free computers to work at home can configure those computers to monitor employee activity.

- If your computer and Internet connection are not properly configured, your name, e-mail address, and other personal data could be stolen from it.

It is only a matter of time before you will have your computer attacked, your privacy compromised, or your critical data destroyed, especially if you are one of the 50% of the U.S. population with Internet access. This means that you need to take steps to ensure your security in an online world.

Some have called the hysteria surrounding security scares on the Internet uncalled for. But, this hysteria has a basis in reality:

- There are more than 50,000 viruses, worms, and Trojan horses on the Internet.
- All software contains bugs and holes that can compromise the security of the computers it is running on.
- Home computers connected to the Internet are routinely probed and attacked.

There is a subculture on the Internet intent on attacking, and gaining access to, computer systems they are not authorized to use. These attackers, known as crackers, feed off a culture that glorifies and sanctifies those who successfully gain control of computers that should be hard to access.

> **NOTE**
>
> More commonly, the term *hacker* is used to refer to attackers; but technically hackers are not attackers.

This book is designed for home Internet users who have broadband or dial-up connections to the Internet and want to secure themselves. If you already use the Internet, this book is for you. It won't teach you how to connect to the Internet or access a Web site, but it will guide you through the nuances of computer security and help you choose the best tools for your home computer security needs.

This book will guide you through the following topics:

- The basics of how computer networks and the Internet work
- Tools for protecting your home computer and network
- Methods for protecting yourself from viruses, worms, and Trojan horses
- Ways to protect your privacy with anonymous Web and e-mail services and the prudent use of Cookies
- Advanced techniques for monitoring and maintaining your computer security

Chapter 1, "Threats from the Internet," will start you on this journey by outlining the types of threats you face when connected to the Internet from viruses to Trojan horses to unauthorized use of your computers.

The Basics

IN THIS PART

Threats From the Internet

IN THIS CHAPTER

In This Chapter

The Internet is a powerful tool, but it is also a dangerous world of viruses and malicious attackers intent on wreaking havoc with the computer systems that are part of it. As a user of the Internet, you should not assume you are immune from these dangers. Instead, assume you are at risk and take some basic steps to protect yourself in the online age. This chapter provides you with a basic overview of the dangers you face in using the Internet.

The Internet Security Hysteria

In the May 28, 2001, issue of *The New Yorker* magazine, technology writer Michael Specter wrote an article about his experience with the Anna Kournikova worm called "The Doomsday Click."

The Anna Kournikova virus is one of the many e-mail[nd]borne worms that have affected computers on the Internet in the late 1990s and the early 21st century. In his article, Specter highlighted the growing security threat faced by companies and individuals alike on the Internet. He points to the capability of teenagers and children to attack sophisticated government and business computer systems, and says it is only a matter of time before an attacker successfully attacks the personal computers of home users the world over.

Many in the Internet community argued that this article was little more than a hysterical reaction to a small Internet worm that attacked Specter's computer. But, this hysteria has a basis in reality:

- There are more than 50,000 viruses, worms and Trojan horses on the Internet.
- All software programs contain bugs and holes that can compromise the security of the computers it is running on.
- Home computers connected to the Internet are routinely probed and attacked.

This doesn't mean you are likely to find your hard drive is erased when you wake up tomorrow. But, as more users join the online revolution, especially using high-speed Internet connections such as cable Internet access or DSL that are connected to the Internet at all times, the need for caution is warranted. The Internet can be enjoyed in relative safety and comfort if you take a few basic steps to protect your computers.

This book will teach you about the threats and guide you through the options you have for protecting yourself, so you can make an informed decision about how to secure your computers.

Security Risks on the Internet

There is a subculture on the Internet intent on attacking and gaining access to computer systems they are not authorized to use. These attackers, known as crackers, feed off a culture that glorifies those who successfully gain control of computers that should be hard to access.

As the Internet has grown and home users such as yourself have joined the high-speed Internet revolution using cable Internet, there has been a noticeable increase in the number of security incidents occurring on the Internet. The CERT Coordination Center, a federally funded research agency at Carnegie Mellon University that tracks security incidents on the Internet, reports a tenfold increase in the number of reported security breaches each year during the 1990s, jumping from about 250 in 1990 to more than 21,000 in 2000.

If you have a computer connected to the Internet, especially with a high-speed cable or DSL connection, you need to think about the various ways that malicious individuals on the Internet can attack your computer and compromise your data. Several risks exist:

- Software vulnerabilities
- Designed vulnerabilities
- Network vulnerabilities

Software Vulnerabilities

The reality is that the running on personal computers and large corporate servers now is much more complex than the software that was running when the early form of the Internet emerged two decades ago. With increasing complexity comes an inevitable problem: more software bugs. Normally, software bugs create small inconsistencies or problems in the way an application operates. However, some bugs can do much more: They can become security holes that enable intent attackers to compromise computer systems running the software.

Examples of this are endless. There have been frequent reports of security vulnerabilities in common software, such as Microsoft Internet Explorer or Microsoft Outlook. Usually, software vendors are quick to release patches that fix the problem, but there is always a time between the discovery of the vulnerability and the fix being released when users are at risk.

Also, each fix can itself contain bugs, creating new security vulnerabilities that attackers eventually discover and take advantage of until yet another new fix is released.

The result of these bugs can range from mild (an attacker might be able to stop an application from running) to catastrophic (an attacker gains complete control of your computer or steals or destroys valuable data).

Imagine what would happen if a hole were discovered in Quicken that enabled attackers to use Quicken's online banking features to gain access to your bank accounts. The attacker could steal all the money in your account in a matter of seconds, and you would be unaware it had happened until you next used your bank account.

It is important to be aware of these vulnerabilities and keep track of the latest fixes for your software. Appendix B, "Resources," lists several Web sites you can refer to for the latest security information, including lists of known software bugs that create security vulnerabilities.

Designed Vulnerabilities

The only completely secure computer is one that is not connected to the Internet or a local area network, has no power connected to it and is stored in a sealed room with no windows, doors or points of access, and that is safe from any type of bomb or explosive. Of course, this computer is useless.

So, true security comes at the expense of utility and functionality. The goal is to find the right compromise between usefulness and security.

The very act of using a computer on the Internet means you are taking certain risks that are inherent in the nature of computers, operating systems and the Internet. For instance, if you want to share files between computers on your home network, you are knowingly allowing other computers to access the hard drive on your computer. Similarly, if you use e-mail software such as Outlook, you are allowing anyone on the Internet to send data to your computer; as the world has learned with e-mail worms such as Melissa, this type of data can, at times, be malicious.

Still, these are risks you knowingly take in order to take advantage of the benefits gained. The key to exposing yourself in this way is to take all possible steps to mitigate any security vulnerabilities you are creating for yourself.

Several chapters in this book guide you through steps you can take to minimize the risk of using the Internet. For instance, Chapter 5, "Securing a Standalone System," and Chapter 7, "Using Personal Firewall Software," offer guidance on various software-based techniques that can help you take advantage of many network services without unnecessary risk. Chapter 12, "Using a Broadband Router," also outlines powerful hardware solutions that can increase your level of protection.

Network Vulnerabilities

Even if you have made your computers as secure as possible, the network, and your connection to it, can be susceptible to attack. A *denial-of-service attack* involves an attacker attempting to deny Internet service to you. A denial-of-service attack's intent is to

- Vandalize your computer or network. The result is loss of service or data.
- Deny service to your network. This results in people attempting to gain access to your network and failing.
- Inundate your computer or network with packets, resulting in your computer or network crashing.

A denial-of-service attack does not usually involve breaking into a computer and gaining access to files. It is mainly for the attacker to deny service to a user or organization.

Although there is not much you can do to stop someone from attacking your Internet connection with a denial-of-service attack, you need to be aware of another aspect of denial-of-service attacks. Attackers waging this type of campaign will first compromise numerous computers belonging to third parties and then launch a denial-of-service attack from those third party systems against the real target. This not only hides the source of the denial-of-service attacks, but also makes it harder for the victim to stop the attack because it seems to originate from numerous third party computers.

This means that you could unwittingly become a party to a denial-of-service attack if the attacker compromises your computer and uses it as part of the attack. Some reports claim that large numbers of home cable and DSL Internet users have been compromised already, and that their systems are sitting dormant, waiting to be used by attackers for future denial-of-service attacks.

For this reason, it is important that you follow the guidance outlined in Chapters 5, 7, and 12 to keep your system safe when connected to the Internet. Following the guidance in these chapters, as well as in Chapter 9, "Vaccinating Your Computer Against Viruses," will ensure that you have the best virus protection you can get. Viruses and Trojan horses can be used to plant the necessary software on your computer to enable an attacker to use it for denial-of-service attacks. It is theoretically possible that your computer has already been compromised in this way, and might even have been used in denial-of-service attacks without your knowledge.

You should also follow the guidance in Chapter 20, "Testing Your Security by Attacking Yourself," to routinely check that your security profile is the way you intend it and to maintain your level of protection as outlined in Chapter 23, "Maintaining Your Protection."

Viruses and Your Computer's Health

A computer virus is simply a malicious program designed to attach itself to other programs and replicate. There are three main types of malicious programs: viruses, worms, and Trojan horses.

A *virus* is any program that replicates itself repeatedly and propagates itself across multiple computers. They can be benign (just replicating for the sake of replicating) or malignant (destroying or stealing data).

Worms are specific types of viruses that replicate themselves through services running on networks such as the Internet. Most modern worms leverage weakness in e-mail software to propagate themselves. Famous worms include the Melissa virus, which attacked thousands of Microsoft Outlook users and brought down e-mail systems at many large companies and organizations.

Generally, modern worms do not actually attack computers, but rather replicate so quickly that they overload e-mail servers and saturate Internet connections to the point of making whole networks or individual computers unusable.

Named after the original Trojan horse from Greek Mythology, A *Trojan horse* "pretends" to be something else (possibly a game or other executable program) and lures you into running it, so that it can perform some malicious act on your machine. Trojan horse programs do not spread from one computer to another, unlike worms and viruses. However, a Trojan horse program is dangerous nonetheless. When activated, this type of malicious program can do a number of destructive deeds—depending on its purpose—such as deleting files from your computer, or creating an entry point to your computer from which others can gain access to your machine, much like a back door into your computer.

The best protection against viruses involves two main steps:

1. Take active and aggressive steps to inoculate your computer against viruses as outlined in Chapter 9.
2. Be cautious: If you don't know the source of an e-mail, don't read it; if you don't know the source of a piece of software or aren't sure if you can trust the source, don't run it. Even Word files can contain viruses; if you don't know where a Microsoft Word file came from, think twice before opening it as well.

Keeping Private in a Wired World

In addition to security and virus risks online, many users are concerned about their privacy when using the Internet. There are several pieces of information that you give away unknowingly when you are connected to the Internet, whether you are browsing Web sites or sending and receiving e-mails. As such, anyone can track you using the following pieces of information:

- Cookies, stored on your machine or in an open browser such as Internet Explorer 5.5 (MSIE) or Netscape 6. With this information, Web sites can maintain records of your behavior and usage of their site.
- IP address of your machine, assigned to you by your Internet Service Provider (ISP). With this information, it is often possible to uniquely identify you. This means Web sites can keep personal records of exactly what you have done on their sites.

- E-mail address, contained in messages you send and receive over the Internet. Your e-mail address can be used to identify you uniquely, and also to send you unsolicited promotional e-mails.

For some, this lack of privacy when online is just a matter of personal concern. For others, it can be critical if they engage in confidential or sensitive work while using the Internet. Chapter 16, "Human Issues in Security," Chapter 17, "Cookies," and Chapter 18, "Anonymous Surfing," all deal with privacy on the Internet.

Summary

In this chapter, you learned about why you are at risk on the Internet and why, even as a lone home user, it is important to be prudent and cautious when using the Internet.

The next chapter will set the stage for the rest of the book by outlining the components of a sound security strategy. This will help you focus your reading and learning in the rest of the book and serve as a checklist for developing your own comprehensive security strategy.

Online Security Strategies

IN THIS CHAPTER

In This Chapter

The last chapter gave you an overview of the types of threats you face by using the Internet, especially with a broadband Internet connection. This chapter takes the next step by providing you with a broad outline of the components of a sound security plan.

Your Security Strategy

A sound security strategy has several components, including

- Securing Your Computer or Network
- Inoculating Your Computer Against Viruses
- Maintaining Physical Security
- Preparing for Disaster
- Ongoing Monitoring and Maintenance

Securing Your Computer or Network

Securing your computer or network involves ensuring that you are only exposing your computers to the degree of risk you want to.

The initial step is to look at the software running on your computer or each computer on your network and verify that it does not create unwanted security vulnerabilities; you want to be sure that you are not running unnecessary software that can create a potential security risk now or in the future. Chapter 5, "Securing a Standalone System," addresses these concerns by discussing security as it relates to each individual machine connected to the Internet.

Next, you need to take steps to secure your Internet connection. This enables you to prevent unwanted connections from the Internet from reaching your computer, and unwanted connections from your computer from reaching the Internet. Typically, this type of filtering and connection blocking is done with *firewalls*. The concept of a firewall is discussed in more detail in Chapter 10, "Overview of Firewalls." A firewall acts as a gateway to your private computer or network, controlling access to it, and what can travel in and out of it. Its main goal is to protect your network from attacks and intruders.

For home users, there are two main types of firewalls:

- Personal firewall software: Personal firewall software runs on each individual computer you have connected to the Internet and acts as a filter, blocking connections to and from that computer. This is the least expensive and most common form of firewall for home use. Chapter 7, "Using Personal Firewall Software," teaches you to select, install, and configure personal firewall software on your computers.

- Broadband routers: Also known as home Internet gateways, broadband routers are physical devices that sit between your Internet connection and your home computers. They have the job of watching all traffic between your computers and the Internet, and deciding what traffic to allow. These are slightly more expensive than personal firewall software, but are generally considered more robust, as they enable you to implement stronger, more secure firewall protection for your Internet connection. Chapter 12, "Using a Broadband Router," helps you select, install, and configure a broadband router for your home network.

Another approach to securing a home Internet connection that is less common than personal firewall software and broadband routers is to implement a proxy server. Like broadband gateways, proxy servers sit between your computers and your Internet connection. But, they do not allow any connections from the Internet to access your computers and vice versa. Instead, they make all connections to the Internet on behalf of your computers. Theoretically, a proxy server can create a much more secure network than either of the firewall solutions outlined previously, if you only need to access the Internet and don't need to allow incoming access to your computers from the Internet. However, they can be harder to configure, and some of your Internet software might not work properly if you use a proxy server. Proxy servers are discussed in Chapter 11, "Implementing a Proxy Server."

Inoculating Your Computer Against Viruses

It is essential to protect your computer against viruses, worms and Trojan horses. This is especially true if you plan to use e-mail, access the World Wide Web, or download software from the Internet. To do this, you need to choose a modern, effective antivirus package as outlined in Chapter 9, "Vaccinating Your Computer Against Viruses."

Maintaining Physical Security

Even if you have the best antivirus software, locked down all your computers, and implemented and configured your firewall, you are still at risk on the Internet. There are several nontechnical steps you can take to increase your level of security that are outlined in Chapter 16, "Human Issues in Security." These include the following:

- Using strong passwords that are hard to guess whenever you have to create an account with a password.

- Being aware of whether you are using a secure or unsecure Web server.

- Being cautious about what information you submit in forms on Web sites and to which Web sites you submit it.

- Taking steps to prevent theft of your credit card information, including using one-time credit card number systems such as those offered by American Express and Discover.

In addition, there are other steps you can take to ensure your privacy on the Internet, including the following:

- Controlling when and whether a Web site can create a cookie on your computer. Cookies are discussed in Chapter 17, "Cookies."

- Using anonymous Web surfing and e-mail services as discussed in Chapter 18, "Anonymous Surfing."

- Encrypting e-mails to hide them from prying eyes as described in Chapter 19, "Encryption."

Preparing for Disaster

Just because you have taken steps to secure your system and prevent viruses doesn't mean something won't go wrong. You can still be attacked successfully, or a new virus can still infect your computer. For this reason, you need to take steps in advance so that you can recover from a disaster. These steps include

- Keeping regular backups of your computer. If your data is destroyed, or you need to reinstall all your software because your system becomes unusable, you will want a backup of all your critical data. Backup strategies are discussed in Chapter 24, "Backup Strategies."

- Keep a clean boot disk for your system so that you can boot up your computer if the system becomes unbootable or your system is infected by a boot-sector virus.

- If your antivirus software offers a boot floppy disk for cleaning infected systems, prepare one and keep it on hand.

Chapter 22, "Recovering from a Disaster," discusses techniques for recovering when disaster hits.

Ongoing Monitoring and Maintenance

Securing your computer is not a one-time task. After you have devised and implemented your security plan, you need to monitor and maintain your security on an ongoing basis; otherwise your security will weaken with time as software changes, bugs are discovered, and new viruses emerge.

There are several steps to this ongoing maintenance:

- Watch for strange behaviors from your computer. This includes software running on your computer that you don't think should be running.

- If possible, monitor and use logs on your computer and firewall to track attempts or successful security breaches. Logs are discussed in Chapter 21, "Managing Your Logs."

- Test your security on a regular basis by attacking your computer from the Internet as outlined in Chapter 20, "Testing Your Security by Attacking Yourself."

- Keep track of regular security updates for your software. Appendix B, "Resources," lists sites you can use to obtain the latest information about security updates.

- Keep your virus software up-to-date, as outlined in Chapter 9, "Vaccinating Your Computer Against Viruses."

Summary

This chapter provided an overview of the components of a sound security strategy, ranging from techniques for securing your Internet connection, to ongoing maintenance and monitoring strategies. This sets the stage for the rest of the book, which provides detailed guidance about building and implementing your security plan.

The next chapter provides you with basic background knowledge about how the Internet really works. This knowledge will help you quickly grasp the security concepts discussed in the rest of the book. If you understand how the network works and the details of how home networks are built, you can jump forward to Part II, "Protecting a Home PC."

2

ONLINE SECURITY STRATEGIES

How the Internet Works

IN THIS CHAPTER

In This Chapter

To understand Internet security, it is necessary to understand how the Internet works and the way your computer or small network relates to the Internet. This chapter provides a basic overview of networking as it relates to the Internet and your Internet connection.

PCs, LANS, and the Internet

Computer networks are any environments in which more than one computer are connected so that they can communicate. You can find numerous examples of networking that we don't normally think of as networking, including the following:

- Two computers communicating through their infrared ports
- Two computers communicating through their parallel ports using a parallel cable
- A computer connected to a *local area network*, or LAN, using Ethernet (Ethernet is a type of network infrastructure, which is discussed in Chapter 4, "Network Infrastructure.")
- A computer connected to the Internet, or even just another network, through a dial-up connection using a modem

All these are examples of small networks or single isolated PCs connected to larger networks. However, there is a concept, which extends beyond the isolated PC or the LAN: the *wide area network*, or WAN.

NOTE

A *local area network*, or LAN, refers to any closed network of computers communicating with each other. These networks cover geographically small areas such as a room, a floor of a building, an entire building, or a self-contained campus. LANs generally do not span multiple large geographic areas such as buildings scattered throughout a city or between multiple cities. The most common implementation of a LAN is an Ethernet network. Ethernet networks are often used in home and small office networks. Types of network infrastructures and implementation are discussed in Chapter 4.

> **NOTE**
>
> A wide area network, or WAN, refers to two or more LANs that are geographically separated and connected together by some type of long distance connection. For instance, a multi-national company might have a LAN in each of its offices around the world, but will connect these LANs together in a WAN. Typically, LANs use high-speed network connection technologies, but the WANs use relatively slower connections because the cost of LAN-speed connections at long distances would be prohibitive.

The idea of a WAN is important because the Internet is the ultimate WAN. The Internet is a large connection of a lot of smaller networks. Some of these smaller networks are corporate, organizational, or even personal LANs, whereas others are private WANs in their own right. The Internet is the ultimate, globe-spanning WAN.

Figure 3.1 illustrates how the Internet is an amalgamation of numerous networks and computers in a large WAN. In this diagram you can see WANs, which themselves are collections of LANs, connected to the Internet network as well as LANs and individual PCs directly connected to the Internet network.

> **NOTE**
>
> It is important to realize that not all connections to the Internet are permanent. It is not uncommon for systems to temporarily connect to the Internet and then disconnect for extended periods of time. The perfect example of this is a dial-up Internet connection. When you dial into the Internet with a modem, your PC creates a new connection to the Internet (imagine your PC being added to the diagram in Figure 3.1). After you disconnect from your Internet service provider (ISP), your PC disappears from the Internet network (imagine your PC vanishing from the diagram).

Of course, for the Internet to work as a large network of networks and computers, there must be a common language of communication among all component networks and computers. This is achieved through TCP/IP (Transmission Control Protocol/Internet Protocol): the protocol used by the Internet. TCP/IP is described in the next section.

3

HOW THE INTERNET WORKS

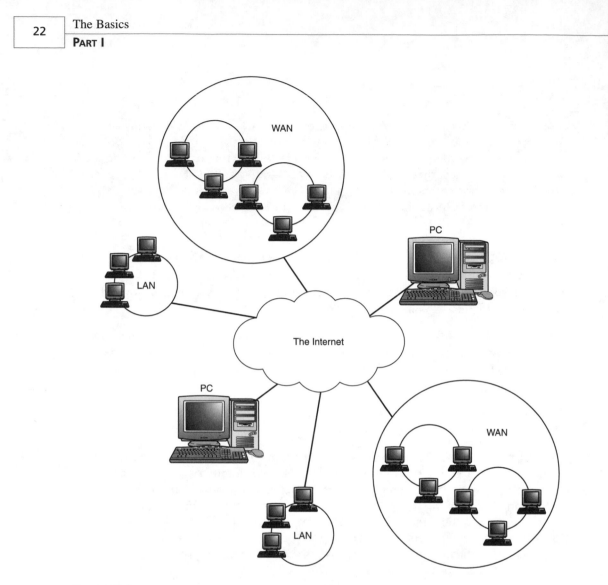

FIGURE 3.1

The Internet is the ultimate WAN connecting numerous WANs, LANs, and PCs.

TCP/IP: The Language of the Internet

TCP/IP is the *protocol* used by all systems connected to the Internet to communicate with other systems on the Internet. It is the basis of all communication on the Internet; without it the Internet would not exist.

NOTE

A *protocol* is a language used to communicate between computers for a particular purpose. Protocols define clear parameters and vocabulary through which communication can occur. Protocols operate at several levels, including protocols that allow networking to occur and protocols that allow services to be performed on the network. Each protocol has a specific purpose. In this chapter we are looking at TCP/IP, which is the basic protocol of the Internet.

NOTE

TCP stands for Transmission Control Protocol and IP stands for Internet Protocol. So, *TCP/IP* is really a pair of protocols working together for the purpose of enabling network communication, but it's easiest to think of TCP/IP as a single protocol.

TCP/IP is one of many networking protocols and is the standard network protocol in Unix, the operating system that was used on most of the original computers on the Internet. TCP/IP is probably the most pervasive networking protocol in the world.

TCP/IP is really two protocols: TCP is a protocol for breaking messages into small parts for transmission on the network, whereas IP handles the job of actually transmitting these message parts. These message parts are known as *packets*. Think of the analogy of letters and the postal service. TCP creates packets that are placed into envelopes. IP then acts as the postal service to deliver the envelopes to their destinations.

NOTE

A *packet* refers to the packages of information transmitted on a TCP/IP network such as the Internet. Typically, large amounts of data are broken down into numerous small packets, and each packet is sent independently to the destination on the network. After the destination computer has received all the packets it requires, it can reassemble a complete message.

TCP/IP can be complicated, but its basics are very simple. The basic concepts that are necessary to understand are

- IP addresses
- Network masks

3

HOW THE INTERNET WORKS

- Broadcast addresses
- Name servers
- Services and ports

IP Addresses

In order for computers on TCP/IP networks such as the Internet to be able to communicate, each unique computer, or *host*, on the network must have a unique address known as an *IP address*. It is important that these addresses are unique; otherwise communication would be impossible. If two machines shared an address, how would it be possible to decide where to send a packet?

TIP

There are techniques for multiple computers on a LAN connected to the Internet to share a single IP address. These technologies include NAT (Network Address Translation), which is used as the basis of many security techniques. NAT is discussed in Chapter 10, "Overview of Firewalls."

IP addresses are entirely numeric and take the form: four numbers separated by dots. Each number can range from 0 to 255; in computer terms this is known as a 1-byte, or 8-bit, integer number. For instance, all the following are valid IP addresses:

- 216.23.79.114
- 194.148.43.194
- 10.10.10.10

NOTE

Although each number in an IP address is 1-byte (which means that 0 and 255 are possible numbers), IP addresses cannot contain a 0 or 255. 0 and 255 are used for special purposes. For instance, 0 is used in network addresses and 255 is used in broadcast addresses. Network and broadcast addresses are discussed later in the section, "Broadcast and Network Addresses."

But, the following are not valid addresses:

- 216.232.79.314 (314 is greater than 255)
- 194.256.43.194 (256 is greater than 255)

- 10.10.10.10.10 (IP addresses consist of exactly four 1-byte numbers; this address has five numbers)

Given this structure of IP addresses, the total possible numbers of addresses is 256 * 256 * 256 * 256 or 4,294,967,296 possible addresses.

> **NOTE**
>
> 4,294,967,296 sounds like a lot of addresses, but the rapid growth of the Internet has put IP addresses at a premium for numerous technical reasons including the way in which addresses are assigned and how they are grouped. Work is underway to upgrade TCP/IP to use 4-byte integers instead of 1-byte integers, which increases the number of available addresses to 340,282,366,920,938,463,463,374,607,431,768,211,456. This change will alleviate the problem of a quickly shrinking pool of available IP addresses.

Network Classes

The more than four billion IP addresses in the current version of TCP/IP are not assigned at random to hosts on the Internet. Instead, there is some structure to the way that they are deployed. The addresses are grouped into three network classes, and addresses are assigned to organizations such as corporations or Internet providers in network class groups. The three network classes are

- Class A networks: Class A networks contain 16,777,214 addresses. In these networks, the first number of the IP addresses identifies the network and the remaining numbers indicate specific machines on a network. For instance, in a Class A network, you might have an address such as 134.X.X.X. 134 identifies the network.

- Class B networks: Class B networks contain 65,534 addresses. In these networks, the first two numbers of the IP addresses identify the network and the remaining numbers indicate specific machines on a network. For instance, in a Class B network, you might have an address such as 134.38.X.X. 134.38 identifies the network.

- Class C networks: Class C networks contain 254 addresses. In these networks, the first three numbers of the IP addresses identify the network and the last number indicates specific machines on a network. For instance, in a Class C network, you might have an address such as 134.38.5.X. 134.38.5 that identifies the network.

Network Masks

You might be wondering how it is possible to know if a specific host's IP address belongs to a
class A, B, or C network. This is done using the *network mask*, also known as a netmask. The
network mask looks like an IP address: four one-byte numbers separated by dots. But, its purpose is different.

Combined with an IP address, the netmask tells you which part of the IP address identifies the
network and which part identifies specific machines on the network. This allows you to identify IP addresses belonging to class A, B, and C networks.

TIP

The discussion of network masks in this section relies on a basic understanding of
binary numbers and binary arithmetic. It is possible to use TCP/IP and implement your
security settings without understanding all this math. However, if you want to learn
the basics of binary math, a useful introduction to binary numbers is on the World
Wide Web at http://www.cs.uregina.ca/~rbm/cs100/notes/binary/binary.html.

If you think of a network mask as four eight-digit binary numbers, you have a number with 32
binary digits. The network mask consists of some number of 1 digits followed by the remainder as 0 digits (remember, 1 and 0 are the only valid binary digits).

Therefore, a network mask might be 11111111.11111111.00000000.00000000 or
11111111.11110000.00000000.00000000 but not 11110000.00000000.00000000.00001111.
If you look at the IP address as binary numbers, for whichever digit is 1 in the netmask, the
corresponding binary digit in the IP address identifies the network whereas for whichever digit
is 0 in the netmask, the corresponding binary digit in the IP address identifies a specific
machine on the network.

Let's look at an example: We have an IP address 194.148.3.162 and a network mask of
255.255.255.0. In binary form, these are

```
11000010.10010100.00000011.10100010 (IP address)
11111111.11111111.11111111.00000000 (netmask)
```

Then, applying the rule described previously, we know that the following part of the address identifies the network:

```
11000010.10010100.00000011.--------
```

This is the first three numbers of the IP address, so we now know that this is an address on the class C network identified by the three numbers 194.148.3 and the last digit, 162, identifies a specific machine on this network.

Things do get a little more complicated. For instance, it is possible to subdivide one of the network classes; for instance, we can split a class C network into two even subnetworks by adding binary one digits to the start of the last number of the netmask: 11111111.1111111.11111111.11110000 (which is a netmask of 255.255.255.240).

TIP

This might sound complicated, but generally you will not need to figure out the appropriate network mask for your computer. Your network administrator or Internet provider will tell you what network mask to use when configuring your PC. However, some advanced security needs require that you understand how IP addresses work with network masks, so it is useful to have at least a basic understanding of the dynamics of netmasks.

Broadcast and Network Addresses

You might have noticed a discrepancy earlier in the section "Network Classes" where the number of IP addresses available in each class was less than what they logically should have been.

For instance, in a class C network, the last number of the address uniquely identifies computers on the network. Because each one-byte number in an IP address theoretically can take 256 possible values (from 0 to 255), it would seem reasonable to assume that 256 host addresses are possible. But, earlier we learned that only 254 addresses were available on a class C network.

This is because there are two special addresses on any network that cannot be assigned to any hosts on the network:

- The *network address* identifies the network and is created by assigning binary 0 digits to all digits identifying hosts on the network. In a class C network, this means that the last number of the address is 0. So, 194.148.3.0 is a network address.

- Each network has a special address that can be used to send a packet to all hosts on the network. This is called the *broadcast address* and is created by assigning binary 1 digits to all digits identifying hosts on the network. In a class C network, this means that the last number of the IP address is 255. So, 194.148.3.255 is an example of a broadcast address.

These two special addresses cannot be assigned to hosts on the network that limits the number of available host IP addresses on a class C network to 254. (Similarly, class A and C networks have two addresses that cannot be assigned to any hosts on the network.)

Name Servers

Throughout this discussion, you will have noticed that all hosts on the Internet are identified by numeric IP addresses. This is how TCP/IP, the protocol driving all Internet traffic, identifies hosts on the network.

However, when you use the Internet you identify hosts (such as Web servers) with descriptive names such as www.bahai.org or www.juxta.com. This means that translation has to occur: When you attempt to contact a host by name, your computer must translate that name into an IP address in order to facilitate the communication.

This translation is handled by the *domain name system (DNS)*. DNS is a network of servers whose job is to translate a hostname such as www.bahai.org into an IP address such as 216.232.79.114. The implementation of DNS servers is not part of the subject matter of this book, but it is important to know the role DNS plays in making TCP/IP work in a user-friendly manner.

TIP

Normally, homes and small offices won't run their own DNS servers. Their IPs provide DNS servers that people can tell their PCs to use to translate hostnames into addresses.

NOTE

The process of translating hostnames to IP addresses is known as *resolving* a hostname.

Services and Ports

Up to this point, you have learned how TCP/IP allows information to travel on the Internet and how individual hosts on the Internet are identified.

The Internet has value because of the services that run on top of the TCP/IP network, however. Examples of these Internet services include the World Wide Web, FTP, Telnet, and E-mail. To enable these services, a server runs a special program called a *daemon* (or server) whose job is to answer requests for a specific type of service. If a host is acting as a Web and E-mail server, it runs a Web daemon and an E-mail daemon.

This poses a problem: When a connection comes from another host, which daemon answers the request? This is addressed through the use of ports. *Ports* are numeric identifiers, and each connection between two machines on the Internet has a port associated with it. The port is used by the daemons to decide which daemon answers the request. All major Internet services have standard ports associated with them such as port 21 for FTP, port 23 for Telnet, port 25 for E-mail, and port 80 for the World Wide Web.

As you will learn in Chapter 10, "Overview of Firewalls," these ports are essential to securing your network. On a port-by-port basis, you can control exactly which services on your network you want to make accessible to the Internet and which you want to make off-limits.

Order in the Chaos: Routing

So far, you have learned how TCP/IP assigns addresses to the host and groups hosts into networks. However, a mechanism is needed so that packets of information can travel from their source host to their destination without getting lost in the Internet.

This is achieved through routing. Routing allows clear routes to be identified for packets to travel on the Internet. Let's consider a simple example: A small LAN is connected to the Internet directly. This scenario resembles the one illustrated in Figure 3.2.

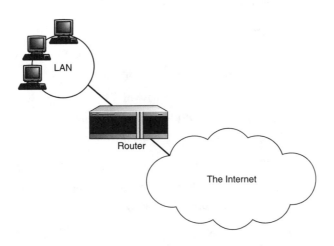

FIGURE 3.2
A LAN connected to the Internet.

Here, the key to everything is the router. The job of the router is to decide how to direct packets. If the router receives a packet for the LAN, it directs it to the LAN. If it receives a packet not addressed for the LAN, it directs it out to the Internet.

Hosts on the LAN are configured with the IP address of the router as their *default gateway*. When a host wants to direct a packet to another host on the LAN, it sends it directly to that host. But, when it wants to send a packet to any other host, it simply sends it to the gateway, and the gateway is responsible for passing the packet on to the destination.

NOTE

A *gateway* is a router connected to at least two networks that plays the role of gatekeeper and traffic director for packets traveling between the two networks.

This description simplifies the reality of how traffic moves on the Internet. In reality, the router in Figure 3.2 is not just connected to the Internet. It is connected to another router at the other end. For instance, if the LAN is connected to the Internet through an Internet service provider, the scenario resembles the one illustrated in Figure 3.3.

As you can see, this extends the picture somewhat from Figure 3.2. Now, the LAN connects to the ISP's network, which contains two routers: Router 1 and Router 2. Router 1 connects to the LAN whereas Router 2 connects the ISP's network to the rest of the Internet.

The two routers work as follows:

- If Router 1 receives a packet for the LAN, it sends it to the LAN's router.
- If Router 1 receives a packet for the ISP's network, it sends it to the destination host.
- If Router 1 receives a packet for any other network, it sends it to Router 2.
- If Router 2 receives a packet for the ISP's network, it sends it to the destination host.
- If Router 2 receives a packet for the LAN, it sends it to Router 1.
- If Router 2 receives a packet for any other network, it sends it to the Internet.

Hosts on the LAN are then configured with two gateways: a gateway for the LAN (Router 1) and a default gateway for all other networks (Router 2).

Ultimately, this design allows packets to find their destination without a host (or a router) having to know explicitly where the destination is located on the network.

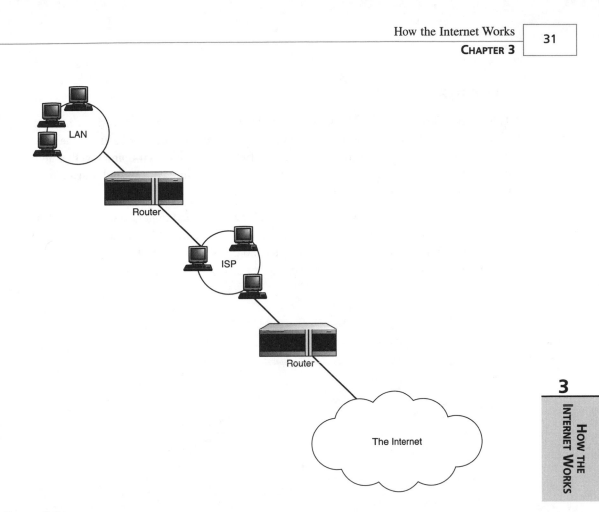

FIGURE 3.3

A LAN connected to the Internet through an ISP.

NOTE

These basic routing concepts are important to understand because routing is a key component of any sound security plan. Chapter 10 discusses how routing fits into the broader security picture.

Summary

This chapter provides you with the basic knowledge of how the Internet works, which you will need to effectively secure yourself on the Internet. TCP/IP provides the basis for the Internet; it offers an addressing scheme (IP Addresses), it offers a scheme for grouping together addresses in blocks (network classes), and it allows data to be broken into packets and transported to their destination anywhere on the Internet using routing.

The next chapter takes the discussion of networking to the next logical step. You will learn about the hardware and infrastructure used to build LANs and WANs, which speak TCP/IP. This will include different network cabling technologies, wireless technology, and various Internet access services that are available.

Network Infrastructure

IN THIS CHAPTER

In This Chapter

This chapter builds on the understanding of networking concepts you gained in the last chapter and discusses some of the options you have for physically building your network in your home.

The network protocols, services and routing discussed in the last chapter need a physical network on which to operate. This infrastructure can be implemented in three main ways for home and small office users:

- Twisted-pair Ethernet
- Phone-line networking
- Wireless networking

In this chapter you will also learn about the various options for broad-band connections to the Internet:

- DSL
- Cable Internet (Modems? Not necessary)
- Wireless and Satellite

Twisted-Pair Ethernet

The most common type of network infrastructure used today is *Ethernet* using twisted-pair cables. These twisted-pair cables are similar to the cables used to connect your telephone to the telephone jack, except that typically your phone cables have six thin colored copper wires running through them, whereas the twisted-pair cables used for Ethernet have eight copper wires running through them. Twisted-pair cables use modular connectors much like those for your telephone. The twisted-pair cable used for Ethernet is similar to what many people have for ISDN telephone connections.

> **Note**
>
> The six-wire twisted-pair cable for telephones uses connectors known as RJ-11; by contrast, Ethernet and ISDN use connectors known as RJ-45. The connectors are similar, but the size is different as illustrated in Figure 4.1.

Figure 4.1 illustrates a typical twisted-pair cable with a modular connector.

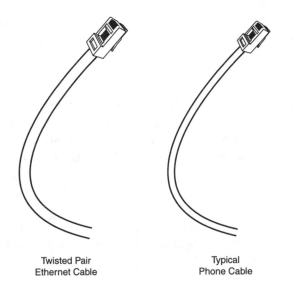

Twisted Pair
Ethernet Cable

Typical
Phone Cable

FIGURE 4.1

A twisted-pair Ethernet cable looks very similar to a typical phone cable except that the cable is thicker and the connector is wider.

> **NOTE**
>
> *Ethernet* is a type of local area network architecture that is actually independent of the physical cabling it runs on. Ethernet implementations run on coaxial cable, twisted-pair cable, and fiber optic cable as well as on wireless connections. The key to Ethernet is how it breaks apart data to send it on the network. These technical details are beyond the scope of this book or any discussion of home Internet security.

4

NETWORK INFRASTRUCTURE

Twisted-pair cable gets its name because the eight wires are paired by colors and then twisted together in pairs inside the cable. The way these wires ultimately connect to the pins in the connector you plug into your computer is the main feature that differentiates twisted-pair cables for Ethernet from those for telephones or ISDN connections: The mapping of the different colored wires in the cable to the pins in the modular connectors varies.

Hardware Requirements

To implement twisted-pair Ethernet in your home requires at least the following basic hardware:

- A twisted-pair Ethernet card for each computer you plan to connect to the network
- An Ethernet hub

- A twisted-pair Ethernet cable for each computer you plan to connect to the network as well as for your broadband Internet connection, if you have one

Network Cards

Network cards come in many varieties, including cards for the ISA bus in older Pentium and 486-based computers, PCI cards for use in more modern Pentium II, III, and IV systems, as well as PCMCIA Card models for use in notebook computers. These cards are available in two speeds, 10 Mb/s and 100 Mb/s, as discussed in the section, "How Fast is Too Fast?" later in this chapter. 100 Mb/s Ethernet is sometimes called Fast Ethernet.

NOTE

Most modern Ethernet cards are a combination of 10 Mb/s and 100 Mb/s cards. They detect the speed of the network they are connected to automatically and cost little more than basic 10 Mb/s Ethernet cards.

NOTE

Mb/s refers to the amount of data that can be transferred on the Ethernet connection in a second; it stands for Megabits per second—that is, 1024 binary digits of information. A Megabit is one-eighth of a Megabyte. It is important to realize that the figures 10 Mb/s and 100 Mb/s are idealistic performance figures. They indicate the amount of raw data that can be transmitted on an uncluttered network in ideal circumstances. In real-world situations, this speed is lower because of congested networks as well as over-head that is introduced when running protocols such as TCP/IP on the network.

NOTE

Twisted-pair Ethernet at 10 Mb/s is referred to as 10 Base-T Ethernet. When running at 100 Mb/s, it is referred to as 100 Base-TX Ethernet.

Typically, it is hard today to find an Ethernet card for your computer that runs at only 10 Mb/s. Almost all cards available operate at both 10 Mb/s or 100 Mb/s and can be used on either type of network. If you are purchasing an ISA bus card for an older computer, you might find that you have the option of a card that runs at only 10 Mb/s, but you might find these more expensive than some of the cheaper PCI cards available that run at both 10 Mb/s and 100 Mb/s.

> **TIP**
>
> Most new Macintosh computers ship with built-in Ethernet capabilities. However, if you own a newer Macintosh computer that doesn't have Ethernet built in but that uses the PCI bus connection for add-on cards, you can probably use most of the PCI cards available on the market. You need to be careful, however, that the necessary drivers are available for the MacOS. If you are not sure about this, consult with your vendor before purchasing.

> **TIP**
>
> If you own an older Macintosh system that uses the NuBUS technology for connecting add-on cards, you will find that not many cards are available, and those that are available can cost as much as five times the cost of entry-level PCI Ethernet cards. To make matters even more complicated, some Macintosh models have special-purpose expansion slots that are neither NuBUS or PCI for which you need to purchase similarly expensive dedicated Ethernet cards. A good discussion of Ethernet for the Macintosh is online at the University of Illinois at Urbana-Champagne at `http://www-commeng.cso.uiuc.edu/nas/nash/mac/ethernet.mac.html`.

A large number of vendors produce Ethernet cards, including the following:

- 3Com (`www.3com.com`): 3Com produces high-quality network cards often recommended for corporate installations where performance and reliability are crucial. This reputation comes with a price: 3Com cards are among the pricier on the market. 3Com cards are among the most commonly used in enterprise settings such as corporations and universities.
- D-Link (`www.dlink.com`): D-Link has built its reputation and following by producing good-quality, value-priced network hardware aimed at the home market.
- Intel (`www.intel.com`): Intel is another company that produces networking equipment aimed at the corporate market which, of course, makes them a more expensive option.
- Linksys (`www.linksys.com`): Linksys is another vendor of networking cards and other hardware aiming to offer competitively-priced quality equipment to the home market.

Of course, there are numerous other vendors of network cards, but these are among the best-known and most widely used brands of network cards.

For the purposes of most home users, the cards produced by well-known, cost-conscious vendors such as D-Link and Linksys provide an unbeatable combination of quality, performance,

4

NETWORK INFRASTRUCTURE

and cost. Although there is no doubt that some of the cards produced by high-end vendors such as 3Com and Intel offer better performance and might offer better reliability and support over the long-term, it is unlikely that you will see the performance difference on a small home network unless you run the most demanding network applications such as some network multimedia or video-conferencing software. If you need to strike the right balance between cost and quality, look at these lower-cost vendors.

TIP

If you are equipping multiple computers with network cards for your home network, it is a good idea to try to buy identical cards for all of your computers, if possible. Of course, if some computers only have ISA bus slots, some have PCI slots, and others are notebooks, this is not going to be possible. But, if you have multiple computers, all with PCI bus slots, for instance, you can use the same network card in each computer. This makes maintaining and configuring networking on each PC easier because you can use the same drivers and installation and configuration software for each computer.

Choosing Your Card

When choosing your cards, it is important to consider which type to buy. For desktop computers, if you have an older computer that only offers ISA bus slots for expansion cards, you have little choice but to buy an ISA bus card. If you can find a dual-speed (10 Mb/s and 100 Mb/s) card for the ISA bus, choose this over a single-speed 10 Mb/s card so that you have room to grow into a faster network.

If your computer has a mix of ISA and PCI bus slots, see if you have room to add another PCI bus card. If you do, choose this over an ISA bus card because the performance will be better. As with ISA bus cards, it is preferable, and not really more expensive, to choose a dual-speed card over one that only works at 10 Mb/s (on top of which, you probably can't find a PCI card that operates at only 10 Mb/s).

With notebook computers, the same speed recommendations apply, but you need to consider another factor: the physical form of the card. Many cards exist that occupy a single PC Card slot. However, most of these use an external attachment to provide the port into which you can plug your twisted-pair Ethernet cable. The disadvantage of this is that it is easy to lose this attachment (called a *dongle*), or the dongle might be inconvenient if you are not using your computer on a flat surface (for instance, if you are working with the notebook computer in your lap).

There are PC Ethernet cards that provide built-in ports to plug network cables directly into the card, but typically these take up two PC Card slots; this means that in return for the convenience of the integrated port, you lose access to one of your slots for additional expansion. Also, some subnotebooks only offer a single PC Card slot, making it impossible to use these double-height cards.

Some newer notebook Ethernet cards come with integrated ports that are designed so that if you place them in the upper slot of a pair of PC card slots, they will not block the lower slot, leaving you free to use that expansion capability. These cards can be used in systems that contain only a single PC card slot.

Ethernet Hubs

If you have only two computers to network together, you can do this by using an Ethernet cable to directly connect the two computers as shown in Figure 4.2.

Crossed Ethernet Cable

FIGURE 4.2

Two computers connected together by an Ethernet cable.

> **NOTE**
>
> Connecting two computers together with a twisted-pair cable requires a special Ethernet cable with different mappings of wires to connector pins than a standard Ethernet cable. These cables are typically referred to as crossed Ethernet cables or computer-to-computer Ethernet cables.

However, this is a limited scenario. Because the Ethernet ports on both computers are connected to this single cable, no additional devices can be connected to the network, including other computers or a broadband Internet connection device, such as a cable or DSL modem.

To solve this problem, the simplest solution is to use an Ethernet hub. A *hub* basically provides a single line into which multiple Ethernet devices can plug. Consider Figure 4.3. This map of a simple network shows how devices such as computers, notebook computers, and broadband connection devices can be connected to a single line known as the *backbone*.

> **NOTE**
>
> The term *backbone* refers to the main communication channel from which smaller communication lines can be linked. In a network diagram, this backbone becomes a central line, which is suggestive of a human back bone.

4

NETWORK INFRASTRUCTURE

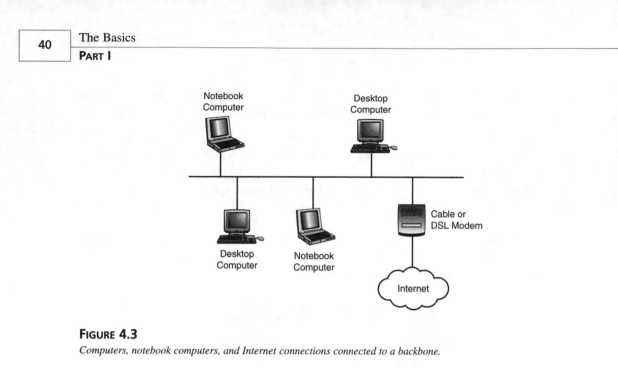

FIGURE 4.3

Computers, notebook computers, and Internet connections connected to a backbone.

Hubs provide a simple backbone for a small network. All devices on the network connect to the hub, which is a small box with multiple Ethernet ports. Inside the hub is the circuitry to act as the backbone communication channel for these devices. Figure 4.4 illustrates the same network as Figure 4.3 connected to a hub.

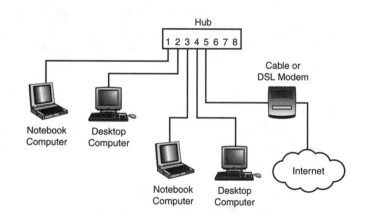

FIGURE 4.4

Hubs provide simple backbone capabilities.

Most modern hubs for home use provide 4, 5, or 8 ports for devices to connect to. It is generally a good idea to choose a device that has at least one more port than you actually need, which provides room for future expansion and daisy-chaining as discussed in the next section, "Daisy-Chaining Hubs."

For instance, if you have two computers and a DSL modem to connect on your network, you can do this with a 4, 5, or 8 port hub. But, if you add a notebook computer to the network, it is advisable to buy a 5 or 8 port hub.

Hubs come in both 10 Mb/s and 10 /100 Mb/s dual-speed varieties. If you are using only 10 Mb/s devices, you can use a simple 10 Mb/s hub. However, if you have some devices with Fast Ethernet ports or expect you might need to upgrade your network to 100 Mb/s in the near future (See the section "How Fast Is too Fast?" later in this chapter for a discussion of speed requirements), it is worth buying a Fast Ethernet hub from the start.

In Fast Ethernet hubs, each port can individually function at 10 Mb/s or 100 Mb/s depending on the device connected to it. The important thing is each port can actually operate at a different speed. For instance, you could have an older computer with a 10 Mb/s Ethernet card connected to one port on the hub, and that port would run at the slower speed, but at the same time a newer computer with a Fast Ethernet card could be connected to another port on the hub, and that port would run at 100 Mb/s.

TIP

The choice of brands for Ethernet hubs is similar to that discussed earlier in this chapter for Ethernet cards. The price points of different brands is also similar. For small, low-volume home networks it is not essential to use more expensive enterprise-quality hubs. You should be able to manage with less expensive hubs from companies such as Linksys or D-Link.

Daisy-Chaining Hubs

Hubs provide an expandability feature called *daisy-chaining*. Each hub has a special port which you can use to connect the hub to another hub, effectively creating a composite hub with more ports than a single hub. For instance, you can connect two five-port hubs together to create a pair of hubs which can effectively connect eight devices to the network as shown in Figure 4.5.

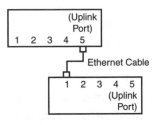

FIGURE 4.5

Daisy-chaining two five-port hubs allows up to eight devices to connect to the network.

4

NETWORK INFRASTRUCTURE

On hubs, the daisy-chain port (also called an uplink port) will be implemented in one of two ways:

One port will be labeled as the uplink port and a switch will change it between a normal port (to which you connect a network device) and an uplink port (to which you connect another hub). The design is illustrated in Figure 4.6.

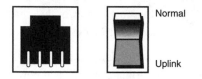

FIGURE 4.6

A single-port uplink port design.

One port will actually be a pair of ports: a normal port or an uplink port; however, only one of the pair can be used at any one time. This is illustrated in Figure 4.7.

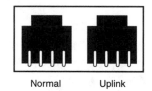

FIGURE 4.7

A dual-port uplink port design.

When daisy-chaining hubs, what you need to do is connect the uplink port to any normal port on the second hub; connecting two uplink ports will not work as illustrated in Figure 4.8.

There are two reasons an uplink port should be connected to a normal port on the second hub:

- Uplink ports swap the wire assignments of some of the pins in the port. This is necessary to create the uplink connection. However, if you connect a cable to two uplink ports, the second uplink port reverses the swapping, effectively creating a situation that is the same as if you had connected a normal port on one hub to a normal port on another.

- You can daisy-chain multiple hubs together. If you connected the uplink ports on two hubs together, then there would be no free uplink ports to add the next hub to the chain. By connecting the uplink port on the first hub of a chain to a normal port on the next hub, you can add a third hub to the chain by connecting the uplink port on the second hub to a normal port on the third hub, as illustrated in Figure 4.9.

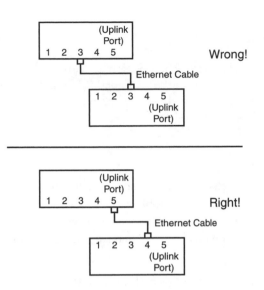

FIGURE 4.8

You cannot daisy-chain two uplink ports; an uplink port must connect to a normal port.

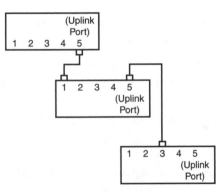

FIGURE 4.9

Multiple hubs can be daisy-chained together.

4

NETWORK
INFRASTRUCTURE

NOTE

There are limits to how many hubs can be daisy-chained together. Some manufacturers recommend you limit the number of hubs in a chain to four. As the number of hubs increases, the chance for collisions on your network increases. Collisions cause computers to resend information they have previously sent which didn't arrive at the destination. As a result, this overhead decreases the performance of your network.

NOTE

The uplink port effectively swaps the position of wires in the same way that a crossed Ethernet cable does. In fact, instead of connecting the uplink port of one hub to a regular port on another, you can also daisy-chain by connecting the regular ports on two hubs using a crossed Ethernet cable.

Should I Get a Switch?

Hubs are a convenient, inexpensive way to create a small home network. However, they do have some limitations that could prove problematic for some users. When you use a hub, every packet of information sent to any network device on the network actually travels out of each port of the hub to each device on the network and each device has to check if the packet is addressed for them.

This creates a shared network. For instance, if five Fast Ethernet devices are connected to a Fast Ethernet hub, the five devices share the 100 Mb/s bandwidth of the hub since all traffic destined for all devices travels out all five ports to all five devices.

For most users this is not important; 10 Mb/s or 100 Mb/s shared between all devices is sufficient and you will not notice the effect of sharing the bandwidth in your daily network use, such as Web browsing or sending and receiving e-mails.

However, if you plan to run bandwidth-intensive tasks internally on your network, the shared architecture of the hub could prove problematic. Examples of bandwidth-intensive applications include

- Multimedia applications such as streaming video
- Video conferencing

Consider the scenario described in Figure 4.10. Here, six computers are connected to the network. Computers 1 and 2 are video conferencing with each other, as are computers 3 and 4 and computers 5 and 6. The difficulty here is that all the video conference traffic between 1 and 2 is seen by computers 3, 4, 5 and 6, which affects the speed of their connections to the hub. Similarly, the video conference traffic between 3 and 4 is seen by the other computers and affects the speed of their connections to the hub. The same is also true for the video conference traffic between 5 and 6.

To solve this problem a solution is needed which segments the traffic so that the cable and port for computer 1 only sees traffic destined for computer 1, and so on for all six computers. This solution comes in the form of a switch. A switch is a specialized hub in which each port only carries traffic for the device connected to that port, as illustrated in Figure 4.11.

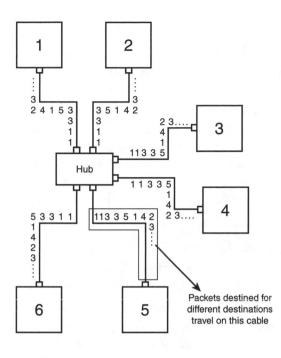

FIGURE 4.10

Video conferencing on a hub.

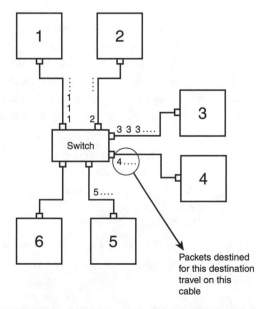

FIGURE 4.11

Packet Transference on a Video conferencing on a hub.

4

NETWORK
INFRASTRUCTURE

Although switches offer improved performance for applications such as multimedia and video conferencing, they do have their drawbacks:

- Switches cost more than hubs. In the entry level market, a switch will be two or more times more expensive than a hub.

- If your main concern is the speed of your Internet connection, moving from a hub to a switch will not make a significant difference because the shared speed of even a 10 Mb/s hub is larger than the maximum speed of most broadband Internet connections. Most broadband connections are limited to about 4 Mb/s. For this reason, moving even from a 10 Mb/s hub to a Fast Ethernet switch will have no noticeable impact on Internet performance because the 4 Mb/s bottleneck of the Internet connection limits Internet connection.

Twisted-Pair Ethernet Cables

Choosing the right cabling for your twisted-pair Ethernet network is essential. There are several things you need to pay attention to in selecting your cables:

- The category of the cable: Twisted-pair Ethernet requires category 5 twisted-pair cable. Other categories of Ethernet cable include category 3, which is sometimes used for voice networks such as telephone systems. It is crucial to use category 5 cable for your Ethernet network. Performance will be poor or non-existent with a lower category of cable. The categories of cabling are differentiated by electrical properties of the cabling such as the resistance.

- Crossed or straight: As mentioned earlier in this chapter, there are two types of cables with respect to the alignment of the cable's wires with the pins on the modular connector at each end of the cable. Straight (or straight-through) cables are used for connection PCs or network devices such as printers and broadband modems to hubs or switches. Crossed cables can be used to directly connect two devices such as two computers or two daisy-chain hubs together. If you use the wrong type of cable, you will not get a connection.

- Cables have a maximum length: Ethernet cables cannot exceed 362 feet. Beyond this length, the signal degrades and many packets of information will be lost on the network, requiring systems to resend packets and seriously degrading network performance. Make sure you keep your cable lengths within the limits, and if you need to exceed the limit, you can use hub daisy-chaining to extend the distance of your network as discussed in the next section, "Only 362 Feet?"

- Built or bulk: You can buy pre-built Ethernet cables in a variety of lengths up to about 100 feet. However, pre-built cables are quite costly. If you want to put in large amounts of cable in your home or use long lengths of cable, you might consider buying cable and connectors in bulk and making your own individual cables. Bulk cable costs a fraction of what pre-built cables usually cost. To do this requires the use of a special tool called a crimping tool and takes some practice, but once mastered is the most cost-effective source of Ethernet cable; it also has the advantage of allowing you to create cables that are exactly the length you want, instead of being forced to choose between pre-built cables that are either too long or too short.

Only 362 Feet?

As mentioned in the previous section, twisted-pair cable lengths should be limited to 362 feet. However, if you are trying to put in an Ethernet network that covers most of a house, you might need your network to span distances longer than 362 feet. To accommodate this, you can use the daisy-chaining features of hubs.

For instance, consider the floor plan of a house to be networked illustrated in Figure 4.12. In this diagram, all the rooms marked with an *X* need to be networked.

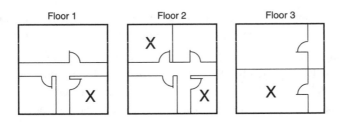

Figure 4.12

A house that needs a network.

To network this home, you can use four hubs. One can go on each of the three floors and be daisy-chained together. By running the Ethernet cables between these hubs through duct work or through walls and ceilings or floors, you can keep the individual cable length well-within 362 feet. Then, a fourth hub can be connected to the hub on the main floor to cross the floor to the fourth room which needs networking. The end result is illustrated in Figure 4.13.

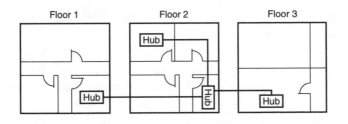

Figure 4.13

A multi-floor Ethernet network.

How Fast Is too Fast?

As mentioned in the section, "Hardware Requirements" earlier in this chapter, twisted-pair Ethernet can run at two possible speeds using the same physical cables: 10 Mb/s or 100 Mb/s. Your choice of speed is largely dependent on your available hardware.

The section indicated that, if possible, you want to buy cards capable of running at both 10 Mb/s and 100 Mb/s. However, this is just a recommendation if you are planning to buy new hardware for your network.

It is important to remember that most network applications you will run on your home network will not require more than 10 Mb/s speed.

Advantages and Disadvantages

Twisted-pair Ethernet networks have several advantages that keep them popular:

- They are inexpensive: With the possible exception of phone-line networking, no current solution costs less to implement in the home than twisted-pair Ethernet.
- They are common: As the most common network infrastructure technology, Ethernet cards are widely supported by all operating systems including Windows, MacOS, and Linux. In addition, there is a wide body of experience in the computer community with respect to installing and configuring Ethernet hardware and networks.
- They are upgradable: Because the same category 5 twisted-pair Ethernet cable can be used to carry both 10 Mb/s and 100 Mb/s traffic, upgrading a 10 Mb/s network can be done by replacing the Ethernet cards, hubs and switches: The network does not need to be rewired with new cables.
- The network is expandable: It is easy and cost-effective to add new nodes to locations that are already wired into the network.

However, twisted-pair Ethernet suffers from some shortcomings which might prevent you from choosing it for your home network:

- High-upfront costs: Because you need to put in place all the cables to cover your network, the installation cost for the network might be expensive, especially if you require professional help to pull the cables through walls or duct work. On networks with lots of computers, this is not an issue because the upfront costs are distributed across many systems. But on a small home network, this can make twisted-pair Ethernet more expensive than some of the other options.
- Inflexibility: You cannot simply move devices to new locations, especially if the new location is not wired on the network; instead, new cable must be laid to reach the location.

- Immobility: If you want to move to a new house, you must tear up all your cabling and then re-cable the new house, or simply leave the existing cables behind in the old house and buy new cables to install a network in your new house.

For many home users, these disadvantages might not be a problem. For instance, their Internet connection might come into a single office where two or three computers are located. A handful of short Ethernet cables and a hub will create a network with no real up-front costs to lay the cables, and without the immobility of cable placed in walls and duct work.

For others, though, these are genuine disadvantages, and serious consideration should be given to the alternative networking technologies described in the rest of this chapter.

Phone-line Networking

In 1998, the Home Phoneline Networking Alliance (HomePNA; www.homepna.org) was formed by eleven companies to establish standards and certification for products seeking to implement networking using existing phone lines in homes.

Home phoneline networking uses the existing phone lines and jacks in your house to allow you to create a network where a computer can connect to the network by plugging in to any phone jack in the house. This networking happens without interfering in any way with the operation of your home phone lines. Home phoneline networking takes advantage of the fact that telephone cables are capable of carrying a wide range of frequency signals. However, voice phone calls only use a small part of this range. Home phoneline networks take a range of high frequencies not used by the telephone signal and manipulate them to carry your home network signal on the same cable at the same time as your telephone service.

By using telephone service, you gain several advantages over adding a new twisted-pair Ethernet network to your home:

- No upfront costs: You do not need to wire your house because your house already has phone cable installed throughout. Wherever you can put a telephone, you can put a computer or other network device with home phoneline networking support.
- Expandability: As long as you have free phone jacks, you can add devices to the network.
- Mobility: To move to a new house, you do not need to tear up your existing cabling and relay new cables in your new home. You simply unplug your network devices from the phone jacks and plug them back into the jacks in the new house.

Home phoneline networking technology comes in two versions: the original version that runs at 1 Mb/s, and the current second-generation technology that gives you 10 Mb/s of performance, comparable to 10 Base-T twisted-pair Ethernet, which also runs at 10 Mb/s. Because the second-generation technology running at 10 Mb/s is emerging as the default standard and the

4

NETWORK
INFRASTRUCTURE

price is not much more than the older 1 Mb/s hardware, it is probably a good idea to use the newer 10 Mb/s home phoneline networking equipment. Eventually the 1 Mb/s equipment will be eliminated from the market. In this chapter we will consider only the 10 Mb/s technology.

The Hardware

To implement a home phoneline network requires, at a minimum, a home phoneline network adapter. These adapters are available in several forms:

- PCI cards for newer desktop computers
- External USB units
- External parallel port units for older computers
- PC cards for notebook computers

Several companies produce network adapters for home phoneline networking:

- 3Com(www.3com.com)
- D-Link (www.dlink.com)
- Intel (www.intel.com)
- Linksys (www.linksys.com)
- Netgear (www.netgear.com)

Many home phoneline network adapters provide two ports so that you can connect two network devices to one phone jack by chaining two network adapters together. Alternately, the second port allows you to plug a telephone into the same phone jack as your computer.

If the card you use doesn't provide a second jack for your telephone, you can use a telephone jack "Y" splitter to plug a telephone and your computer into the same phone jack.

Home Phoneline Network Kits

Several vendors sell home phoneline network kits that bundle together all the hardware and software you need to set up a small home phoneline network in your residence. Typically, these kits will contain two home phoneline network adapters, all necessary cables including telephone cables, and any necessary software such as drivers for the network adapters. Because many homes will typically network an average of two computers if they need networking, one of these kits provides a convenient, single-box networking solution.

Examples of home phoneline networking kits include

- D-Link 10 Mb USB Phoneline Network in a Box
- Linksys HomeLink Phoneline 10M Network Starter Kit
- 3Com HomeConnect Home Network 10 Mbps Phoneline PCI Kit

Home Phoneline to Ethernet Bridges and Internet Gateways

Often, it is necessary to integrate a traditional 10 Mb/s or 100 Mb/s twisted-pair Ethernet network with a home phoneline network. For instance, you might have created a small 10 Mb/s Ethernet network in one room of your home, and now would like to provide network access throughout the rest of your house. To do this, you can use a home phoneline-to-Ethernet bridge, which effectively connects an Ethernet network to a home phoneline network and makes them function as one larger network.

Typically, a bridge has two ports in it: one port to connect to a telephone jack and another to plug into a twisted-pair Ethernet hub or switch running at either 10 Mb/s or 100 Mb/s. The devices themselves require little or no configuration and provide a true out-of-the-box solution.

A popular use of these bridges is to connect a broadband modem for a cable, DSL or satellite Internet connection to a home phoneline network spanning a home. Typically, these modems provide a single twisted-pair Ethernet port to connect to your home computer or network. You can connect this port to the Ethernet port of a home phoneline to Ethernet bridge and then connect the bridge to your home phoneline network. This will provide access to your Internet connection to your home phoneline network.

CAUTION

Connecting your home phoneline network to an Ethernet network might not be secure enough for your needs. In this case, you might want to look at home phoneline Internet gateways like those discussed in Chapter 12, "Using a Broadband Router," which provide gateway security features while connecting your Internet connection to your home phoneline network.

Wireless Networking

In 2000, wireless networking emerged as a viable alternative for the home user. Wireless technology is extremely attractive, especially for users of portable devices such as notebooks. It uses high frequency radio signals at frequencies similar to those used in some cordless phones to connect devices on the network.

It also takes overall network convenience one step further than a home phoneline network does by allowing devices to be placed anywhere in the home without regard for the location of existing twisted-pair hubs or phone jacks. This provides the ultimate freedom.

Of course, this freedom doesn't come without a price. Wireless technology can be much more expensive than either twisted-pair Ethernet or home phoneline networks with similar levels of performance.

4

NETWORK INFRASTRUCTURE

Two standards exist for wireless networks in the home:

- HomeRF (www.homerf.org): HomeRF is a standard originally designed to bring low-cost wireless networking to home users. The current HomeRF standard runs at 1.6 Mb/s. An upcoming standard promises 10 Mb/s. Outside of the home, HomeRF is not widely used. Vendors of HomeRF technology include Intel, Compaq, Motorola and Proxim.

- Wireless Ethernet: The 802.11b wireless Ethernet standard emerged originally as the high-end wireless technology aimed at the office setting. However, its price has dropped considerably, putting it within the reach of many households even as home networking vendors such as Linksys and D-link have opted to enter the wireless Ethernet market instead of the HomeRF market. Wireless Ethernet runs at 11 Mb/s. Vendors of 802.11b wireless Ethernet hardware include 3Com, Intel, Linksys, and D-link.

> **NOTE**
>
> The consensus of many analysts is that 802.11b-based wireless Ethernet will emerge as the de facto standard because it is already deployed in large offices as well as many homes and is already running at 11 Mb/s, whereas HomeRF has not yet reached 10 Mb/s. In addition, HomeRF has a distance range rated at about half that of 802.11b systems, which means that in larger sites HomeRF might be impractical.

The Hardware

To implement a wireless network requires, at a minimum, a wireless network adapter. These adapters are available in several forms:

- PCI cards for newer desktop computers
- External USB units
- PC cards for notebook computers

Several vendors sell wireless network kits which bundle together all the hardware and software you need to set up a small wireless network in your residence. Typically, these kits will contain one or two wireless network adapters, an access point (access points are discussed in the next section, any necessary cables, and any necessary software such as drivers for the network adapters. Because many homes will typically network an average of two computers if they need networking, many of these kits provide a convenient, single-box networking solution.

Wireless Network Access Points

Wireless networks operate in two ways:

A point-to-point mode, sometimes called ad hoc mode, in which two devices communicate directly with each other.

An infrastructure mode in which multiple devices communicate with each other through a base station known as an access point.

For most home wireless networking needs, an access point is essential even if only two devices will be used on the network; with an access point the range is improved, and your wireless network can be integrated with an existing twisted-pair Ethernet network, or connected to the Ethernet point of a broadband modem for your cable, DSL, or satellite Internet connection.

Access Points will include a single twisted-pair Ethernet port and high-powered antennas for communicating with wireless Ethernet devices in your home.

CAUTION

Connecting your wireless network to an Ethernet network might not be secure enough for your needs. In this case, you might want to look at wireless Internet gateways like those discussed in Chapter 12, "Using a Broadband Router," which provide gateway security features while connecting your Internet connection to your wireless network.

Summary

This chapter wraps up our discussion of networking basics. By now you should understand your home networking options including wireless, home phoneline and twisted-pair Ethernet cabling options and have chosen the best for your home.

The next chapter marks the transition from discussing networking basics to addressing real security issues. You will learn about steps you can take, without purchasing any additional software, to protect your PC as much as possible while it is connected to the Internet. These techniques include ensuring that unnecessary network services are not running and checking permissions and file and printer sharing settings on your computer.

4

NETWORK
INFRASTRUCTURE

Protecting a Home PC

IN THIS PART

Securing a Standalone System

IN THIS CHAPTER

In This Chapter

In this chapter we will look at how we can secure a standalone computer connected to the Internet. The main focus will be on how to properly configure a Microsoft Windows 98/Me computer to be connected to the Internet safely. We will look at Windows 9x/Me and its networking components because it is a very popular operating system and it contains a number of elements that can potentially become security problems when configured improperly.

The Windows 9x/Me's networking technologies are based on older proprietary networking technologies used in earlier versions of Windows. When the Internet became popular and Internet networking technologies were needed for Windows 9x/Me, instead of developing new networking technologies for the operating system, the older proprietary networking technologies were instead adapted for Internet use. This allowed Microsoft to keep all its networked platforms compatible and interoperable. However, not designed with the Internet in mind, these older network technologies adapted for Internet use contain a number of security liabilities.

In comparison, the Apple, Linux and even Windows 2000/XP platforms do not have such potential security issues, mainly because they have not continued to support older proprietary networking technologies, and rather have developed new networking technologies for the Internet.

Hence, we must always remember that the Internet is sometimes called the "Information Superhighway" for a reason. It is similar to an auto highway, in that traffic moves in both directions. You must be aware that if you can access a remote Web server somewhere on the Internet, at the same time, someone else can access your computer.

NOTE

It should also be noted, that even if the computer is properly configured for the Internet, it cannot provide the complete security a network firewall can provide. More information about network firewalls will be discussed in Chapter 6.

Security Liabilities of the Windows Networking Platform

Although we are focusing on the Windows networking platform, what we will discuss in this section is still applicable to other operating systems you are currently using or plan to use. The problems discussed in this chapter arise because an older existing networking technology was adapted to a new emerging technology, the Internet. This occurs frequently in the computer world, and in this case and like many others, the security of the technology is overlooked.

The Windows networking platform is based on a protocol called Network Basic Input/Output System (NetBIOS). NetBIOS was developed by IBM and adopted and incorporated into one the earliest Windows operating systems by Microsoft.

NetBIOS provides the capability to enable a number of computers to connect to each other to create a local area network (LAN). However, the key to the protocol is that it was designed for local use. NetBIOS was meant to be used in an office setting where colleagues and associates can share files and printers easily. A certain amount of trust between all users was required for the concept of this LAN to succeed, and in most cases it did work.

NOTE

If you have not read Chapter 3 on how the Internet works, it is best to go back and review it now. This section deals with how the NetBIOS protocol was adapted for the Internet.

However, when the Internet began to emerge as a killer application, and everyone wanted access to it, Microsoft decided to integrate the Internet into its existing networking platform.

However, there lies the origin of the security liabilities caused by this networking platform. NetBIOS is a non-routable protocol whereby all the devices in the local area network has a single unique text name identifier. This single namespace technique works fine for small local area networks, but does not pair up easily with the Internet, where there exist millions of computers. The Internet uses a hierarchical namespace system to guard against computers having the same name.

And although NetBIOS is non-routable, the protocol of the Internet, TCP/IP; provides network addresses that are fully routable. TCP/IP addresses describe the route needed to reach the destination address. This routable address is assisted by the hierarchical namespace system.

To solve these differences, the Windows networking platform was bridged to work with TCP/IP. The NetBIOS protocol was bound onto the top of TCP/IP, where NetBIOS would be used for the local area network, and TCP/IP would be used for the transport across the Internet. This was called "NetBIOS over TCP/IP."

However, this binding of NetBIOS to TCP/IP produces a glaring security issue. The NetBIOS protocol enables users to share files and printers by making each individual computer a file and/or printer server. This allows every computer on the private LAN to be able to share, store, and print files using a shared service from another computer.

5

SECURING A STANDALONE SYSTEM

However, by binding NetBIOS to TCP/IP, it also makes the private shared LAN a part of the entire Internet, or conversely, it makes the Internet a part of the shared LAN. This results in allowing any computer on the public Internet to be able to share and print files from the computers on the private shared LAN.

But many will argue that the Windows platform does provide security protection for their operating system and networking technology. Every computer is password protected and a user must be authenticated before given access to the shared resources.

Nonetheless, for this security to work, every user must follow the practice of using their username and password, but it is very common for people to ignore the authentication, because they are the lone physical users of their computers and would rather have fast access to their computers. Many users do not see the intrusion threat coming from the Internet, but rather worry more about physical intruders.

But even if the users of the computers do use password authentication, it is still possible for intruders to gain access to the computers. The NetBIOS protocol inherently leaks out information to the network. This information contains the computer's workgroup, name, and the current user logged on. This information is enough to give an intruder the tools to attempt to access your computer. It enables an intruder to grab a username, and use a password-scanning tool to try to access the computer. In the old days of dialup connections, this might have not worked because the shared LAN would not be connected fulltime to the Internet. But with today's always-on-broadband connections, the network can always be connected to the Internet. An intruder now has time on his side, and can just set up his password-scanning tool to attempt access to your computer until he gains access. And unlike other operating systems, the windows platform does not refuse authentication after a certain number of failed attempts. Hence the intruder can use the password-scanning tool to attempt login as many times as is necessary.

Password-scanning tools usually attempt multiple simultaneous logins to decrease the time it takes to crack the password, and the windows platform also does not refuse simultaneous attempts. Hence, with the username information provided, an intruder can usually crack a password in a matter of hours depending on the strength of the password. Of course this intrusion all occurs unannounced to the user, as no alerts or signals of login occur.

But there are defenses against these Windows platform security issues. In the next section we will discuss how to configure a Windows 9x computer to protect itself from such intrusions. But first we will discuss two pieces of advice for all users, not just Windows platform users.

First, always use a strong password. A strong password is defined as a password with more than eight characters, including numbers, letters (upper- and lowercase) and punctuation characters. In addition, you should never use words that can be found in the dictionary.

Second, always turn off services and resources on your computer that do not need to access the Internet. Leaving services available to be accessed from the Internet provides the window for an intruder to gain access. It is best to disable all unused services.

In the case of the Windows 9x/Me platform, Windows networking technologies are not needed to access the Internet. Hence, if you are a using a standalone computer, and do not need to share files or printers, it is best to disable the built-in network technologies. Applications such as telnet, Web browsers, e-mail, ftp, and other Internet applications never use the Windows networking NetBIOS protocol, because they directly communicate with TCP/IP.

Proper Configuration of a Windows 9x/Me Standalone System

In this section, we will discuss how to safely configure Windows 9x/Me to be connected onto the Internet. The primary configuration required is to unbind the windows networking from the TCP/IP transport layer.

By default, when Windows 9x or Me is installed, the network technologies are installed and enabled. This configuration includes file and printer sharing being enabled and NetBIOS being bound to TCP/IP, as shown from the Network window dialog box shown in Figure 5.1. The Network window dialog box can be found by selecting Start, Settings, the Control Panel and choosing Network.

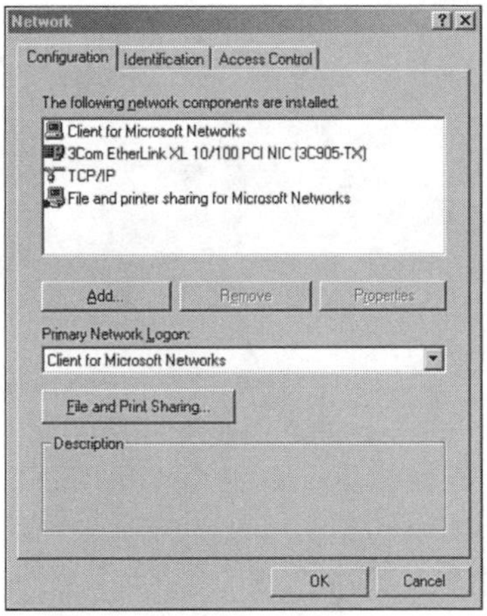

FIGURE 5.1
The Network window dialog box.

Now, there are three possible configurations:

- Internet access with no windows networking
- Internet access with local windows networking
- Internet access with Internet windows networking

Configuration 1: No Windows Networking

The first configuration includes Internet access and no windows networking. Because the default configuration already provides the Internet enabled, all that is required is the disabling of the windows networking. To do this, we must disable both Client for Microsoft Networks and File and Printer Sharing for Microsoft Networks. To disable file and printer sharing, we select the File and Print Sharing button on the Network dialog box. From the File and Print Sharing window, we deselect the two choices for enabling access to files and printers as seen in Figure 5.2.

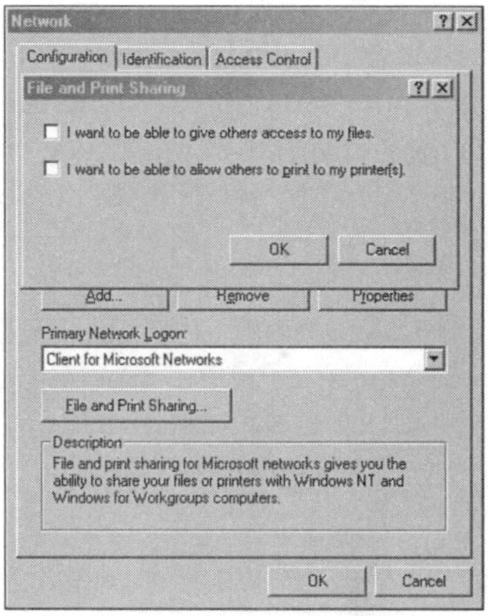

FIGURE 5.2
File and Print Sharing window with deselected options.

After this is performed, the Network dialog box loses the File and Printer sharing component as shown in Figure 5.3. File and Printer sharing is now disabled and unbound from TCP/IP.

Now, to disable Client for Microsoft Networks, it must be unbound from TCP/IP. First, select the TCP/IP component, and select the Properties button, as shown in Figure 5.4.

The TCP/IP Properties window dialog box will appear, as shown in Figure 5.5.

Select the Bindings tab as shown in Figure 5.6, and deselect Client for Microsoft Networks.

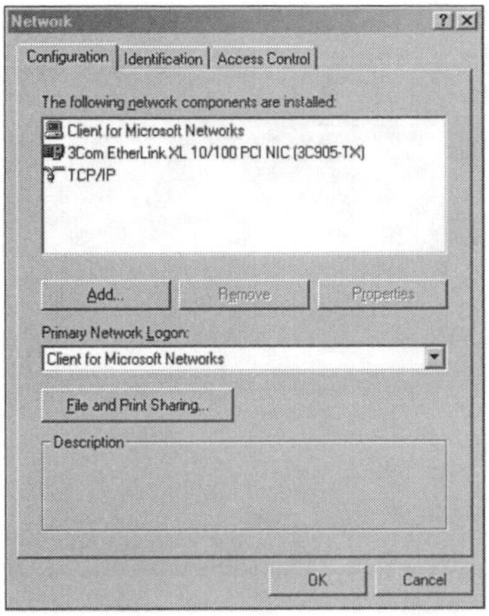

FIGURE 5.3

File and Print Sharing component no longer exists in the Network dialog box.

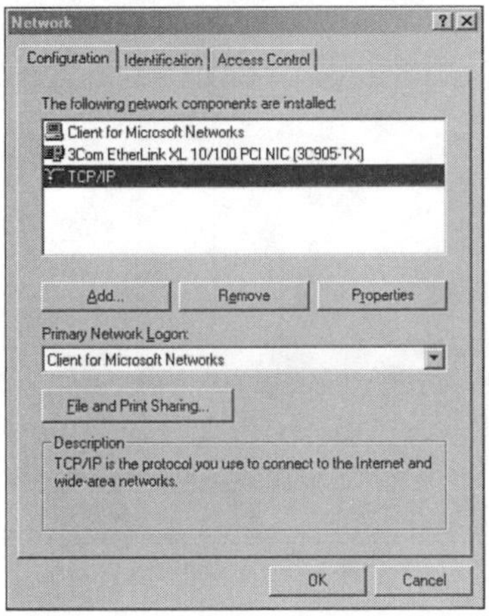

FIGURE 5.4

Selecting the TCP/IP component.

When the OK button is pressed, the system will ask whether TCP/IP should be bound to any drivers. Select No and reboot the computer. After the computer reboots, Windows networking will be completely unbound and disabled.

5

SECURING A STANDALONE SYSTEM

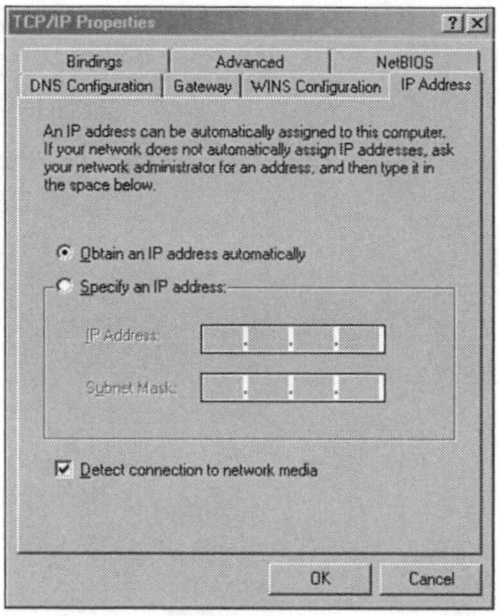

Figure 5.5

The TCP/IP Properties dialog box, with the IP Address tab selected.

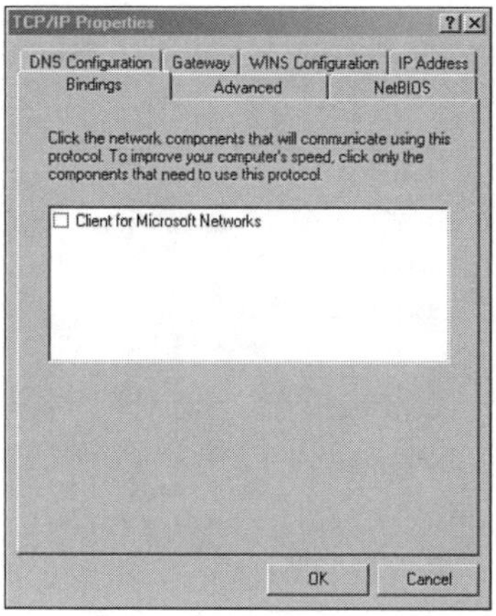

Figure 5.6

The Binding tab and the deselected Client for Microsoft Networks.

However, there is a problem with this configuration, as some Windows platforms expect the Windows networking component to exist. Windows might report an error message stating the network is not complete. This does not interfere with access to the Internet and can be ignored. But if you prefer not to have these errors, you might want to try the next configuration, Internet access with local windows networking. This provides Internet access with windows networking bound to a local protocol for the LAN.

Configuration 2: With Local Windows Networking

In this configuration, access to the Internet is provided in addition to Windows networking. Windows networking is installed to allow sharing of files and printers for computers attached to the private local area network. This configuration is achieved by replacing the TCP/IP transport layer for Windows networking with NetBEUI, the local windows transport protocol.

The first step involves installing the NetBEUI transport protocol onto the computer. Select the Add button from the Network windows dialog box as shown in Figure 5.7.

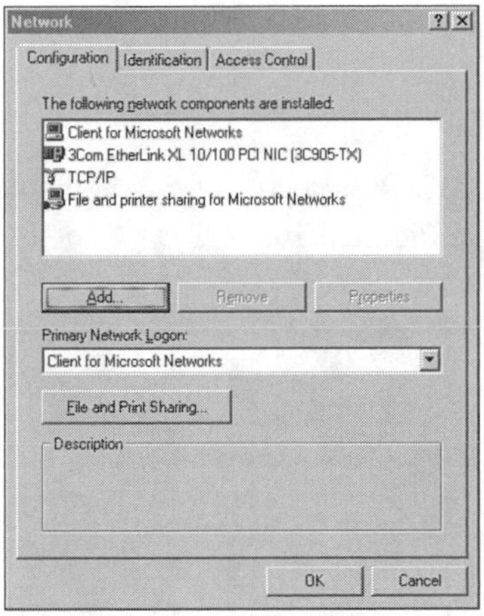

FIGURE 5.7
The Network windows dialog box.

When the Add button is selected, the Network Component Type dialog box appears as shown in Figure 5.8. Select the Protocol component and click the Add button.

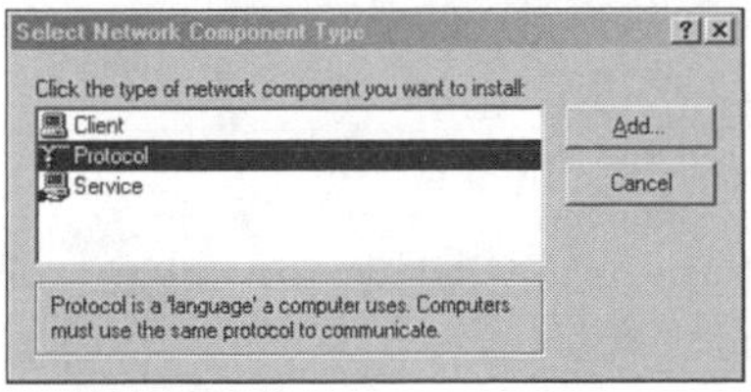

FIGURE 5.8
Select Protocol from the Network Component Type dialog box.

From the Network Protocol dialog box as shown in Figure 5.9, select Microsoft and NetBEUI and click the OK button.

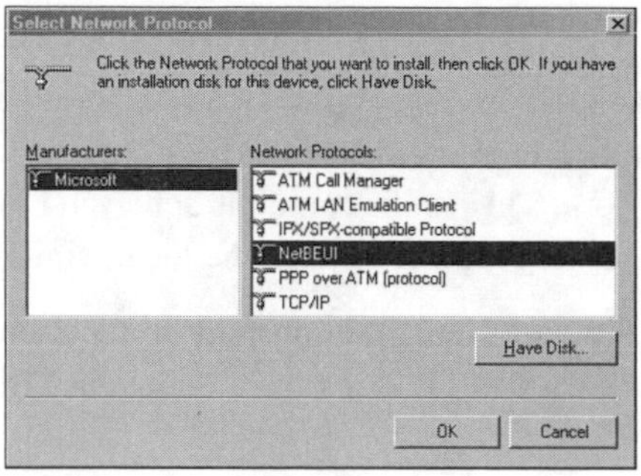

FIGURE 5.9
Select Microsoft and Net BEUI from the Network dialog box.

When this is completed, the NetBEUI protocol appears in the network components of the Network dialog box, as shown in Figure 5.10.

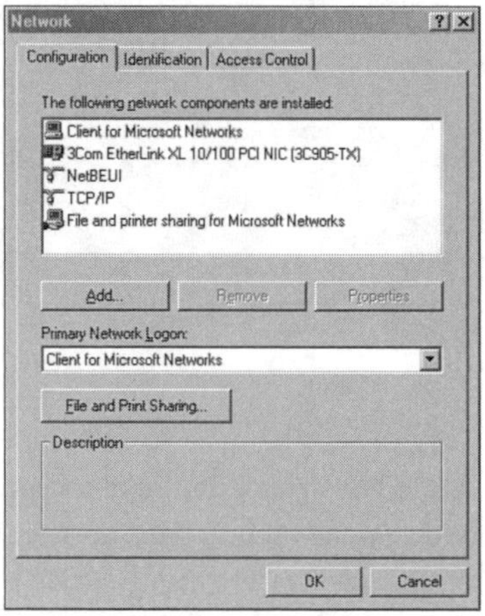

FIGURE 5.10
The Network dialog box with the newly added NetBEUI protocol.

Now before unbinding TCP/IP from the windows networking components, it is best to check that NetBEUI is bound to windows networking. Select NetBEUI from the Network dialog box and press the Properties button. As can be seen in Figure 5.11, NetBEUI is indeed bound to the windows networking components. Press Cancel to return to the Network dialog box.

To unbind TCP/IP from the windows networking components, we perform similar actions as in configuration 1. We select TCP/IP from the Network dialog box and press Properties. We select the Bindings tab and deselect all components, in this case, both Client for Microsoft Networks and File and Printer Sharing for Microsoft Networks as shown in Figure 5.12.

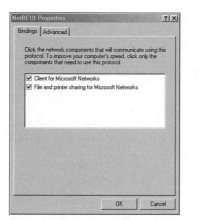

FIGURE 5.11

NetBEUI is bound to the Windows networking components.

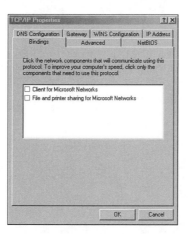

FIGURE 5.12

TCP/IP Bindings Properties: Both Client for Microsoft Networks and File and printer sharing for Microsoft Networks are deselected.

Again, Windows will ask whether TCP/IP should be bound to any drivers. Simply click No and the computer will request that you reboot. Reboot the computer, and the computer will be configured to access the Internet safely and have local file and printer sharing enabled. The local sharing is conducted using the NetBEUI protocol and is not accessible by the Internet.

Configuration 3: With Internet Windows Networking

This configuration is basically the default configuration provided by Windows. It is very insecure and highly unadvised. Some believe that making shared resources hidden or invisible will deter intruders, but that is not the case. The NetBIOS protocol leaks connection information and also leaks information about the services and resources a connected computer provides. The only secure way to use windows networking over the Internet, to share files and printers on the Internet, is to use a firewall to protect your system.

Summary

In this chapter, you learned about securing a standalone computer, and more specifically, securing a Windows 9x/Me computer.

It is recommended that users of Windows 9x/Me platform machines at minimum follow either configuration 1 or 2 described in this chapter. Enabling a computer to access the Internet with Windows networking enabled, as in configuration 3, is very insecure and ill advised.

You should continue on to the next chapter regarding firewalls for more information about further protecting your computer and network.

Wireless Ethernet Security

IN THIS CHAPTER

In This Chapter

In this chapter, we will discuss one of the latest home and small office networking technologies, wireless local area network (LAN) networking and more specifically, wireless Ethernet LANs.

This chapter will focus on the security considerations needed for wireless Ethernet LAN technology. Unlike ordinary wired Ethernet, where access to the network can be secured by limiting access to the physical cable, wireless Ethernet uses a shared radio transmission medium, and hence cannot control access to the network. Any device within the same radio proximity of the transmitting device can potentially eavesdrop. Consequently, security is a very important component of wireless Ethernet. The objective of wireless Ethernet is to make wireless LAN technology as safe as wired LAN technology.

In this chapter, we will begin by discussing the basic ideas underlying wireless Ethernet. This will be followed by a review of the three primary security methods used by wireless Ethernet:

- Shared Key
- Wired Equivalent Privacy (WEP)
- MAC Address Control

At the end of this chapter, we will discuss briefly the hardware alternatives users have when deciding on installing wireless Ethernet in the home or small office.

Wireless Ethernet Technology

There are several wireless networking technologies currently on the market, but Wireless Ethernet has become the de facto standard. Wireless Ethernet is often referred to by its standard protocol name, IEEE 802.11b, and generally offers a data bandwidth of 11 Megabits per second and operates in the 2.4 GHz frequency range of the radio spectrum.

NOTE

Later in 2001, the successor to the 802.11b standard will be finalized and products based on this standard should start to ship. This new standard will be called 802.11a and promises speeds of 54 Mb/s, almost 5 times what is offered by the current 802.11b. This new standard will move from using 2.4 GHz to 5 GHz radio and will imply several changes to networks: Range distances will reduce even as the total number of users who can be supported will increase. Also, the price point of 802.11a hardware will likely keep it to corporate environments initially, whereas 802.11b will remain the popular choice for home wireless networking for some time.

The 802.11b protocol has gained wide popularity because of its similarity to the wired Ethernet protocol, IEEE 802.3. In most cases, with the exception of the low-level hardware drivers for wireless Ethernet network cards, wired and wireless Ethernet function in the same manner, and therefore operating systems and network tools do not need to treat them differently. This enables users and system administrators to add a wireless Ethernet LAN to their existing wired Ethernet LAN without much effort. Additionally, the compatibility with wired Ethernet allows for existing higher-level protection mechanisms such as firewalls and other network security mechanisms to fully function.

The cost for wireless LAN technology has recently dropped as large businesses and corporations have begun adopting the technology in the workplace. Additionally, secondary manufacturers have begun marketing hardware targeted for the home and small office. The hardware targeted for the home is usually less performance oriented, and in some ways, less secure. However, in most cases involving technology, the home user must decide between the cost of technology and the security that is really required. The remaining sections of this chapter will inform the user on making the best decision in his or her personal case.

As discussed earlier, whereas wired Ethernet technology can be access controlled by limiting physical access to the hubs, switches, cabling, or even the physical space the network resides in, wireless Ethernet cannot. The data is transmitted through the space by radio signal, and in most cases is broadcast outside the physical space that it is intended for. Consequently, security is a core element of wireless Ethernet technology. The main objective of the wireless security mechanisms is to provide a level of security equivalent to what wired Ethernet can provide. In the next three sections, we will discuss the three most commonly implemented security mechanisms.

NOTE

More information about wireless Ethernet can be found at: http://www.wi-fi.com, the Wireless Ethernet Compatibility Alliance homepage.

Shared Key

A basic security mechanism used by 802.11b is the use of a shared key. Basically, a shared password controls access to the network, and every device must have the same shared key to be able to communicate with each other. In most cases, a wireless Ethernet access point will have a defined shared key, sometimes called the Extended Service Set ID (ESSID). Without the defined shared key, wireless network cards cannot communicate with the access point or access the network.

> **NOTE**
>
> A *wireless access point* is a stationary network bridge that provides a wireless Ethernet extension to a wired Ethernet network. An access point enables wireless devices to access the wired Internet by forwarding packets to the wired LAN connection. An access point is sometimes referred to as a base station.

The shared key can be a combination of letters and numbers. A private network should have a unique private ESSID created, and the default key should never be used. In early deployments, system administrators would leave the ESSID as the manufacturer default, and leave their networks open to wireless intrusion. The ESSID should be treated as a password and not freely given out. As for intrusions, it is possible for intruders to attempt to scan for the ESSID, and therefore shared key security should be used in conjunction with other security mechanisms.

Wired Equivalent Privacy

Wired Equivalent Privacy (WEP) performs two security functions. It encrypts the data being transmitted over the network, guarding against eavesdropping, and it also provides access control to the network. WEP uses a secret key that is shared between the access point and a wireless device. The secret key is used to encrypt packets before being transmitted across the network, and a verification integrity check is performed at the destination to ensure no modifications have occurred during the transmission. The key also provides access control because without the key, packets will fail the verification test at the destination site. For functional use, at least one secret key must be entered into each device and the network's access point. However, there is support for a group of secret keys that allow for modification of keys over time without hindering the daily use of the network.

WEP encryption has two strengths, 64-bit and 128-bit secret keys, the stronger being the 128-bit key. The actual secret key is made up of either a 40-bit or 104-bit user-defined key, and a 24-bit initialization vector defined by the devices. Most devices do support both levels of encryption; however, note that some manufacturers separate the two strengths into separate products. A network must run the same level of encryption on all its devices; hence, 64-bit and 128-bit encryption cannot be mixed in the same network. The encryption level of a network is defined by setting the encryption level at the access point and for the network cards being used on the network.

> **NOTE**
>
> 64-bit encryption is sometimes marketed as 40-bit encryption, 40-bits coming from the 40-bit user-defined key.

However, WEP encryption does not come free, technology-wise. In some cases, it does affect the performance of the network. This is usually because of the implementation of WEP on the networking device or access point. In most cases, a hardware-based WEP product will outperform a software-based implementation, and this should be studied when purchasing equipment.

It also must be noted that WEP has recently come under media and security scrutiny. It has been found that WEP can be attacked, and intruders can add and decrypt a small number of packets to the communication stream. The industry is working on a solution, but because WEP is an integral part of the 802.11b protocol, solutions to this problem are not simple. It also must be stated that these intrusions were conducted by research labs, and corporations continue to use and have confidence in 802.11b and WEP even after these findings were released.

When buying wireless Ethernet hardware, you should pay attention to the WEP capabilities of both the network cards and access points you buy. For instance, some companies offer access points capable of both 64-bit and 128-bit WEP security, whereas the network cards they sell only provide 64-bit security. With other companies, the situation is reversed with the access point topping out at 64-bit and the network cards having 128-bit capability.

Also, some companies' hardware doesn't include 128-bit security out of the box but offers firmware upgrades you can download and install to increase the capabilities of the hardware to support 128-bit WEP security.

You should consider your present needs and future needs in judging this aspect of the hardware. Also, when buying wireless Ethernet cards, consider whether you will use those cards on other wireless networks, such as a corporate wireless network or a partner's network, where you are required to use 128-bit security.

MAC Address Control

A third security mechanism found in wireless Ethernet is the use of MAC address filtering. A Media Access Control (MAC) address is a computer's unique hardware number. In many wired Ethernet networks, MAC addresses are filtered to prevent unauthorized computer access to certain resources and services. And because wireless Ethernet is fully compatible with wired Ethernet, MAC addresses are also used for the same purpose on wireless LANs.

Many higher end commercial access points provide MAC address-based hardware access control and some software routers systems provide this similar restrictive filtering mechanism.

However, this is not a mechanism without flaws. Most wireless devices provide a method to change the MAC address, so it is not impossible to figure out the MAC addresses that are allowed to access a certain resource and modify a wireless device to gain access.

> **NOTE**
>
> If an attacker does attempt to gain access to your network by configuring a wireless device to mimic the MAC address of an authorized device on your network, it is likely you will notice this attempt fairly quickly. If two devices on a network share the same MAC address, hosts and routers on the network won't know how to deliver packets because networks expect unique MAC addresses for each network device. It is likely that the device with the MAC address, which the attacker is mimicking, will either lose the ability to communicate on the network or will have intermittent ability to communicate.

Choices in Wireless Ethernet Technology

Recently, the market has been flooded with wireless access points and PC cards from most networking manufacturers. In most cases, obtaining an access point and plugging it in to your existing network will provide your network with an automatic wireless extension.

The prices are dropping as supply and demand increases; however, one must still be aware of the types of security mechanisms provided by these devices. In most commercial products, shared key, 128-bit encryption and MAC address access control mechanisms are all standard features. However, these devices are usually out of the budget of the home or small business user. For units marketed towards the home, manufacturers have mainly been including shared key and 64-bit WEP, and no MAC address control. This level of security should be enough for the common home user, but if you do require more security, look at the commercial units on the market. It is also best to determine how a manufacturer implements WEP on the networking devices.

Another recent trend by manufacturers is to build the wireless access point and the Internet firewall router together into one unit. This enables the home user to share the Internet with a number of wireless devices. These combined units provide the same functionality as the separate units; however, this might limit the placement of your wireless access point because it is tied to the location of your router. Wireless access point placement is sometimes important when trying to provide your space with full wireless coverage.

Table 6.1 provides an overview of the features of popular home-oriented wireless network products from vendors targeting the home and small office market.

TABLE 6.1 Wireless Ethernet Hardware for the SOHO Market

Vendor	Access Point?	Network Card?	WEP
2Wire	Yes	No	64-bit
3Com	Yes	Yes	64-bit
D-Link	Yes	Yes	64-bit
Farallon	Yes	Yes	64-bit and 128-bit (requires purchase of different network card to get 128-bit support)
Linksys	Yes	Yes	64-bit and 128-bit (Access point requires a firmware upgrade for 128-bit support; network card includes 128-bit support)
Orinoco	Yes	Yes	64-bit and 128-bit (requires purchase of different network card to get 128-bit support)
Xircom	Yes	Yes	64-bit

Summary

In this chapter you learned about the basic principles of Wireless Ethernet and the security issues involved in taking network traffic and putting it out on radio spectrum communication. You learned about the use of shared keys as well as WEP and MAC-address filtering to secure the network transmissions and limit access to the network, and considered how these factors should influence a decision to purchase wireless network hardware.

The next chapter takes the discussion into what is known as Personal Firewall Software. In this chapter, you learned about wireless Ethernet and the security mechanisms it provides at the lower network layer.

Using Personal Firewall Software

IN THIS CHAPTER

In This Chapter

In this chapter we will discuss what to look for when purchasing a personal firewall, and the kinds of protection a personal firewall software package can provide.

The remaining part of the chapter will examine personal firewall software and how it is properly installed, configured, and maintained. During this discussion, we will use an existing personal firewall software package (Zone Lab's Zone Alarm) to demonstrate the methods used to set up and maintain a personal firewall.

In this chapter you will learn:

What to Look For in a Personal Firewall

Before downloading or purchasing your personal firewall, verify your computer's current hardware and software and determine whether your computer can support personal firewall software.

For example, system requirements for Symantec's Norton Personal Firewall 2001 for Windows 95/98 include the following:

- Pentium class or higher processor
- Windows 95, Windows 98, Windows 98 SE
- 32 MB of RAM (48 MB recommended)
- 35 MB of available hard disk space
- CD-ROM drive
- Microsoft Windows Internet support

After determining that your computer can support a personal firewall, you must decide on the protective features you need.

> **TIP**
>
> At this time, if you are unfamiliar with how firewalls work, you might want to skip to Chapter 10, "Overview of Firewalls," and learn the theory behind firewalls.

Personal firewalls usually provide a number of different protection mechanisms to protect your computer against numerous known methods of attack. These protection mechanisms include the following:

- Stealth Mode: Provides your computer with stealth or invisibility on the Internet. This helps protect you from intruders and hackers because they cannot see or find your computer.

- Monitors: Performs data and traffic logging, letting you know what or who has attempted to access your computer, and alerts you of suspicious connections.

- Secure File Share Utilities: Enables you to share files with other known hosts and people that use your computer.

- Internet Locks: Enables you to block your computer from the Internet manually, or on a schedule. This prevents attacks because your computer is blocked from connecting to the Internet.

- Application Scanning: Scans applications' unique signatures as they attempt to access the Internet. This is to prevent Trojan horses masquerading as real applications from accessing the Internet. This in turn prevents an intruder from renaming a Trojan horse to a real application in an attempt to trick you into using their hidden software.

- Port Blocking: Blocks all ports on your computer that are not being used. This prevents intruders and attackers from using these ports or "doors" to gain entry into your computer.

- Trusted Groups: Support for trusted groups, based on trusted networks that permit you to exchange data freely and connect with these trusted hosts.

- Security Levels: Enables you to easily choose the security level of your personal firewall. These are predefined security settings that can be customized for the more experienced user.

- Web Protection: Provides protection against scripts and active content from the Web that might include hidden scripts that could damage your computer.

- Antivirus: Virus scanning tools to guard against virus and other malicious files sent to your computer.

- Privacy: Software to protect your identity and block the transmission of private data. Some Internet applications contain Spyware, malicious software that secretly communicates with the distributor of the application. Spyware usually steals personal data from your computer and sends it to the developer of the application.

Remember that personal firewalls are intended to protect a single standalone computer, so many developers of firewall software package the firewall with other required protection mechanisms, such as privacy and antivirus software.

7

USING PERSONAL FIREWALL SOFTWARE

However, keep in mind as well that personal firewalls cannot provide total protection. The user must still have the knowledge about what intruders and attackers can do, and be diligent in their own computer security. However, in some cases, personal firewalls actually conflict with other applications you use. In fact, many users often complain about numerous false alarms the firewall reports about attacks and intruders. We will talk later about personal firewall configuration, which, when done properly, will reduce the amount of false alarms reported.

Personal firewalls have no control of what Internet applications and programs do on your computer. Applications and operating systems often have security holes, and these might provide back doors for intruders to gain access to your computer, even when you are protected by a personal firewall. Always patch security holes in your applications and operating system after the developer or manufacturer releases a security patch.

NOTE

Here is an example of a recently discovered security hole. The deception involved a malicious user or rogue program deleting a commonly used Internet application and replacing it with a fake intrusive application. The key to this deception was that the fake application's name was exactly that of the deleted program, and in some cases actually functioned and appeared to be the same. Because many firewalls used to only check the names of applications attempting to connect to the Internet, the malicious application could easily gain access to the Internet posing as one of the common Internet applications. Once connected, it would communicate with its home and grant the deployer of the malicious program access into your system or files. Most personal firewall applications have patched this security hole, but it is always a good idea to make sure that your personal firewall does not just use application names during application filtering, but also checks an application's unique signature or fingerprint.

As for recommendations for personal firewall software, any personal firewall software that provides you with a majority of the protection mechanisms discussed previously will be able to protect your computer system. But, be mindful of how your computer is functioning on a day-to-day basis, proceed carefully when installing applications from unknown sources, and never give out your password. Security cannot be realized by just using a firewall application; it is simply a way of working safely on the Internet.

It is best to check that the personal firewall developer provides updates to the code when a security hole is found in the software, and that it is compatible with your Internet applications.

In regard to freeware/shareware versus commercially purchased software, most personal firewalls provided via the Internet do a good job. However, it is always smart to download your

Internet applications from reputable download sites, and to use software developed by reputable manufacturers. In the appendix, there is a list of a number of personal firewall packages, some that are freeware or shareware available on the Internet, and others that can be purchased online or at your local retailer. The difference between freeware and purchaseware usually is in the support and service provided. If you are quite familiar with Internet applications, you might not need the documentation and support, so the freeware or shareware might be best for you. If you are a new user, a purchased personal firewall might be better for you, as they usually include manuals and technical support.

How to Install a Personal Firewall

If you have not already chosen and obtained your firewall software, one option is to download or purchase one of the following suggested firewalls. For our example, we will be using Zone Labs' ZoneAlarm.

- Zone Labs' ZoneAlarm Firewall can be downloaded for free at `http://www.zonelabs.com/products/za/index.html`. As this book was published, the most current version was 2.6.
- Tiny Software's Tiny Personal Firewall can be downloaded for free at `http://www.tinysoftware.com`.
- Symantec's Norton Personal Firewall 2001 can be purchased at `http://www.symantec.com/sabu/nis/npf/`.

When you have obtained the firewall software, you are ready to install it on your computer. In the remaining parts of this chapter, we will be using the Zone Labs' ZoneAlarm firewall to work through the process of installing, configuring and maintaining a personal firewall. In most cases, personal firewall software packages will work in a manner similar to our sample application; however, in cases of differences, it is best to rely on the application's documentation, as an incorrectly installed, misconfigured, or unmaintained firewall can compromise your computer system's security. Nevertheless, even if you do select a different personal firewall, this chapter will be of benefit to you, as you will learn how in general terms a personal firewall is installed, configured and maintained.

In Appendix B, "Resources," a list of popular personal firewall sites is provided.

Installing ZoneAlarm

In this section, we will go through the process of setting up Zone Labs' ZoneAlarm on a computer. To keep this section brief, only the parts of the installation relevant to security have been included. The other parts of the installation process can be reviewed in the user manual or the help provided on the setup dialog box. Let's begin the installation.

In the case of Zone Labs' ZoneAlarm, clicking the downloaded installation file zonalm26.exe will start the ZoneAlarm setup program.

After the initial dialog box, an information and help dialog box will be presented, followed by a registration dialog box. Registration with Zone Labs permits them to notify you if problems are found with the ZoneAlarm firewall, or if new versions are available.

After registration is complete, the setup program requests that you agree with the Zone Labs license agreement, and asks where to install the software.

In addition, ZoneAlarm attempts to automatically configure itself to enable your default Web browser to access the Internet through the firewall, as seen in Figure 7.1. This step is for your convenience, and can actually be skipped until firewall configuration.

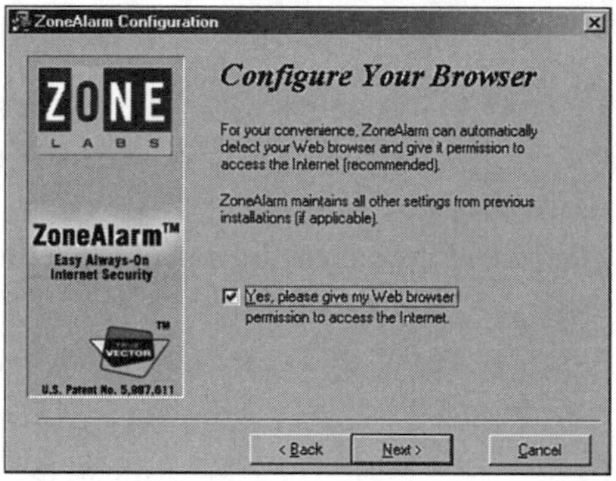

FIGURE 7.1

Configure ZoneAlarm to enable your Web browser to access the Internet.

After navigating through the setup dialog boxes, the ZoneAlarm software will be installed on your computer and a user survey dialog will appear. Complete the survey and click the Finish button.

Finally, the setup program will provide a setup confirmation dialog box, as shown in Figure 7.2, that asks to start ZoneAlarm. Click Yes.

FIGURE 7.2

The setup confirmation dialog window.

ZoneAlarm is now installed.

How to Properly Configure a Personal Firewall

In this section, we will discuss how to properly configure Zone Labs' ZoneAlarm. Proper installation of a firewall is important, but proper configuration is extremely vital. An improperly configured firewall can cause two problems: It might not protect your computer system from outside intruders, or permit you and your applications to access the Internet.

The following is the process used to properly configure the ZoneAlarm firewall.

Configuring ZoneAlarm

When you first start the application, the startup dialog box shown in Figure 7.3 is displayed. ZoneAlarm is by default configured in *stealth* mode, indicating it is configured to be invisible to the rest of the Internet.

FIGURE 7.3
The ZoneAlarm startup dialog box.

ZoneAlarm provides two default user interfaces: the ZoneAlarm tray icon and the Control Center panel dialog box.

The ZoneAlarm task tray icon, as shown in Figure 7.4, enables the user to lock the firewall and restore the ZoneAlarm Control Center when minimized.

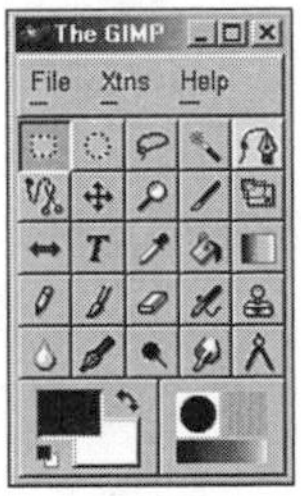

FIGURE 7.4
The ZoneAlarm task tray icon.

The ZoneAlarm Control Center panel, as shown in Figure 7.5, provides a number of display panels for the user. Each panel provides a different set of configuration tools. The panels, from left to right, include: Alerts, Lock, Security, Programs, and Configure. We will begin on the far right and describe the Configure panel first.

FIGURE 7.5
The ZoneAlarm Control Center.

Configure Panel

The Configure panel presents a large ZoneAlarm Help button. This button brings up the Help page in a local Web browser. When you click on the Configure button, the Configure panel also expands to display the full Configure dialog box, as shown in Figure 7.6.

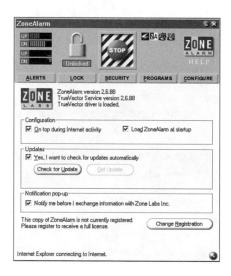

FIGURE 7.6
The ZoneAlarm Configure panel.

The Configure panel provides version information and permits you to set how ZoneAlarm is run. Furthermore, this panel enables you to check with Zone Labs for updates to the software. If you prefer, you can set ZoneAlarm to notify you when an update is available.

To the left of the Configure panel is the Programs panel. The Programs panel presents the current programs (the application's icon) that are accessing the Internet. When you click the Programs button, the ZoneAlarm Programs panel is expanded, as shown in Figure 7.7.

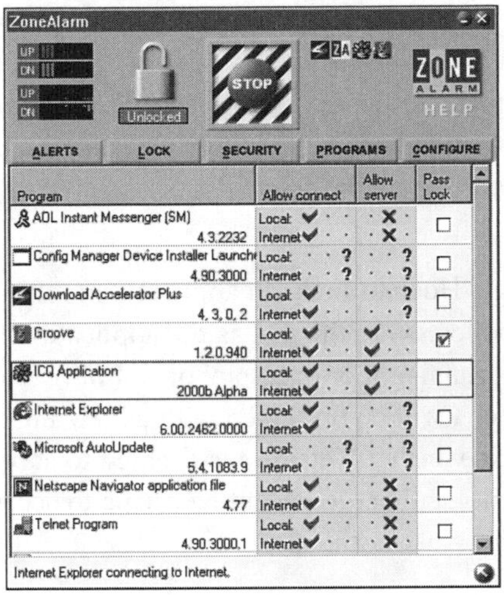

FIGURE 7.7

The ZoneAlarm Programs panel.

The Programs panel enables you to define the access rights for each individual application on your computer that accesses the Internet. In this panel, you can define whether a program can access the Internet, or a local area network called your Local Zone.

In this table, each application is listed, along with the permission for it to access the Internet and your Local Zone. The three possible settings are Allow, Disallow and Ask. Allow, signified by the green check mark, permits the application to access the Internet or Local Zone. Disallow, denoted by a red X, prevents the corresponding application to access the Internet or Local Zone. The final setting, Ask, represented by a question mark, asks you for the current appropriate action (Allow or Disallow).

Additionally, each application is configured on whether it can act as a server. Again, the three settings are Allow, Disallow, and Ask. When an application is allowed to be a server, it is allowed to wait for connection requests and allow outside entities to connect to the application. Use this setting cautiously, as a poorly developed server application can become a potential opportunity for intruders to gain access to your computer. Permit only well-known applications to become servers. In most cases, when a security flaw is found in a well-developed server, security patches are published as soon as a security hole is found.

7

USING PERSONAL FIREWALL SOFTWARE

An application can also be configured to bypass the Automatic Internet Lock. The Automatic Internet Lock is applied to the firewall whenever your computer is connected to the Internet and not being used (idle). This prevents intrusion and access to the computer when unattended. When applied, the Automatic Lock does not allow any applications to connect to the Internet except for those applications that have been configured to bypass the lock. The Automatic Internet Lock is useful for allowing servers to continue to connect to the Internet even when you are away from the computer. It must be noted that the Automatic Lock is not the same as the Internet Lock. The Automatic Internet Lock is applied automatically, whereas the Internet Lock is applied manually. More about the Internet Lock will be discussed when the Lock panel is discussed.

But now you must be asking, "How do I add an application to this Programs list?" Good question! ZoneAlarm adds an application to this list as the application first tries to access the Internet while ZoneAlarm is running. For example, once I have ZoneAlarm running, the first time I run Netscape Navigator I will be presented with a New Program Alert dialog box, as shown in Figure 7.8, that asks whether Netscape is enabled to access the Internet and whether ZoneAlarm will remember this setting. To permit Netscape to access the Internet, I select Yes and select the Remember This Answer the Next Time I Use This Program option.

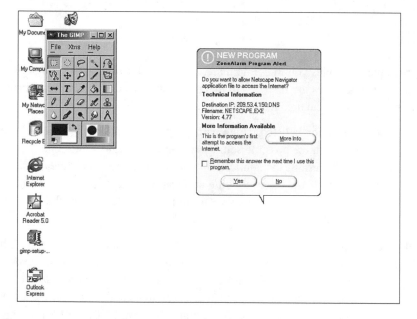

FIGURE 7.8

The New Program Alert dialog box.

Consequently, when a server program first accesses the Internet, you are presented with a Server Program Alert dialog box. As shown in Figure 7.9, the Groove application is trying to act as a server.

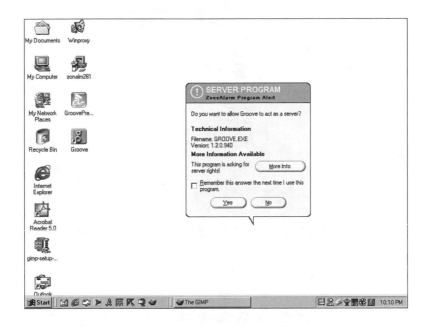

FIGURE 7.9
The Server Program Alert dialog box.

In cases when you do not select the Remember This Answer the Next Time I Use This Program option, when an application tries to access the Internet for a second time, you are presented with a Repeat Program Alert, as displayed in Figure 7.10. If you no longer want to receive these Program Alerts, you need to either select the Remember This Answer the Next Time I Use This Program option or configure this application's permissions in the Programs panel.

Security Panel

To the left of the Programs panel is the Security panel. The first thing that stands out in this panel is the Stop button. The Stop button is for emergencies, in cases when you know someone or an application is accessing your computer without your authorization. When the Stop button is clicked, the transmission of all data is immediately prevented from traveling through the firewall.

Like the other panels, when the Security button on the Security panel is clicked, the expanded Security Settings panel is displayed, as shown in Figure 7.11.

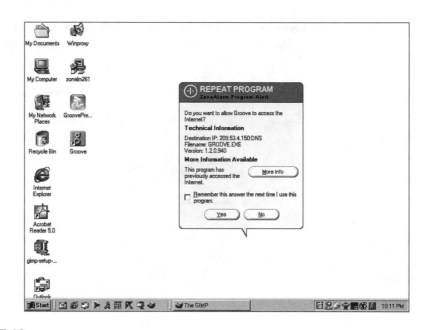

FIGURE 7.10

The Repeat Program Alert dialog box.

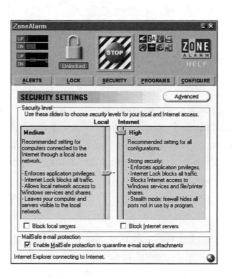

FIGURE 7.11

The expanded Security Settings panel.

This panel contains what Zone Labs calls the security level selector. Zone Labs has made the configuration of the ZoneAlarm firewall simpler by grouping security mechanisms together. ZoneAlarm has three group security settings: High, Medium, and Low.

- High security includes enforcing program and application access permissions, blocking all traffic when the Internet Lock is enabled, blocking access to all window services and sharing, and places the firewall in stealth mode, hiding all ports that are not in use.
- Medium security includes enforcing program and application access permissions, blocking all traffic when the Internet Lock is applied, blocking all access to all window services and sharing, but leaves your computer visible to the Internet.
- Low security includes only enforcing program access permissions and Internet Lock settings, the Internet Lock only blocks application traffic, granting access to windows services and sharing, and leaves your computer visible to the Internet.

ZoneAlarm also creates two security zones. The Local Zone consists of the computers on your local area network, and any computers you want to manually add. The Internet Zone consists of all computers not in the Local Zone. You must be very cautious in adding computers to your Local Zone, as this provides the added computers with potentially more access to your computer. Of course, the differentiation between the Local Zone and the Internet Zone can be configured. If you prefer that the Local and Internet Zones have the same High security settings, it can be configured this way. However, the separation enables you to give more access to computers that you trust. By default, the Internet Zone is given High security and the Local Zone is given Medium security.

Note that cable modem users should not lower their security setting below Medium. Cable networks are implemented by creating local area networks with their neighbors. Setting your Local Zone to Low would grant your neighbors access to your computer.

In addition to the security level selector, the Security panel provides an Advanced menu that enables you to add computers to your Local Zone. The Security panel also provides the following three optional choices:

- Block local servers: This blocks all application servers from accessing the Local Zone.
- Block Internet servers: This blocks all application servers from accessing the Internet Zone.
- Enable MailSafe: Enables filtering of e-mails containing scripts.

The two blocking options permit you to easily stop servers from accessing the Internet; however, application servers can be individually configured in the Program panel.

Lock Panel

The information display to the left of Security is the Lock panel. The Lock enables you to control access for data traveling in and out of your computer. You can manually lock and unlock your computer by clicking on the large Lock button on the top of the Lock panel.

- When locked, the Lock is graphically locked and the box is red. In this mode, no data can travel in or out of your computer.
- When unlocked, the Lock is graphically unlocked and the box is green. In this mode, data can travel in and out of your computer. The data travel is limited to your program configuration settings.

Again, when you select the Lock button, the Lock Panel expands, as seen in Figure 7.12. In the Lock panel, you can configure how the Automatic Lock is run. The Automatic Lock is an automatic lock that turns on when your computer is inactive. However, if your application has Pass Lock enabled (from the Programs Panel), the program can continue to access the Internet even while an Automatic Lock is applied. The Pass Lock setting does not work with a manually set Lock.

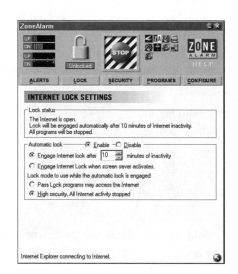

FIGURE 7.12
The ZoneAlarm Lock panel.

Alerts Panel

Finally, the far left panel, titled Alerts, displays the current Internet activity. The two sets of graphs show the data traveling through the firewall to the Internet. The red bar shows data sent to the Internet, whereas the green bar shows the data being received from the Internet. The top graph shows the current live activity through the firewall, and the bottom graph shows the past history of activity.

When you click the Alerts button, the expanded Alerts panel is displayed, as seen in Figure 7.13. This panel displays the total amount of data traffic passing through the firewall. An Alert is a notification to you that an unknown outside entity has tried to access your computer, or an application from your computer has tried to access the Internet without permission.

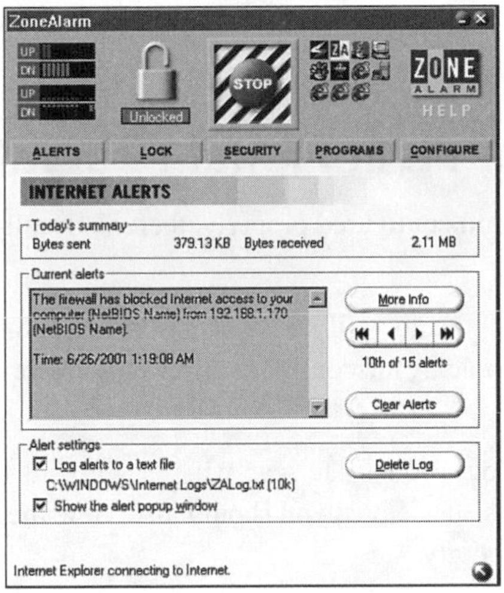

FIGURE 7.13

The ZoneAlarm Alerts panel.

A list of current alerts is provided for review in the Alert panel. In addition, a log file is configured in this panel and is kept to store all Alerts. The purpose of this is to let you review the past Alert history of the firewall and determine who has been attempting to access your computer. By default, all the preceding Alert settings are on, and should be kept on.

In addition to this panel, ZoneAlarm will sometimes display an Alert window as shown in Figure 7.14. This window warns the user of intrusions as they occur.

Now that we have reviewed all the parts of the configuration of ZoneAlarm, you're ready to configure your firewall. ZoneAlarm is by default configured in such a way as to provide security for your system.

If you choose a different firewall, you now have a good idea what is required to configure a firewall. In most cases, firewalls are preconfigured to be in a secure state.

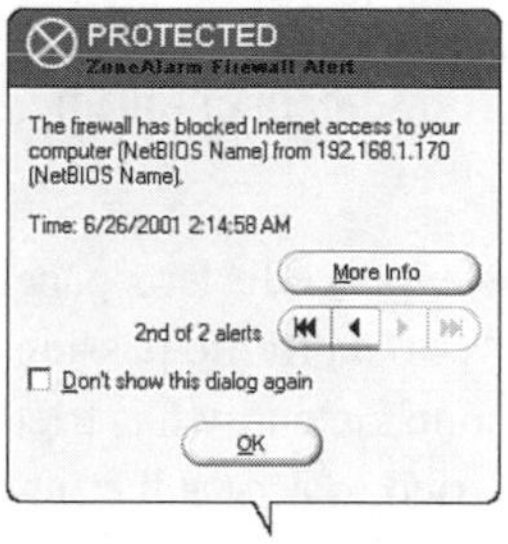

FIGURE 7.14
The ZoneAlarm Alert Window.

How to Maintain a Personal Firewall

After a firewall is installed and configured properly, there is usually little maintenance required to keep it running.

However, it is always a good idea to verify your firewall configuration, especially if your computer is used by multiple people. A misconfigured firewall can create security holes and make your system less usable.

Also, check the Alerts page occasionally to scan what or who has been trying to access your computer. If something looks suspicious, you should also view the alerts security log and look for a pattern of suspicious activity.

Finally, firewalls must be continually updated to be fully effective. They are similar to antivirus software packages, in that when attackers devise new methods to gain access to your computer or reduce your network connectivity, patches or updates must be downloaded and applied to your firewall to increase protection.

Maintaining ZoneAlarm

Specific to ZoneAlarm, Zone Labs has a Security Resource Center located at http://www.zonelabs.com/CS/security.html. This page provides you with updates and a collection of documents that can help increase your security knowledge.

Additionally, another useful support document for ZoneAlarm is the Service and Support FAQ page, located at http://www.zonelabs.com/services/support_za_all_faq.htm and the full user manual for ZoneAlarm can be found at http://www.zonelabs.com/zonealarm/help/ZoneAlarmHelp.htm.

It is always important to remember to review what is accessing your computer by viewing your Alerts and Alert log. Furthermore, it is not a bad idea to run the Automatic Lock when the computer is not in use.

CHAPTER 7

Summary

In this chapter you learned how to choose, configure, and maintain a personal firewall software application. Hopefully it has shown that setting up a personal firewall is simple, and that it can provide a high level of security. However, it must be remembered that just running a personal firewall is not enough. To provide protection, a personal security firewall must be properly configured and maintained, and the users of the computer system must continue to practice secure computing.

The next chapter covers viruses and the dangers found on the Internet. This is an important partner to firewall protection because firewalls can only protect your computer's perimeter from outside intruders; virus protection provides security against intrusion from the inside by rogue programs.

7

USING PERSONAL
FIREWALL
SOFTWARE

The Dangers of Viruses on the Internet

IN THIS CHAPTER

In This Chapter

To understand how to keep your computer—and all the information stored in it—healthy and virus-free, you must understand the danger that viruses and other malicious programs pose to computers. This chapter provides an overview of the dangers of viruses on the Internet.

What Is a Malicious Program?

A malicious program, or *malware* (malicious-logic software), is designed to attach itself to other programs and replicate. Three main types of malicious programs are as follows:

- Trojan horse
- Worm
- Virus

Although all malicious programs have properties in common, namely, that they are designed for the purpose of doing something bad, they do not all act in the same manner or have the same purpose.

What Is a Trojan Horse?

This type of malicious code is named a *Trojan horse* after the original Trojan horse from Greek Mythology. This type of program pretends to be something else (possibly a game or other executable program) and lures you into running it, so that it can perform some malicious act on your machine. Trojan horse programs do not spread from one computer to another, unlike worms and viruses. However, a Trojan horse program is dangerous nonetheless. When activated, this type of malicious program can do a number of destructive deeds—depending on its purpose—such as deleting files from your computer, or creating an entry point to your computer from which others can gain access to your machine, much like a back door into your computer.

> **NOTE**
>
> For more information about Trojan horse programs, see the following Web site:
> `http://www.networkice.com/Advice/Phauna/Trojan_Horse/default.htm`.

What Is a Worm?

Like a virus, a worm is a self-replicating malicious program. However, the purpose of a worm is not to infect, alter, or delete files. A worm lives in a computer's memory and copies itself to and from floppy disks or over network connections. Worms use up a computer or network's resources, and can go unnoticed until they have consumed system resources to the point where other tasks are slowed or stopped.

Types of Viruses

Although thousands of viruses roam machines and networks all over the world, most have common traits that can be categorized into one of the following groups:

- Boot sector viruses
- File infector viruses
- Macro viruses

NOTE

There are many possible additions and exceptions to these categories of viruses, such as *multipartite* viruses, which are a combination of boot sector and file infector viruses.

What These Viruses Do

Virus code must be executed in order to have any effect. As such, data files are not capable of infecting your computer. That means that opening a text file (.txt), a sound file (.mp3), or simply viewing a graphics file (.jpg, .gif) will not cause your computer to become infected with the virus. The following sections list the categories of viruses, with a brief explanation of what the viruses do.

Boot Sector Viruses

Boot sector viruses—also known as infectors—only live in specific parts of a computer known as the *boot sector*. The boot sector of a hard drive is the area where files and programs (executables) are stored to be read and executed by the computer when it is turned on. The virus sits in the boot sector of your computer's hard drive and gets loaded into memory, before the system files are loaded, when the computer is restarted or turned on. The virus can also delete or move the original contents from the boot sector.

File Infector Viruses

File infector viruses, or parasitic viruses, attach themselves to an executable file. File infectors usually infect files with the following extensions: .com, .exe, .drv, .bin, .ovl, .sys. These viruses are activated whenever an infected file is executed (opened), and will copy themselves into other executable files.

Macro Viruses

Macro viruses account for the majority of viruses today. This group is not only the largest, but also the fastest growing virus type. Macro viruses are transmitted primarily through e-mail attachments, but are also transmitted through floppy disks, file transfers, and Web downloads.

The reason macro viruses are so widespread is because they do not require a specific operating system, such as Microsoft Windows 98 or Unix. However, macro viruses are program (or application) specific. Therefore, a Microsoft Word macro virus will infect other Word documents, but will not be able to infect a Microsoft Access document.

Macro viruses can infect all open files in the same application, and can eventually infect all files of that type on your machine if left undetected. Depending on the specifics of the virus, macro viruses can infect your files at varying times during the file's use, such as when the file is opened, closed, saved, or deleted. Unfortunately, this type of virus is very easy to create using Visual Basic (VB) .

How Do You Get a Virus?

Most viruses today are transmitted through the Internet. The macro virus is the fastest spreading virus because it is usually transferred from machine to machine via e-mail attachments. However, viruses can also be transmitted through floppy disks, file transfers, and Web downloads. In addition, macro viruses infect all open files of a specific application.

Therefore, if your machine has a Microsoft Word macro virus, it will infect all Word documents that are open on your machine. If you save those infected files to a floppy disk, you will transfer the infection along with the file when you copy it to another hard drive, or open it on another machine using the same application.

In addition, using the Web to download files is another common way to get a virus. Sites that allow users to share information over the Internet, such as Napster and Gnutella, are a potential breeding ground for computer viruses, much like real-world viruses breed in high traffic areas such as malls and schools.

CAUTION

It is possible for your computer to be infected with a virus through HTML documents containing JavaScript or another type of executable code, such as ActiveX.

How Do You Avoid a Virus?

The best way to avoid getting a computer virus is to be careful. It is always better to be safe than sorry. All of these typically cliché phrases are practical ways to approach computer safety.

In order to protect your computer, and all the valuable data stored in it, you need to install antivirus software and use it. This topic is covered in detail in Chapter 9, "Vaccinating Your Computer Against Viruses." Without antivirus software, you really have no way of knowing what you are putting on your machine when you open an e-mail attachment or download a file from a file-sharing Web site.

But just having antivirus software is not enough. According to Cyber Sentry (`www.cyber-sentry.com`), an online virus protection provider, over 600 variant and new viruses are created and released over the Internet each month. As a result, you need to be able to update your software regularly to catch all the different strains of viruses.

In addition, you need to have a preventative attitude towards viruses. It isn't enough to maintain up-to-date software. You need to think of every attachment that gets to your inbox as a potential threat to the security of your system and/or network. Instead of randomly opening every attachment that crosses your path and opening yourself up to attacks from viruses, a better approach is to open only those attachments that are expected, and are scanned by Anti-Virus software before they are opened.

Beyond the steps outlined previously, you need to be aware of attachments with the following extensions: .com, .exe, .drv, .bin, .ovl, .sys. These files are generally the ones that can be infected with, and carry, viruses. But just watching out for the file extension isn't enough either because macro viruses are transmitted through application files.

8

THE DANGERS OF VIRUSES ON THE INTERNET

TIP

If you use Microsoft applications and want to prevent against the threat of macro viruses, be sure that the Macro Virus Protection is ON. Doing so will prevent the application from automatically executing the virus code, by turning off the macro auto-execute feature (which is ON by default). You can turn on Macro Virus Protection in Word 97 by opening the Tools menu, Options window, General tab, and setting virus protection to ON. For Word 2000, open the Tools menu, Macro sub-menu, Security window, and set your macro security to Medium or High.

Another potential virus problem has to do with certain e-mail programs, such as Outlook Express. Some of these e-mail programs are configured by default to automatically execute VB scripts. But these VB scripts can be viruses, or contain viruses within them. This was the case with the "I Love You" virus. Users would download the e-mail to their computer and open it in an e-mail program, and the software would automatically open the virus that was attached to the e-mail. This is very similar to the way macro viruses work. To prevent the software from automatically opening attachments, change the settings in Outlook and other e-mail programs.

TIP

To learn more about the potential security holes in Outlook 98 and 2000, and to download the security patch, visit the following Web site: http://www.zdnet.com/zdhelp/stories/main/0,5594,2585925,00.html.

The Melissa Virus

The W97M/Melissa.A virus, also know as the Melissa virus, was first discovered on March 26, 1999. The Melissa virus is a macro virus that infects Microsoft Word documents using VBA (Visual Basic for Applications). Once your machine has contracted the Melissa virus, it has three main actions: the Melissa virus will infect Microsoft Word and all Word documents that are open; the virus will alter the Normal.dot document template file to increase the ease of infection; and the virus uses Microsoft Outlook to e-mail the virus to addresses in your address book.

By altering the Normal.dot file, the Melissa virus ensures its survival. By changing this file, the virus guarantees that your Word installation is infected, which in turn will infect future documents or templates that you create. In addition, this change to the document template file will cause the virus code to be executed each time you open or close a document.

You can visit the following Web site for more information on the Melissa virus, how to protect your computer from this virus, and what to do if your machine is infected: http://www.zdnet.com/zdnn/stories/news/0,4586,2233116,00.html.

The Melissa virus affected many people across the world in a very short period of time because of its capability to send out e-mails bearing your name to e-mail addresses stored in your address book. As a result, many company networks were forced to shut down because of the enormous volume of e-mails that were being sent in and out of the computers. This virus even had the power to cause havoc in the home offices of the Microsoft Corporation.

Although this virus did not delete any data from computers, it did drastically slow down networks—causing many to come to a grinding halt—and the virus was difficult to get rid of because of the number of files it infected and because of the changes the virus made to the Microsoft Word settings.

The History of Viruses

The first viruses were reported in the mid-1980s. At that time, neither computers nor the Internet were readily available for the public yet. But back in 1986, several people separately created the first viruses.

Two people going by the names Amjad and Basit discovered a way to take advantage of the fact that a boot disk contains executable code that is run whenever a computer is started up with a disk. They replaced this code with their own, creating a memory resident program that could install a copy of itself onto any 360kb disk that the computer accessed. They called this program a virus, though it was rather harmless.

At the same time, a programmer by the name of Ralf Burger created a virus named VIRDEM, after realizing that a file could be made to copy itself and attach that copy to other files. VIRDEM would copy and attach itself to any .COM file, but VIRDEM was also fairly harmless.

In the next few years, many others created their own viruses. Vienna, Charlie, and Israel (also called Italy) were three of the more familiar viruses created during that time. But it wasn't until the late 1980's that viruses began to be recognized for their potential harm. At that time, personal computers became more widespread in businesses, homes, and college campuses. In addition, people began to use dial-up modems to connect to bulletin boards to download games and other programs. This was when the potential for spreading viruses began to rapidly increase, thus driving more people to create viruses.

Virus Hoaxes

A virus hoax is a false threat created by someone with the intent of playing on peoples' fears and lack of knowledge about viruses. Usually, when someone hears about a virus—whether it is real or not—they automatically forward a warning message to every e-mail address in their address book. Although this seems like the right thing to do (I know I'm guilty of this), it isn't. What this does is slow down the Internet or network you are using, propagates someone's false threat, and gives a sense of satisfaction to the person, or persons, who created the phony threat.

How to Find Out If You've Got a Virus Hoax

Instead of just forwarding the warning on, it would be better to go to a virus hoax Web site, where thousands of real and hoax viruses are listed in a virus database or on a virus bulletin, and verify (or disprove) the validity of the claim. The following Web sites have a database of known viruses and/or a virus hoax bulletin:

- http://www.virus.com/

- http://www.virusbtn.com/

- http://www.mcafee.com/anti-virus/default.asp?

- http://www.symantec.com/avcenter/hoax.html

- http://www.vmyths.com/

- http://www.datafellows.com/v-descs/

Summary

This chapter provides you with the basic understanding of what malicious programs are, what they do, and how they are transmitted. While all malicious programs have similarities, the three main types are the Trojan horse, Worm, and Virus. The Virus is the most common, but all malicious programs have the potential to cause harm to your machine or your data.

The next chapter discusses how to vaccinate your computer against viruses. In this chapter you learned about viruses and other malicious programs, what they are, the different types, the history of viruses, and also about virus hoaxes. In the next chapter, you will learn how to vaccinate your computer. This will include discussions on what types of antivirus software are available, and how to install and configure your antivirus software.

Vaccinating Your Computer Against Viruses

IN THIS CHAPTER

In This Chapter

In the previous chapter, you learned about the dangers of viruses on the Internet. This chapter will give you an understanding of antivirus software, and will help you develop a plan for preventing viruses from infecting your computer.

In this chapter you will learn about the following topics:

- Scanning techniques
- Antivirus software packages
- Installation and configuration of antivirus software

Scanning Techniques

When using antivirus software, there are several scanning strategies. *Background scanning* is the scanning of a file (or e-mail) whenever it is opened or closed. Background scanning is a useful "everyday" virus protection strategy. *Full scanning* involves the scanning of all files and programs on your hard drive. This process is far more time- and resource-consuming because the antivirus software scans everything on your machine, and requires a significant amount of system memory and processing power. As a result, full scanning is usually done occasionally, such as once a week or at the end of the month.

Most antivirus software used for home computing is now *transparent*. This means that the program goes about its business with little or no input from the user. The program is generally always on, but sitting idle on your machine waiting for a file to be scanned. By making the antivirus program transparent to the user, the intention is to simplify the product and thereby make it easier to use.

Virus Signatures

Generally, antivirus programs require updates to ensure that the software is current and capable of discovering viruses when they arrive on your machine. In order to have the best possible defense against viruses—and other malicious programs—it is essential to have the latest *virus signatures*, also called virus definitions. Virus signatures are identifiers that the antivirus software uses to search for viruses on your machine. Many antivirus software companies have a database of known viruses that are usually updated daily, or weekly, on their Web sites. Because hundreds of new viruses are found every month, it is vital that your antivirus program is updated for new signatures often.

There are several methods of updating the virus signatures for your antivirus software from a company's Web site. Depending on the software you are using, you can choose from the following:

- Auto-update: Enabling this feature will enable the antivirus software to automatically visit the appropriate Web site, check for any new virus threats, and then update your software with new virus signatures.

- Remind: By enabling this feature and setting up a designated reminder time, the antivirus software will ensure that you don't forget to visit the Web site to check for new virus signatures.

- Manual: This feature requires that the user remember to check regularly for updates on the Web site. This feature is used occasionally in addition to the auto-update or remind feature.

Antivirus Software Packages

Many different antivirus software packages are being offered these days, and many companies are using the Internet to sell their antivirus software. Some companies offer their software in two formats: packaged (delivered) and downloadable. The following is a list of some of the better-known antivirus packages currently available.

Norton AntiVirus 2001 PRO

Norton AntiVirus 2001 PRO is a comprehensive antivirus software package that includes automatic updating of virus definitions. Norton AntiVirus also protects your computer from Internet and e-mail viruses by scanning files you download, and e-mail attachments before they are opened on your machine. This product sells for $59.95 on the Symantec Web site (http://www.symantec.com), or $39.95 for an upgrade.

McAfee VirusScan 5.16

McAfee VirusScan 5.16 is a complete antivirus solution. This product can detect ActiveX and Java applets that are unknowingly downloaded from the Internet, and will quarantine infected and suspicious files to prevent further spreading of viruses. In addition, this product can be easily updated from the Web site. VirusScan 5.16 sells for $29.95 on the McAfee Web site (http://www.mcafee.com).

F-Secure Anti-Virus for Workstations 5.22

F-Secure Anti-Virus for Workstations 5.22 uses multiple scanning engines to ensure the safety of your computer or network. F-Secure Anti-Virus automatically updates virus signatures daily. F-Secure can be purchased from the Web site (http://www.datafellows.com), at a cost of $125.00 for 1 license. Although this product is suitable for a standalone computer, it includes advanced features such as setting the User Interface, which are more suited for a network of computers.

Dr. Solomon's Anti-Virus 8.5

Dr. Solomon's Anti-Virus 8.5 takes advantage of automatic virus detection and deletion to protect your computer. Dr. Solomon's Anti-Virus also detects ActiveX and Java applets that are
unknowingly downloaded from the Internet to keep your computer safe from harm. This
antivirus product sells for $29.95 on the Web site (http://www.mcafee.com).

Installation and Configuration of Antivirus Software

Although many adequate antivirus programs are currently available, the following section will
only cover the installation of Norton AntiVirus 2001 PRO and McAfee VirusScan 5.16.

Installation and Configuration of Norton AntiVirus 2001 PRO

To install Norton AntiVirus, run the setup program. If you are using the CD-ROM version,
simply insert the disk and the setup program will auto-run. If the setup program doesn't auto-
run from the CD-ROM, open the setup file from your CD drive. If you are using the downloaded version, you can open the installation program by accessing it from the location on your
hard drive where you originally saved the download. By default, this file is located in the
Windows directory in the Vbox subdirectory.

TIP

You can download a free trial version of Norton AntiVirus 2001 at http://
software.symantec.com/dr/v2/ec_dynamic.main?cat_id=7&pn=16&sid=27674.

Installing Norton AntiVirus

To install Norton AntiVirus, use the following steps:

1. Run the installation program from the CD-ROM, or open the file from your hard drive.
    The name of the installation file is Setup, with the following default path (on your hard
    drive, using C as your default drive letter): C:\WINDOWS\Vbox\Installers\
    Symantec_Norton AntiVirus 2001_7.0_en-us\Nav9xME

2. Before installation will begin, you must accept the License Agreement by clicking the
    Yes button at the bottom of the installation window, as illustrated in Figure 9.1.

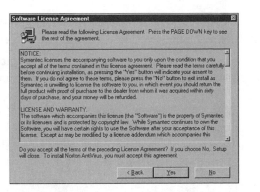

FIGURE 9.1

The Software License Agreement.

3. You will be prompted to begin installation by selecting the location where you want the program to be stored, as shown in Figure 9.2. The default location is: C:\Program Files\ Norton AntiVirus. You can change the location of the antivirus program by clicking the Browse button. Otherwise, click the Next button to continue the installation to the default destination folder.

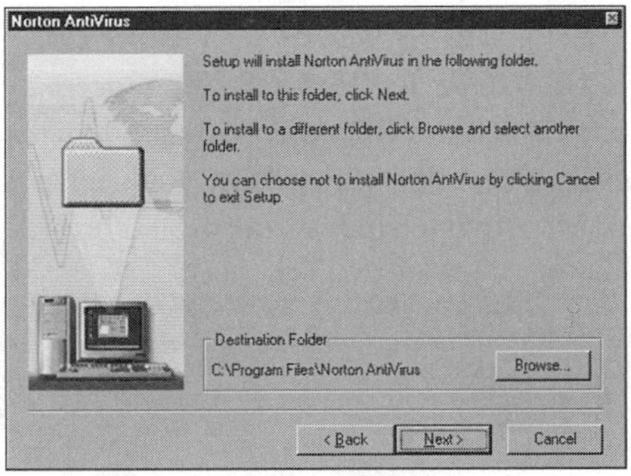

FIGURE 9.2

The Destination Folder.

4. Figure 9.3 illustrates the next screen during installation, which provides the following options:

- Enable Auto-Protect at startup (Recommended)—This option will enable the antivirus software to continually watch over your computer for viruses and other malicious code.

- Schedule weekly scans of local hard drives—This option provides additional protection by automatically scanning your entire system once a week.
- Scan at startup—This option enables Norton AntiVirus to automatically scan critical files and memory for viruses every time you start your computer.

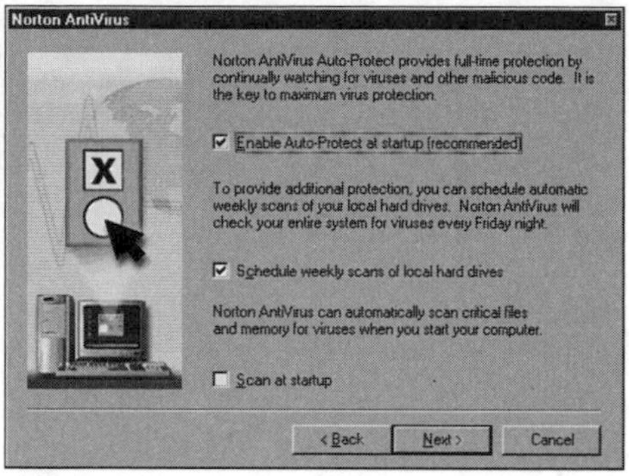

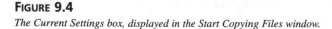

FIGURE 9.3

Select the options you want installed.

5. After you have selected the option(s) you want to activate on the antivirus program, click the Next button to continue with the installation process.

6. At this point, you are asked to begin the installation process by clicking the Next button after you verify the current settings from the Current Settings box, from within the Start Copying Files window as shown in Figure 9.4. If you decide that you want to change any of the settings or options on the previous installation screens, click the Back button.

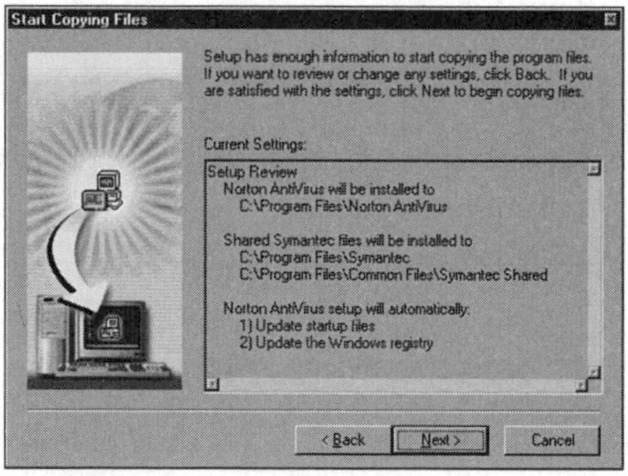

FIGURE 9.4

The Current Settings box, displayed in the Start Copying Files window.

7. At this point, Norton will begin the installation of AntiVirus on your machine. During the installation process, you will be prompted to register your copy of Norton AntiVirus, as demonstrated in Figure 9.5. You have the choice to complete the registration process or skip it entirely. If you choose to skip the registration process, you will be prompted to verify your selection. Click Yes to continue.

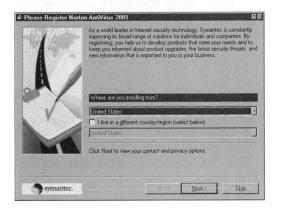

FIGURE 9.5
Norton AntiVirus 2001 Registration window.

8. Figure 9.6 illustrates the following prompt (after registration) that asks you to Enable E-mail Protection by checking the box. This feature will enable the antivirus software to scan your e-mails before they are delivered to your machine.

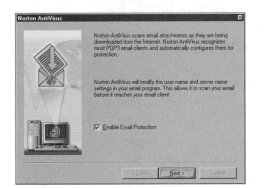

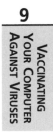

FIGURE 9.6
Enable Email Protection prompt.

9

VACCINATING
YOUR COMPUTER
AGAINST VIRUSES

9. The next screen asks you to Enable Automatic LiveUpdate at Startup, as shown in Figure 9.7; if selected, you are required to choose how LiveUpdate works by selecting either Apply Updates Without Interrupting me, or Notify Me When Updates Are Available.

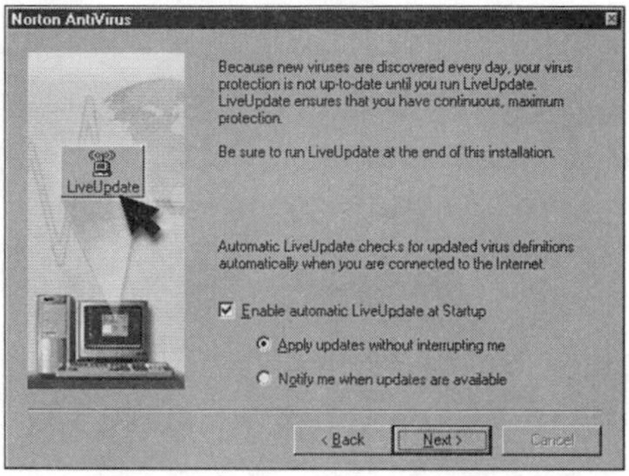

FIGURE 9.7

Enabling LiveUpdate prompt.

10. The screen shown in Figure 9.8 has two options (after you choose, click Next to continue):

- Create a Norton AntiVirus Shortcut on My Desktop—This option will place a shortcut icon on your desktop that will enable you to access the program more easily.

- View the Readme File when Setup Is Done—This option will automatically open the Readme file when the installation process is completed.

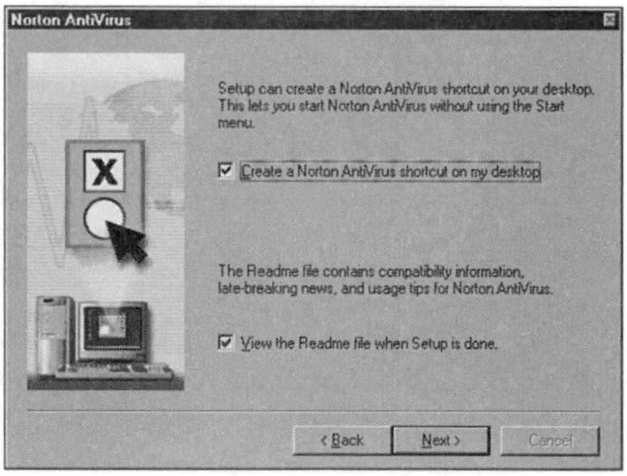

FIGURE 9.8

Create a Norton AntiVirus shortcut on the desktop and view the Readme file when the setup is done.

11. The screen illustrated in Figure 9.9 prompts you to select the following recommended options (click Next to continue):

- Run LiveUpdate After Installation: LiveUpdate is used to download new virus signatures and updates to Norton AntiVirus through the Internet from Symantec.

- Create a Rescue Disk Set: A rescue disk set can be used to check your system for viruses where you can't, or don't want to, boot your system directly. Instead, you can boot from the rescue disk set and scan your system.

- Scan for Viruses after Restart: Scanning for viruses after restarting your computer is a good way to ensure that your system is clean before using it.

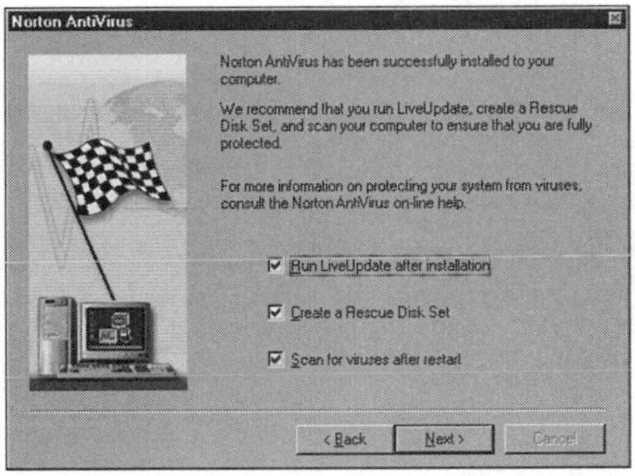

FIGURE 9.9
Recommended Options prompt.

12. The final step in the installation process is to select what to do after the installation is complete, in the Setup Complete window. You are prompted to choose either Yes, I Want to Restart My Computer Now or No, I Will Restart My Computer Later, as demonstrated in Figure 9.10. Before the program can begin protecting your machine from viruses, you must restart your computer.

CAUTION

You must restart your computer at some point after the installation process to activate the antivirus software.

13. Click the Finish button to complete the installation of Norton AntiVirus.

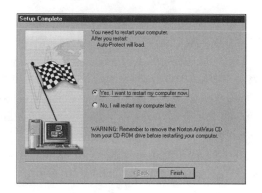

FIGURE 9.10
The Setup Complete window.

TIP

You can uninstall Norton AntiVirus at any time by selecting Uninstall Norton AntiVirus from the following default location: Start Menu/Programs/Norton AntiVirus/Uninstall Norton AntiVirus.

Configuring Norton AntiVirus

After you have installed Norton AntiVirus, there are several steps you can take to ensure that your software is up-to-date and running efficiently. This section deals with configuring your Norton AntiVirus software. Specifically, you will learn how to do the following:

- Configure automatic scans
- Perform a one-time scan
- Update virus signature files

TIP

If the Norton AntiVirus icon is present in the system tray (next to the clock on the Start bar), you can right-click on the icon and select Open Norton AntiVirus to open the Norton AntiVirus window, or select Configure Norton AntiVirus to open the Options for Norton AntiVirus window. This method is faster than opening the program from the Start menu and Programs sub-menu.

How to Configure Automatic Scans

To enable the automatic scanning feature, click the Start menu, activate the Programs menu, activate the Norton AntiVirus menu, and select Norton AntiVirus 2001. From the Norton AntiVirus window, click the Options button. The Options for Norton AntiVirus window will appear. Select Auto-Protect from the System options tree in the left side of the window. Make sure that the following options are checked in the right side of the window:

- Start Auto-Protect when Windows starts up (recommended)
- Run or opened
- Created or downloaded

Setting the preceding options will enable Norton AntiVirus to perform a scan of files when they are run, opened, created, or downloaded. Click the OK button to end automatic scan configuration.

How to Perform a One-Time Scan

To perform a scan of your system at any time, click the Start menu, activate the Programs menu, activate the Norton AntiVirus menu, and select Norton AntiVirus 2001. From the Norton AntiVirus window, click the Scan for Viruses option. From the right side of the screen, select the appropriate icon from the What Do You Want to Scan? window. You can scan your hard drive, a disk in the floppy drive, or selected files and folders on your machine. To begin the scan, click the Run Scan Now button at the bottom of the window.

How to Update Virus Signature Files

To update the virus signature files, as well as any other Norton AntiVirus components, click the Start menu, activate the Programs menu, activate the Norton AntiVirus menu, and select Norton AntiVirus 2001. From the Norton AntiVirus window, click the LiveUpdate button. The Welcome to LiveUpdate window will appear to guide you through the update process; click the Next button to advance. The software will search for updates and will install the updates if necessary. If Norton AntiVirus determines that updates are available, you can click the Next button to begin updating. After the installation is complete, click the OK button to end the installation process.

Installation and Configuration of McAfee VirusScan 5.16

To install McAfee VirusScan, run the setup program. If you are using the CD-ROM version, simply insert the disk and the setup program will auto-run. If the setup program doesn't auto-run from the CD-ROM, open the setup file from your CD drive. If you are using the downloaded version, you can open the installation program by accessing it from the location on your hard drive where you originally saved the download.

> **TIP**
>
> You can download a free trial version of McAfee VirusScan 5.1 and read a product review at the CNET Web site: `http://download.cnet.com/downloads/0-10093-108-16992.html`; or you can download a trial version directly from the McAfee Web site: `http://download.mcafee.com/eval/evaluate2.asp`

McAfee VirusScan uses an InstallShield Wizard to guide you through the installation process.

Installing McAfee VirusScan

To install McAfee VirusScan, use the following steps:

1. Run the installation program from the CD-ROM, or open the file from your hard drive. The name of the installation file is Setup. If you are using the trial or downloaded version, open the application from its location on your hard drive (where you originally saved it to).

2. You will be prompted to begin installation by selecting the location where you want the program to be stored, as shown in Figure 9.11. The default location is: C:\Program Files\ McAfee VirusScan. You can change the location of the antivirus program by clicking the Change button. Otherwise, click the Next button to continue the installation to the default destination folder.

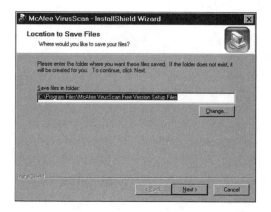

FIGURE 9.11
Location to Save Files window.

3. You are then prompted to review the Product Information window, as illustrated in Figure 9.12. You must click the Next button to advance.

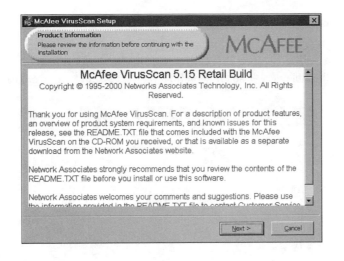

FIGURE 9.12

The Product Information window.

4. Figure 9.13 illustrates the License Agreement window. You must accept the License Agreement by clicking the I Agree to the Terms of the License Agreement option at the bottom of the installation window before you can continue. Then click the Next button to advance.

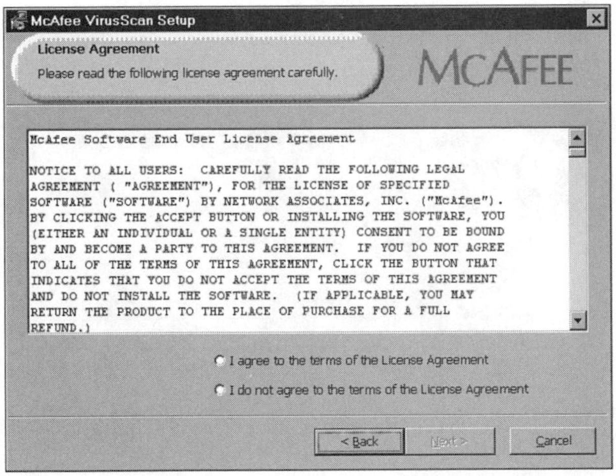

FIGURE 9.13

The License Agreement window.

5. Now you must choose the Setup Type, as shown in Figure 9.14:

- Typical Installation— This is the recommended choice, and selecting this will install the most commonly used features.

- Custom Installation —This is recommended for advanced users, and selecting this option will enable you to select which features to install and where to install them.

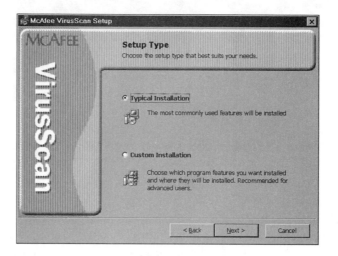

FIGURE 9.14

Setup Type window.

6. Figure 9.15 demonstrates the Ready to Install the Program window. Click Install to continue with the installation process.

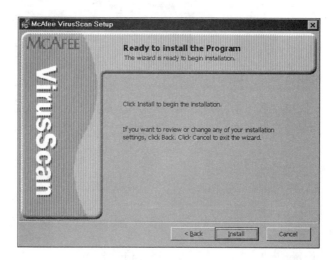

FIGURE 9.15

Ready to Install the Program prompt.

> **TIP**

You can press the Back button to change or review any of the installation settings.

7. After VirusScan is installed, the Completing the McAfee VirusScan Setup Wizard window will pop up, as shown in Figure 9.16. You must now click the Configure button to complete the installation process, or you can skip the configuration step by clicking the Skip Config button.

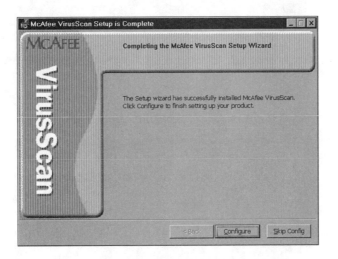

FIGURE 9.16

McAfee VirusScan Setup Is Complete window.

8. During VirusScan configuration, you will be prompted to set the Scan at Startup option, as illustrated in Figure 9.17. Click the box next to Scan Boot Record at Startup to activate this option. Then click Next to continue with the configuration process.

9. The next VirusScan Configuration screen, shown in Figure 9.18, provides the following options:

   • Safe & Sound—This option will enable the antivirus software to create a backup of all files in use. Click the box next to Configure Safe & Sound to activate this feature.

   • VirusScan Maintenance—This enables the software to Run VirusScan Update and Create a Rescue Disk Set. By selecting these two options, you will further protect your computer from viruses and other malicious programs.

9

VACCINATING
YOUR COMPUTER
AGAINST VIRUSES

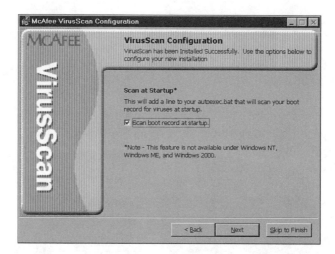

FIGURE 9.17

Scan at Startup option.

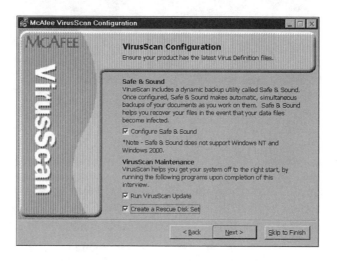

FIGURE 9.18

Options prompt.

10. Click the Next button to continue. You can click Back to return to the previous screen, or click the Skip to Finish button to skip the configuration process.

11. Figure 9.19 illustrates the Enable McAfee VirusScan Protection option. Click the box next to this option to enable it. Click Finish to complete the installation and configuration process.

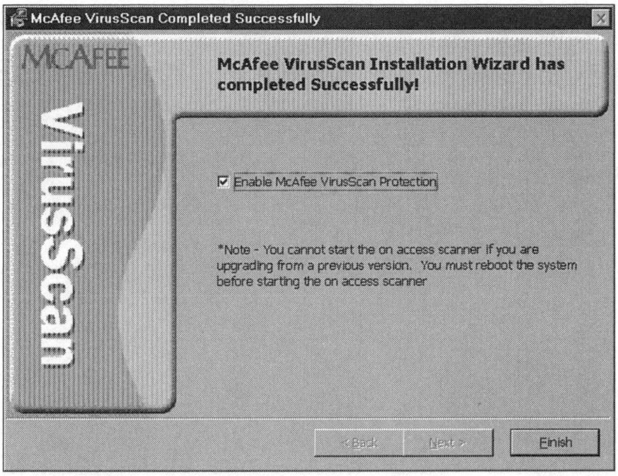

FIGURE 9.19

Enable McAfee VirusScan Protection option.

12. The final step in the installation process is to select what to do after the installation is complete. You are prompted to either restart your computer immediately, or to restart later. Before the program can begin protecting your machine from viruses, you must restart your computer.

CAUTION

You must restart your computer at some point after the installation process in order to activate the antivirus software.

TIP

You can uninstall McAfee VirusScan at anytime by re-running the Installation program and selecting Remove from the McAfee Program Maintenance window. You can also modify the current settings by selecting Modify from the same prompt, as illustrated in Figure 9.20.

9

VACCINATING YOUR COMPUTER AGAINST VIRUSES

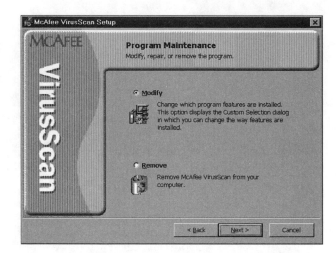

Figure 9.20
McAfee Program Maintenance window.

Summary

This chapter provides you with the necessary information to understand, install, and use antivirus software. Several antivirus programs are discussed in this chapter, and you are given step-by-step installation instructions for two of the most popular antivirus titles, Norton and McAfee.

The next chapter delves into some of the issues surrounding network security for your home by providing an overview of firewalls, the core component of any network security plan.

Securing a Home Network

IN THIS PART

Overview of Firewalls

IN THIS CHAPTER

In This Chapter

To improve the security of your home computer and network, it is necessary to understand how a firewall works and the protection it provides. This chapter provides an overview of firewalls.

> **TIP**
>
> At this point, if you have not read Chapters 3, "How the Internet Works," and 4, "Network Infrastructure," and are not familiar with how networks work, it would be a good time to go back and review those chapters. This chapter's discussion requires that you have an understanding of how networks work.

Introduction to Firewalls

The term firewall is used in several areas of our normal everyday lives. In a house, a firewall is a wall built of inflammable material that helps prevent fires from traveling through it. In a car, a firewall is a metal plate placed between the main passenger cabin and the engine compartment. In case of a fire, the firewall protects the passengers in the car by not permitting an engine fire to enter the passenger cabin.

A computer firewall functions similarly to a house or car firewall. It prevents approaching fires from spreading, but in this case, the fire is a malicious attacker trying to do one of the following:

- Obtain access to your network
- Vandalize your network or computer
- Crash your network or computer
- Steal data from your computer

A firewall acts as a gateway to your private computer or network, controlling access to it, and what can travel in and out of it. Its main goal is to protect your network from attacks and intruders.

NOTE

A *gateway* is a node (computing device) on a network that acts as an entrance to a different network. For security, firewalls are usually placed at gateway nodes to protect the internal network from the outside network.

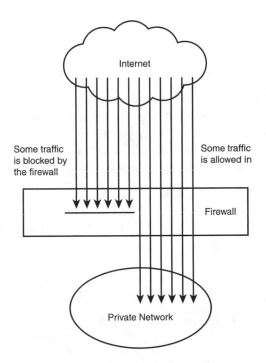

FIGURE 10.1

A private network connected to the Internet using a firewall.

The firewall protects your network by examining all the network traffic routed between your private network and the Internet, as shown in Figure 10.1.

TIP

In some instances, a firewall can be used to protect two private networks from each other.

During the examination of packets, the firewall acts as a sieve, filtering the packets entering and leaving your network. If a packet is flagged as not accepted, it is not allowed through the firewall. The firewall contains an *access control policy* that defines what enters and leaves the network. An access control policy is a list of acceptance statements defining what type of packets can travel through the firewall. In addition, the access control policy can define what privileges specific users have and authentication rules to use for connecting to the network or computer.

Firewalls have two sets of policies:

- What is kept out of the network
- What is kept in the network

Additionally, a firewall provides protection to a network by closing access to ports open by computers residing within the network. A computer's port is usually opened by an application to await or initiate a connection to another computer. The firewall prevents unknown connections by closing all access to these internal open ports. To protect the network from tampering, a firewall usually also blocks all access to its own unused ports.

As well as closing ports, some firewalls actually hide the ports from external view. This prevents intruders from discovering these ports. If an intruder discovers the existence of closed ports, they might continually scan them with the hope that the closed ports will be open. A hidden port is often called a "stealth" port.

> **NOTE**
>
> A *port* refers to a logical location, where a server program waits for a client to communicate with it.

Firewalls can be implemented in several ways in the home or small business environment. The easiest way to implement a firewall is to either use an off-the-shelf hardware firewall, or a software firewall application. A software firewall application is often known as personal firewall software, and is usually run on the lone computer it is protecting. The alternative is to use a hardware firewall that can be either a turnkey off-the-shelf hardware solution, or a separate PC running a software firewall. Linux is a popular operating system used to run standalone firewalls.

> **NOTE**
>
> A *turnkey hardware* solution refers to a hardware device that is ready for immediate use once purchased and installed. These types of devices are developed for a specific purpose and produced in large quantities for market sale.

The main element of a network firewall (excluding personal firewall software) is that there are two independent network interfaces: one connected to the Internet, and the other to your home or small business network. The firewall keeps the two networks separated, and when an attack is executed on your network, the only device that experiences the attack is the firewall, not your internal networked computers.

Network firewalls are implemented in or attached to a network router. In the case of a router with a firewall, the router directs traffic, as well as hiding the computers behind the router from the outside world. In fact, the firewall router machine is the only device on your network that can be seen from the Internet.

Typically, a combined firewall-router unit will use a technology called *network address translation (NAT)*. NAT hides the network addresses of the internal network from the outside world. This provides your internal network with anonymity from the outside; because hosts outside the internal network do not know what is inside your network, NAT effectively decreases the opportunities for an intruder to attempt to attack or vandalize your network because they lack critical knowledge about your network they normally would use in an attack.

When using NAT on a firewall-router, the firewall-router is typically called a *bastion host*.

> **NOTE**
>
> A bastion host refers to the single host computer that a network enables to be addressed directly from a public network (the Internet), and is designed to be a firewall and hide the existence of the network to the outside world. Some bastion hosts run NAT.

Why You Need a Firewall

In the previous section we introduced what a firewall is, but why do you need one? It is becoming increasingly clear that computers and networks are becoming the targets of crime.

10

The techno-savvy criminals are realizing that it is not necessary to attack the large government agencies and corporations to obtain services and assets. They have realized that although the small business and home users have less to steal and use, they also have less security to stop them.

Many people work from home in today's economy, and others store private data on their home computers. In addition, small businesses are increasingly using the Internet to conduct business. These are all potential scenarios that attackers and intruders are targeting. Potential dangers from attackers and intruders include the following:

- Gaining access to your network and PC, and stealing your confidential information
- Gaining access to your PC, and then masquerading as you on the Internet
- Crashing your computer or network, therefore not permitting you to do your work or obtaining your information
- Vandalizing your PC or network, thus requiring you to repair them
- Corrupting your data

Home and small business users must realize that a computer or network should be viewed as your home or office, where you store all your valuables and possessions. A firewall can be viewed as having locked doors and windows on your house; you can control what enters and leaves your house, while still being able to live in it. A firewall can protect against unauthorized logins and use of services, and also block traffic entering from the outside and from leaving the inside. This protects the network from outside intruders and attackers.

Shortcoming of Firewalls

Firewalls can protect you from attackers and intruders; however, they are not autonomous to inside and outside sources.

Users of your computer and network must be educated about how your firewall works. If users do not know about the firewall and how it works, they might give out their private login information, how your network is setup, what Internet services your computers run, or even the type of firewall you are running. All this information can help an attacker or intruder gain access or attack your network or computer.

In addition, most firewalls provide logging and auditing services. These services log the types of activities that travel through your firewall, users gaining access or the type of data traffic passing through. Having a firewall without occasionally checking the log, or not being notified automatically by the logging services of suspicious activity, diminishes its usefulness. Attackers or intruders could be staking out your network or computer, looking for cracks in the firewall over a period of time.

Finally, firewalls might protect your network and computers from attack, but the presence of your network on the Internet still exists, as the firewall is still visible. Thus, even though an attacker cannot view what is behind your firewall, your network can still be a potential victim. Firewalls do not provide total anonymity on the Internet.

TIP

Users must remember that firewalls provide protection for your computer or network, but you must also remember to help your network and firewall by educating your users and not provide motivation for an attacker or intruder to attack your network.

Potential Attacks and Intrusions

Many home and small business users today use broadband connections, either DSL or cable networks. A security risk involved with these services is that they provide a user with a permanent, static IP address. A static IP address can be viewed as a permanently known home address on the Internet. Just as an intruder can repeatedly visit your house once he knows your home address, a permanent IP address provides intruders and attackers a method to find your network repeatedly.

Even if you are assigned a dynamically allocated IP address, it does not provide anonymity, because it might still be possible for an attacker to determine your address. For instance, you can still become a target of malicious attackers who randomly *sniff* for active IP addresses and ports for an unprotected victim.

NOTE

Sniffing is the act of monitoring or analyzing network traffic. This can be used for legitimate purposes, such as analyzing network performance. This can also be used for illegitimate purposes, such as searching for passwords.

When an attacker or intruder can find your IP address and the location of your network, there are numerous types of attacks they can perform. However, as most attacks involve the use of the ports on your computer, they can poll the ports to find open ones. After an open port is found, an attacker can attempt to determine the type of service that is provided by that port and

10

either gain access to your system using that port or obtain services from that port. Other methods of attack involve sniffing all the packets entering and leaving your network, the intruder might then find user information and also view the data traveling in and out of your network.

The attacker's main objectives when attacking your network are

- To obtain the user authentication for your own and other systems
- To steal your private files
- To vandalize your network by wreaking havoc on your computers and corrupting your data
- to terrorize you by denying you service to the Internet

There are many reasons why someone might attack your system, from having a purpose to just vandalism for its own sake, because it is possible and you are not prepared for it.

In addition, currently the Internet is plagued by *distributed denial of service* attacks. A denial of service attack involves an attacker denying Internet service to a victim target. A target can be a home network or a large corporate private network. The key to these attacks is that third-party computers are used to wage the attack on the victim from multiple locations. In most instances, the third parties do not even know they are waging the attack until it is too late. Furthermore, it is very difficult to track down the originator of the attack because the third parties executed the attack unknowingly.

A denial of service attack's intent is to do one of the following:

- Vandalize your computer or network. The result is loss of service or data.
- Deny service to your network. This results in people attempting to gain access to your network and failing.
- Inundating your computer or network with packets, resulting in your computer or network crashing. Sometimes this is referred to as a packet storm, or packet flood.

A denial of service attack does not usually involve breaking into a computer and gaining access to files. Its main intent is for the attacker to deny service to a user or organization.

As shown in Figure 10.2, third party computers, often referred to as *attack daemons*, attack the victim target. A master control is used to initiate the attack from a remote location, preventing the disclosure of the attacker's location. A distributed denial of service attack is hard to prevent because its distributed nature prevents networks from guarding against certain Internet hosts.

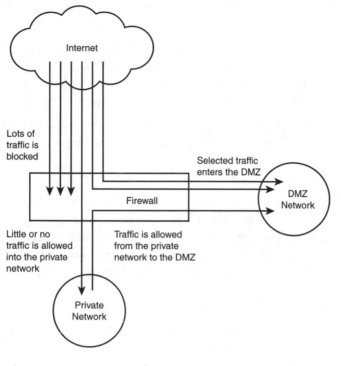

Figure 10.2

Figure 10.2: A distributed denial of service attack.

How Do Firewalls Work?

This section outlines some of the techniques that firewalls use. Firewalls might use some or all the following techniques to protect your computer or network:

- Packet filtering
- Circuit level gateway
- Application level proxies
- NAT: Network Address Translation

Packet Filtering

A *packet filtering* firewall looks at each packet entering and leaving the firewall, and accepts or rejects the packet depending on predefined access control policy rules. Since this type of filtering occurs at the packet level, packet filtering is usually implemented as part of a router. Each packet is compared against a predefined criteria. Comparison criteria can include: source and destination IP addresses, source and destination ports, and type of protocol used.

The advantage of packet filtering is that it is low-cost and has a low impact on the network performance. However, a packet filtering firewall is difficult to configure so that it provides strong protection against attacks, because it looks at the properties of packets other than their content or purpose in determining whether they should reach the internal network.

Packet filtering can be viewed as a cheap low-level initial defense for your network or computer, although this type of firewall is vulnerable to denial of service attacks.

Circuit Level Gateway

A Circuit level gateway monitors the initial TCP dialog for illegitimate session requests. It also acts as a session request proxy, making TCP session requests to outside systems on behalf of computers on your internal network. This helps hide the details of the internal network. Although inexpensive and efficient to deploy, circuit level gateways offer no packet filtering on their own, because they only operate at the start of TCP interactions.

Application Level Proxies

Using an application proxy is a way for a network to secure itself by creating an intermediary for all applications that connect to the Internet. A proxy server operates on an application-by-application basis, providing support for a specific set of applications, such as the World Wide Web, Telnet and e-mail. If a proxy does not contain configuration information for a particular Internet application, the application is disallowed to connect to the Internet. The proxy server performs a number of security duties including verifying that applications are correctly using a network, caching data, and only authenticated users can access the Internet.

When an internal computer on your network attempts to connect to a server on the Internet, the proxy server actually performs the connection on behalf of the internal computer, and then returns the results of the request to the internal computer after performing optional filtering of the data itself.

An application level proxy can affect the performance of a network, because internal machines no longer directly contact the Internet, but instead all rely on the single proxy server to perform these actions on their behalf. The proxy can then easily become a bottleneck in connecting to the Internet.

Other Firewall Technologies

This section describes the following three other firewall technologies that a user should know about:

- SOCKS
- Network Address Translation (NAT)
- Demilitarized Zone (DMZ)

SOCKS

SOCKS is a network proxy protocol that enables a proxy server to give full access to the Internet or vice versa to computers residing in the private network, regardless of the specific application users on the private network want to use. Unlike application level proxies, discussed in the previous section of this chapter, SOCKS proxy servers do not require explicit built-in support for each network application users might want to use.

SOCKS does this by redirecting requests for services and can provide this service without disclosing the network addresses (IP address) of the requesting internal computer.

The SOCKS proxy server authenticates and authorizes the requests, establishes a proxy connection, and relays data for any application. The only caveat is that the applications used on internal computers need to support the SOCKS proxy standard (as many do).

NAT: Network Address Translation

Network Address Translation (NAT) is the translation of an IP address used in one network (the Internet) to a different address in a private network. This is implemented in routers and helps provide security because each outgoing or incoming request must be translated. This process enables a private network's structure to be hidden from the Internet. In addition, it permits the network traffic to be authenticated during the translation.

NAT is a sub-form of packet filtering. NAT routers offer the advantages of packet filtering firewalls, but can also hide the IP addresses of computers behind the firewall, and offer a level of circuit-based filtering.

Demilitarized Zone (DMZ)

A *Demilitarized Zone (DMZ)* is one or more machines on a pseudo-internal network. Your internal network permits no incoming access from the Internet or the DMZ. The DMZ permits limited incoming access from the Internet. The DMZ can then be used for public servers, such as Web servers and mail servers. If an attacker succeeds in compromising systems in the DMZ, they still cannot compromise systems on the internal network.

The term DMZ comes from the DMZ formed between North and South Korea, the neutral area between the two countries that acts as a neutral border area. Your DMZ computer acts as a neutral border area between the two networks.

Hardware Versus Software

When selecting a firewall to install for your home or small business, there are a variety of firewall solutions to choose from and each of these different firewall solutions have their positives and their negatives. In this section, we will discuss the different firewall solutions available to the home and small office user.

There are three possible types of firewalls for the home and small business user:

- A software-based firewall that runs on the same computer it protects. This is sometimes called personal firewall software because it only protects your single personal computer.
- A hardware-based firewall that is an off-the-shelf product, often including a built-in network router.
- A software-based firewall running on a separate machine. Software firewalls are available for various operating systems, including Windows and Linux.

Personal Firewall Software

Personal Firewall Software is the cheapest solution to provide your computer some protection. To set up, you are required to install it on your personal computer, and in most cases it automatically configures itself. However, this type of solution has its drawbacks. First, it can only protect the single computer unless you are using some sort of Internet-sharing, and are protecting the Internet-sharing computer. In addition, a personal firewall relies on the operating system on which it is based; if there are security flaws in the operating system, it will affect the firewall. Furthermore, when an attack is targeted towards your personal computer, the attack is made directly on your computer because there is no buffer. No buffer exists because the firewall resides on the same computer it is attempting to protect. Total anonymity for your computer is not possible, as your computer is connected directly to the Internet. These types of firewalls usually include both TCP layer-filtering and some sort of application filtering. In addition, there is not much configuration available to the user. However, this is the main benefit for this type of firewall. To a novice user, this is probably the best possible solution without the need to learn more about firewall and networking technology. It will not provide the best protection for a user, but taking into account the cost, security, and user experience level, this is the least common denominator solution.

Off-the-Shelf Hardware Firewalls

The simplest of the three solutions is the off-the-shelf hardware firewall. All that is necessary is to plug in the firewall between your network or computer and the outside Internet connection. It provides reliable and substantial security with a very simple setup. In the past, however, the cost of one of these devices was a major limiting factor, but recently the prices of these devices have dropped to about $100.

A hardware-based off-the-shelf product provides a solution that can be attached to a network or between your personal computer and the router. It provides an easy turnkey hardware solution, just plug it in and turn it on. Drawbacks include its limited configurations, and most do not permit some features, such as a Demilitarized Zone. This is an easy solution for a user with little knowledge of firewall technology who needs to protect an entire network.

In addition to providing firewall protection, most off-the-shelf hardware solutions provide network translation and routing. This allows the device to share a single Internet connection with an entire network. Off-the-shelf hardware firewalls are often referred to as *broadband routers* or *Internet gateways*.

Most hardware-based firewalls provide port blocking and forwarding, network-based translation, and data logging. In most cases, these units do not provide application proxy services.

Standalone Hardware Firewalls

The last firewall solution is the software-based computer firewall. This is typically an older computer, dedicated as the firewall machine. The firewall computer has two network adapters, running a basic operating system and firewall software. This dedicated firewall machine is intended to protect an entire network, rather than a lone machine.

Depending on what types of operating systems you use, such as Windows, Linux, or something else, firewall software can range in price from free to $100. Hence, this can be a cheap solution if you have an old PC sitting around the office or home, and can use free open source software such as Linux, coupled with one of numerous free open source firewalls. The advantages are that you can configure and do anything you like with the firewall. However, a disadvantage is that any problems in the lower-level operating system with security will be needed to be patched. But for the Linux operating system, patches are available quite readily, and in most cases very up-to-date. This leads to the main caveat: This solution requires a lot of configuration and knowledge of the lower-level operating system and firewall software. The user must be comfortable with scripts, configuration of operating systems and software, and in some cases compilation of code.

Firewall Comparisons

Software-based firewalls protect your computer from attackers flooding your ports and stop intruders from polling your computer(s) for open ports from which they can try to gain services and access. In addition to this lower-level protection, most software-based firewalls also provide application proxy services that guard against high-level attacks, such as Trojan applications and denial of service attacks using applications masquerading as commonly known Internet applications.

10

OVERVIEW OF
FIREWALLS

Most hardware firewalls protect the lower level of the network, controlling access and protecting the open network ports. Additionally, because hardware firewalls are dedicated machines, when an attack does occur on your network, your private network of computers is not affected, as the brunt of the attack is incurred on the firewall. In most cases, the firewall will need to be rebooted after the attack.

The advantages of software-based standalone hardware firewalls are that they are a cheap alternative to the off-the-shelf, hardware-based firewalls, and they are just as useful. The Linux operating system is a very popular platform on which to base a firewall service. The disadvantages of software-based, standalone firewalls are that they are difficult to configure and require understanding the security features of the software firewall and the limitations of the underlying operating system.

Summary

This chapter began by introducing firewall technology followed by a discussion focusing on why firewalls are needed and how they are implemented. Three firewall solutions were compared: personal firewall software, an off-the-shelf hardware firewall, and a standalone firewall. Each firewall solution has its advantages and disadvantages, and you should decide on a solution that best fits your needs and resources.

The next chapter takes this discussion of network firewalls to implementation. We will go through the process of setting up a software-based standalone proxy firewall.

Implementing a
Proxy Server

IN THIS CHAPTER

In This Chapter

An alternative solution to a standalone hardware firewall or a personal firewall application is a proxy server, which provides both the functionality of a hardware firewall and network router and the application protection a personal firewall offers. For the home or small office, all that is needed to setup a proxy server is

- One personal computer
- Two network interface cards (NIC)
- One network hub
- Network proxy software

The personal computer can be an existing computer already on the network, which consequently reduces costs for this type of security solution. Once it is set up and configured, a proxy server acts as a network router and firewall for a connection to the Internet. The proxy server provides two services because it permits the sharing of a single broadband connection between a network of computers and protects the computers on the network from intrusion and attack from the Internet.

A proxy server solution is best suited for situations that require the sharing of a broadband connection between an existing group of networked computers; additionally this type of solution is beneficial for situations that have special configuration requirements because proxy servers are extremely configurable. Last, this solution is most appropriate when application level firewall filtering is needed for a network of computers. A proxy server can provide application level filtering for a group of computers without the need to install firewalls and filters on each individual machine; the proxy server handles all the application filtering for the network.

NOTE
This chapter discusses firewalls and methods of implementation. If you have not read Chapter 10, "Overview of Firewalls," and are unfamiliar with firewall technology, it might be a good idea to review Chapter 10 before progressing further.

What a Proxy Server Does

A proxy server operates as an intermediary between a private network and the Internet. A proxy computer has two physical network interfaces cards (NIC), as shown in Figure 11.1, and allows the two networks to be separate.

- Network card 1 connects to the public Internet.
- Network card 2 connects to the private network.

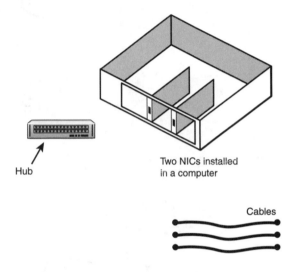

Hub

Two NICs installed
in a computer

Cables

FIGURE 11.1

A computer with two NIC cards installed. To set up a proxy, a hub and extra Ethernet cables are also required.

The two networks are kept apart but bridged by the proxy server. As shown in Figure 11.2, the proxy server bridges the two networks: It connects to the Internet using one NIC, and to the private network using the other NIC.

The proxy server software provides the logic and functionality behind a proxy server. Proxy software is composed of two key security components:

- A network router
- A firewall

Shown in Figure 11.3 are the components of proxy server software.

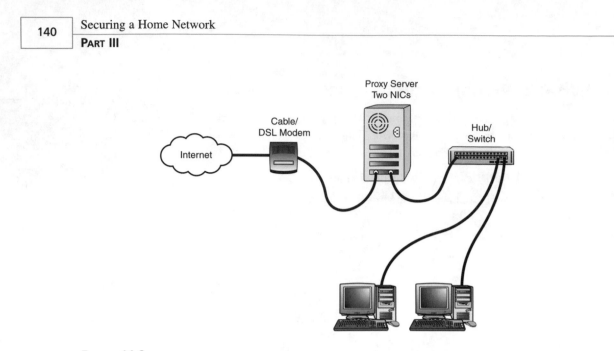

FIGURE 11.2

A proxy server connecting a private network to the Internet.

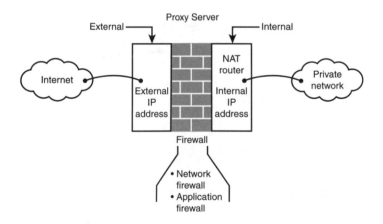

FIGURE 11.3

Proxy server software architecture.

The network router software component allows a proxy server to share a single broadband connection among a group of networked computers. This is usually performed using Network Address Translation (NAT). Implementing NAT as a method to share the Internet itself provides a mechanism of security because connections can only be initialized from the private network out to the Internet. Connections cannot be initialized originating from the Internet because the address translation only functions for outbound traffic. This prevents malicious scripts and applications hosted by computers on the Internet from connecting to computers inside the private network.

The Proxy as a Firewall

The second key security component of the proxy server is a firewall. Most proxy servers implement two levels of firewall security:

- Network level firewall
- Application level firewall

The network level firewall is a packet inspection filter that inspects every packet passing through the proxy server. This function is closely tied with the NAT router because both services inspect the data traffic. Whether a packet is allowed to travel through the firewall is usually based on source and destination addresses and ports. Most proxy servers provide *stateful* packet filtering: This allows for connections to the Internet to be established based on earlier traffic patterns. The network level firewall also provides port blocking, which can close unused ports and make them invisible to the outside world. Ports that are made invisible are often referred to as *stealth* ports.

The application level firewall provides security at a higher level. Instead of looking at packets, IP addresses, and ports, the application level firewall studies application sessions and the context in which packets are sent and received for those applications. Applications can be limited to rules defined by the administrator of the proxy server for the entire network. This application level firewall protection is similar to the functionality provided by a personal firewall software package because it provides application specific security control.

In most cases, a combination of both levels of firewall technology is implemented in a proxy server to provide the most optimal security solution.

In addition to network sharing and firewall protection, many proxy software packages also include other useful functions. These added components include

- Logging
- Virus scanning
- Site filtering
- Data caching

Data logs records of attempted intrusions to the network and traffic patterns. These logs can be used to study user patterns of the network and to assist in determining sources of attacks on the network. An integrated antivirus software application allows scanning of viruses and Trojan applications before they enter the private network. This reduces maintenance because there is less need to install antivirus software on each individual computer. Site filtering allows the network administrator to filter out sites that he thinks are inappropriate. This is a great component for home networks, where children frequently surf the Internet. And finally, proxy servers are best known for providing caching of Web data and information. This saves bandwidth for the network and faster response times to frequently visited sites.

A key difference between a proxy server implementation and a standalone hardware firewall router is the amount of configuration allowed. In a standalone firewall, everything is implemented in hardware with a small ROM for configuration data. An advantage of standalone hardware firewalls is that they are easy to set up; however, with a small ROM, they are very limited in configurable options. Whereas with a proxy server implementation, everything is implemented in software running on a computer, and hence allows for greater configuration of the entire software package.

In the next section, we will discuss the base requirements for running a proxy server and the software packages currently available.

Proxy Server Software Currently on the Market

A number of proxy server software packages are currently available on the market aimed for the home or small office user. Most of these software packages include the functionality and elements we discussed in the previous section. An added benefit of these software packages is that they provide a 30-day trial version, which allows you to evaluate a fully functional proxy server on your own home or office network before purchasing the software.

The minimum computer requirements to run a proxy server include

- 90MHz Pentium PC
- Microsoft Windows 95, 98, ME, 2000, or NT
- 32MB of ram
- 30MB of disk space
- 1 network interface card (NIC) for the internal network connection
- 1 Internet connection (Dial-up Adapter or NIC)

These are general base requirements, and you should definitely check the requirements of specific proxy server software packages. But as shown by these requirements, a proxy server does not need to be a top-of-the-line computer. In fact, for home or small office use, a proxy server can fully function using an older Pentium machine.

Many proxy server packages are currently on the market, and they range in price from $40 to $120 depending on the options required. Most of these packages provide three to five client user licenses. Client licenses determine the number of computers that can connect to the proxy server at one time. For a home or small office, three to five computers is about right; however, all the manufacturers do sell packages with more licenses if needed.

In the next section, we will work through the setup of a proxy server. We will be using the server proxy WinProxy by Ositis Software.

However, it is best to evaluate a number of proxy server packages and determine what best fits your needs. Listed later is a number of proxy server applications that provide free 30-day trial applications.

All three solutions in the following list require server software. The network clients themselves do not need any extra software, just some specific networking configuration. This feature requires less setup and maintenance for your private network.

- Winproxy, developed by Ositis Software, can be found at `http://www.winproxy.com`.
- WinGate, developed by Deerfield.com, can be found at `http://wingate.deerfield.com`.
- WinRoute, developed by Tiny Software, can be found at `http://www.tinysoftware.com`.

How to Set Up a Proxy Server

In this section, we will go through the process of implementing a proxy server on a Windows based machine.

Before installing the proxy server software, the proxy computer must be properly set up. This includes installing the two network interface cards, and configuring windows networking. As shown in Figure 11.4, two NICs should be configured and bound to TCP/IP.

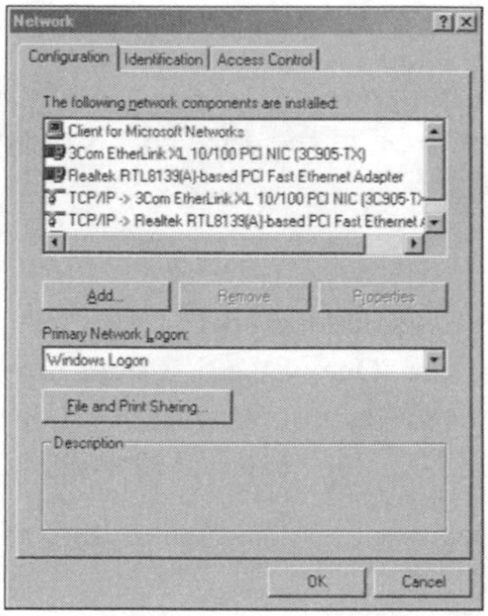

FIGURE 11.4
Two NICs installed and bound to TCP/IP.

NOTE

If you have not read Chapter 5, "Securing a Standalone System," I would recommend you do so. Chapter 5 covers securing the base windows networking technologies like TCP/IP, discussed previously.

For the NIC connected to your broadband connection, set up the TCP/IP settings as specified by your Internet service provider, including IP address, Gateway, and DNS. For the NIC connected to your internal network, if you do not have a pre-existing network, assign it a static IP of 90.0.0.1, with a netmask of 255.255.255.0. However, if you already have a private network functioning, assign it an IP in the range you are already using.

Once the windows networking is set up, the networks should be physically connected, and the proxy server software installed.

If you do not already have an existing private network, the client computers for this new private network should also be configured. Again, TCP/IP should be installed and configured. As for IP address assignment, you have a decision to make: You can configure the proxy server to act as a DHCP server and have the server assign IP addresses dynamically, consequently setting the client machines to obtain a dynamic IP address; or you can simply assign a static IP address to each client computer. If you used 90.0.0.1 as the proxy server, client IP addresses can range from 90.0.0.2 to 90.0.0.254, where the last digit changes. The submask should be 255.255.255.0 and the Gateway and DNS server should also be assigned to 90.0.0.1.

NOTE

In our examples, our pre-existing network uses an internal IP range of 192.168.1.X, hence our proxy server is set to be in the 192.168.1.X range (192.168.1.171) rather than the 90.0.0.X.

Once the network is physically set up and the proxy server installed, the first time the server is initialized, it will run a Setup wizard. One of the first steps it will conduct is to confirm the internal and external IP addresses for the proxy server. As shown in Figure 11.5, the internal IP address is defined as 192.168.1.171 and the external IP assigned by the ISP is 11.3.6.9.

And after the wizard is complete, it will test the functionality of the proxy server, as shown in Figure 11.6.

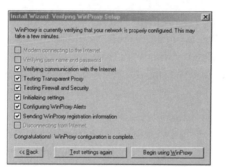

FIGURE 11.5

Internal and external IP address confirmation.

FIGURE 11.6

Verification of proxy setup.

After this wizard is complete, the proxy server should be running and functioning. The proxy server provides a window dialog, as shown in Figure 11.7, and a task tray icon as shown in Figure 11.8.

In the case of WinProxy specifically, after the Setup wizard has run, it creates a customized text file called WinProxy.cfg, which provides configuration information for the clients on your specific private network.

Selecting File and Show Client Configuration from the WinProxy window dialog can retrieve this text file.

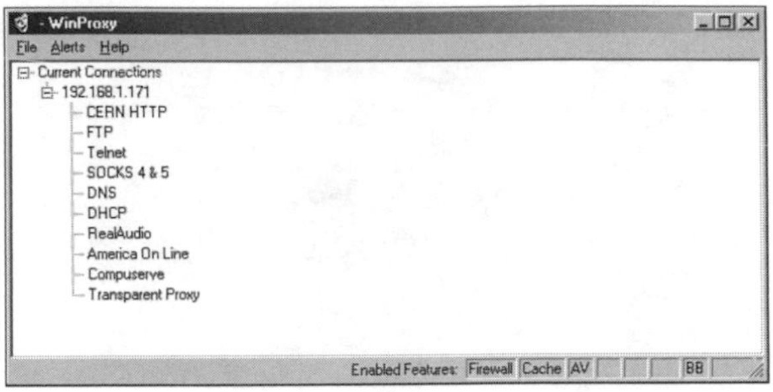

FIGURE 11.7

The WinProxy window.

FIGURE 11.8

The WinProxy task icon.

After you have configured the proxy server and the client computers, you should test your newly connected network. The client computers should be able to access the Internet with no trouble. However, try accessing your network from the Internet. You should now find you cannot access your private network; the firewall is working. Also attempt to scan your networks ports using Shields Up from http://www.grc.com: You should find that all your ports are closed.

For basic security use, the previously mentioned configuration is enough, but if a more specific configuration is needed, further advanced configurations can be performed. In the case of WinProxy, it provides three advanced configuration tools:

- Properties Wizard
- Settings
- Advanced Settings

The Properties Wizard walks you through an advanced configuration of the proxy, including configuration of Internet protocols, logging, caching, proxy services, and antivirus packages. As shown in Figure 11.9, Internet protocols can be enabled and disabled.

The Settings Window dialog box allows you to directly configure each setting the Properties Wizard walks you through. This is best used when you know exactly what you need to configure. As shown in Figure 11.10, this dialog box allows you to directly configure the Internet protocols and their settings.

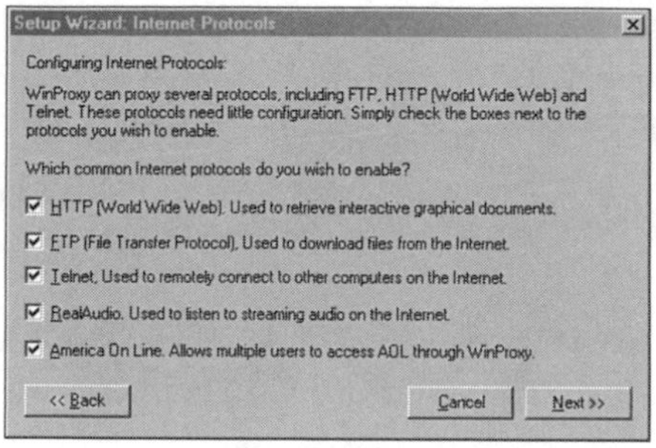

FIGURE 11.9
Internet Protocol Properties Wizard.

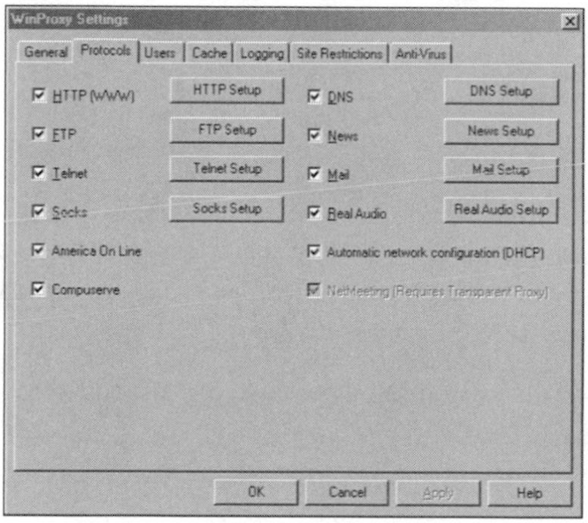

FIGURE 11.10
Internet Protocol direct configuration.

Finally, the Advanced Settings allows you to directly configure the firewall itself. This includes the mechanisms the firewall uses: network level or application level firewall, the filtering of specific applications and ports, and the methods with which the client computers on the private network can access the Internet. As shown in Figure 11.11, specific applications can be filtered.

All three of these selections can be found from the File menu of the WinProxy dialog box.

For more advanced configuration of your proxy server, it is always best to reference the documentation for your specific proxy server software.

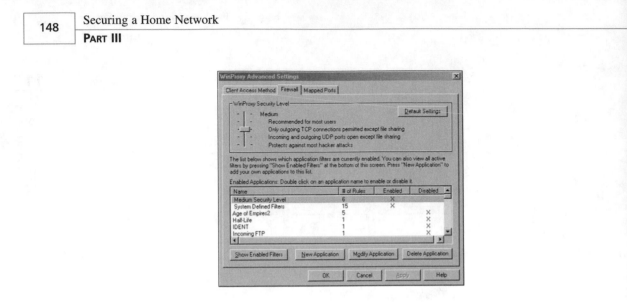

FIGURE 11.11

Application level firewall filtering.

Summary

In this chapter you learned the role that a proxy server can play as a viable alternative to a firewall or broadband gateway or router. You also learned the basics of installing and configuring a proxy server using the popular WinProxy software.

The next chapter takes our discussion into how to set up a broadband gateway, a standalone hardware firewall solution.

Using a Broadband Router

IN THIS CHAPTER

In This Chapter

In this chapter we will look at how to use a hardware broadband router, often referred to as a home Internet gateway or a standalone hardware firewall. We will discuss the different types of broadband routers on the market, how to set up a broadband router, and discuss the types of protection it can provide.

Broadband routers provide two services: security for your home network, and the capability to share the Internet with your LAN, enabling all your computers to access the Internet using a single cable or DSL connection. Broadband routers provide a drop-in independent solution for your home network security needs.

Broadband Routers Currently On the Market

Currently, there are numerous broadband routers on the market. Depending on the security features you require, common broadband routers can range in price from $80 to $500. However, most broadband routers marketed towards the home market cost between $100 and $150. Broadband routers found in this price category by and large provide the same security features. In this section we will focus on three popular broadband routers found in this price category. However, there are more expensive routers that provide more security mechanisms, but based on the added cost and configuration needed, they are inappropriate for the basic home user.

The following three broadband routers are similar in price and function:

- Linksys BEFSR41 EtherFast Cable/DSL Router, a 4-port 10/100 switch with router and NAT firewall. More information about the BEFSR41 can be found at `http://www.linksys.com/`.
- NETGEAR RT314 Internet Gateway Router, also a 4-port 10/100 switch, router and NAT firewall. NETGEAR's Web site is located at `http://www.netgear.com`.
- SMC Networks SMC7004BR Barricade 4-Port 10/100 Broadband Router, a 4-port 10/100 switch, with built-in router, NAT firewall and printer server. SMC is located at `http://www.smc.com`.

All three of these broadband routers provide similar security features, NAT firewalls and security access control. The SMC Barricade has an additional printer server that differentiates it from the others. Configuration for each of the units is performed similarly using a Web interface. The NETGEAR also provides a telnet and serial console configuration interface, and the SMC provides a secondary serial console for limited configuration. The Web interface provides a simple method for home users to configure their internal networks, and allows for multiple platforms to be able to use these hardware broadband routers. The Web interfaces work with Internet Explorer, Netscape, and most other compatible Web browsers.

Advantages of using a hardware broadband router solution include

- Read-only files: Attackers and intruders that compromise your firewall have nothing to modify because everything is burned into the onboard *read-only memory (ROM)*.

- Less maintenance: After it is configured and set up, your broadband router is set. From time to time the router's manufacturer might provide an up-to-date ROM flash that would require the user to flash the ROM onto the router.

- No computer required: The router is a mini computer in itself. Personal firewall software requires a computer to implement the firewall.

However, there are disadvantages in using one of these broadband routers, and you should be aware of them when deciding on a broadband router solution.

Disadvantages include

- Incompatible applications: The router might not allow various applications to function, such as some games, Internet chats, and file transfer utilities. The problem is usually caused by applications using network protocols or ports that are blocked by the hardware firewall. It is best to check with the manufacturer of the router for incompatibility issues.

- Higher cost: Even with the reduction in prices, the purchase of a hardware router in most cases is more expensive than the purchase of a personal firewall software package.

- Additional network configuration: A hardware broadband router requires more configuration than a personal firewall software package. In most cases, personal firewall applications are installed on lone computers requiring little network setup. Conversely, hardware router setup requires knowledge of networking concepts and techniques.

Initial configuration is a big part of the broadband router, and most importantly, authentication with your DSL or cable Internet provider. Authentication is done by many methods, including: MAC address filtering, login and password authentication, or a specific defined host and domain name. You should check with your provider to determine which type of authentication is used by your service. The preceding three routers provide access for all three methods; however, some routers do not, so research is important before you buy.

Alternatively, there are other routers priced below and above your chosen home category. Newer firewalls include the NETGEAR FR314 and the SonicWall SOHO2. These routers cost more, but also provide more security mechanisms, including defenses against distributed denial

12

USING A BROADBAND ROUTER

of service attacks. However, these routers range in price from $200 to $500. But for a lower price, if you already have a pre-existing LAN or do not need to share the Internet, a router with the same features as the three discussed previously can be bought for between $75 and $100. This router will not have the built-in 4-port switch, but will still provide the same security mechanisms.

How to Set Up a Broadband Router

In this section, we will discuss going about setting up a broadband router, including the physical setup and the proper configuration. It is best to check out the manual or quick install guides for complete details regarding your specific router.

In this chapter, we will go about setting up the Linksys BEFSR41 EtherFast 4-Port Cable/DSL router. We will first discuss setting up the physical device and cabling, followed by the configuration required.

Installing the Broadband Router

For our discussion about the physical installation of the broadband router, we will assume that your computer or network is already connected to your cable or DSL connection. Your network could be currently set up in a few different ways; you might have a single computer connected to a cable or DSL modem, as seen in Figure 12.1.

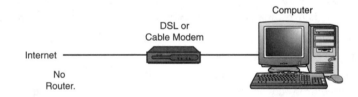

FIGURE 12.1

A single computer with a cable or DSL Internet connection.

Alternatively, you could currently be sharing your cable or DSL connection by using a network hub or switch. This most likely involves obtaining more than one IP address from your *Internet service provider (ISP)*. As shown in Figure 12.2, two computers are connected to the Internet simultaneously using a switch and modem.

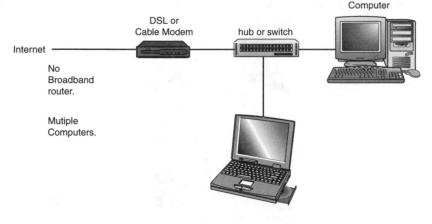

FIGURE 12.2

Multiple computers connected to the cable or DSL Internet connection using a hub or switch.

Before you obtain your broadband modem, there are a few choices you can make. If the situation matches the preceding scenarios, you have two alternatives: you can purchase a broadband router with a 4-port switch and not use the existing hub or switch, or just buy the 1-port broadband router and use your existing hub or switch. Both alternatives will function the same and offer the same level of security. If you currently only have a cable or DSL modem and a single computer, you should decide whether you will be obtaining more computers in the near future; if you are, a good economical choice would be to obtain the built-in 4-port switch. But if you do decide on the 1-port version, a switch or hub can always be purchased later for expansion to your network.

After you have obtained your router, there are a few different setup scenarios, depending on your current network. For the one-computer scenario, you would set up the broadband router between your modem and your computer, as shown in Figure 12.3. On the router, you would connect the modem to the WAN port. This is sometimes also referred to as the Internet port, or the cable/DSL port. Then attach the Ethernet cable attached to your computer to the LAN port on the router. If you have bought the 4-port switched version, any of the four LAN ports can be used.

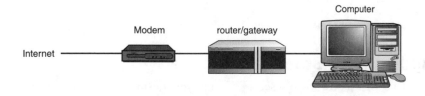

FIGURE 12.3

A single computer connected to the broadband router.

In the case of an existing shared connection using a switch, the router is placed between the modem and the switch, as shown in Figure 12.4.

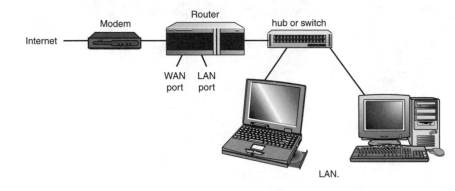

FIGURE 12.4

Multiple computers connected to the broadband router via an external switch.

In the case of a single broadband router with a built-in 4-port switch, security and Internet connectivity can both be provided to a number of computers by a small integrated device. Shown in Figure 12.5 is a broadband router providing Internet connections to two computers.

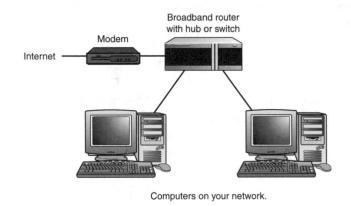

FIGURE 12.5

Multiple computers connected to the Internet using a broadband router.

Configuring the Broadband Router

When you have your hardware in place and set up, you must configure the broadband router. It is probably best to now consult your quick install guide or user reference guide. For our example, the process of installing a Linksys for the Internet will be described.

The first step requires that you configure your computer's network setup. For Windows Millennium, selecting Network from the Windows Control Panel will bring up the Network window dialog as shown in Figure 12.6.

> **NOTE**
>
> Before configuring your computer, it is prudent to write down the existing TCP/IP settings. If your provider assigns you a static IP address and DNS and gateway hosts, it is best to write them down, as the router will need them.

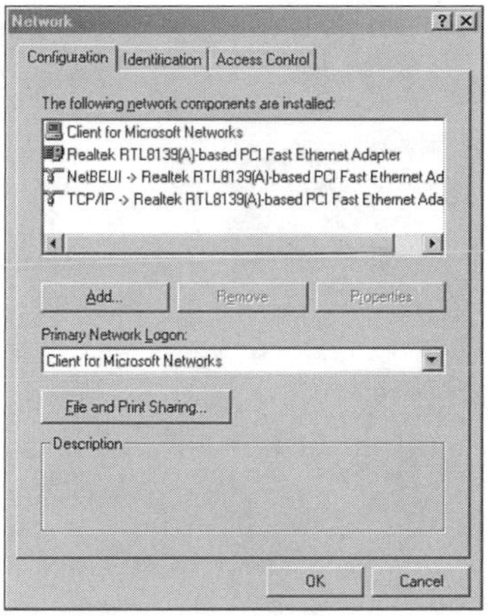

FIGURE 12.6
The Network dialog window.

From this window, you should select the TCP/IP protocol linked to the Ethernet card; in this case, the Realtek RTL8939. You are then presented with the TCP/IP properties dialog window. For use with the Linksys router, the computer must be configured to obtain an IP address, as shown in Figure 12.7.

In addition, there should be no gateways installed, as shown in Figure 12.8, and the DNS lookup should be disabled as shown in Figure 12.9. These features are all disabled because the computer will obtain all these settings from the router when the computer obtains its IP address.

This is the entire configuration needed on the computer; repeat the same steps on the other computers you plan to attach to the router. The computers are configured this way so that when they connect to the router, the router will assign them an internal IP address, DNS and Gateway.

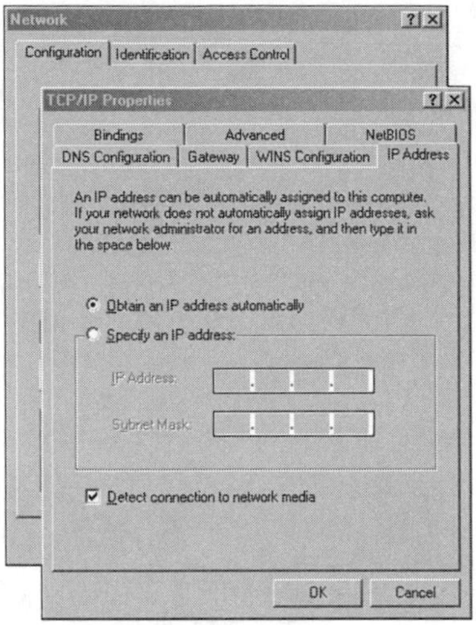

FIGURE 12.7
The TCP/IP Properties dialog box.

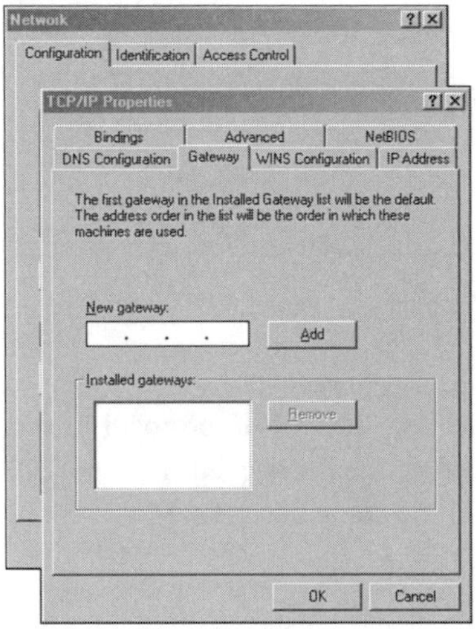

FIGURE 12.8
TCP/IP Properties dialog box defining no gateways.

Now with the computers properly configured, the router must be configured to communicate with the Internet. In the case of the Linksys router, the router is by default located at the IP address 192.168.1.1. As shown in Figure 12.10, you can enter the IP address in a Web browser and are then presented with a login dialog window asking for the username and password of the router. By default, the username and password are "admin" for the Linksys router.

FIGURE 12.9

Disabling the DNS.

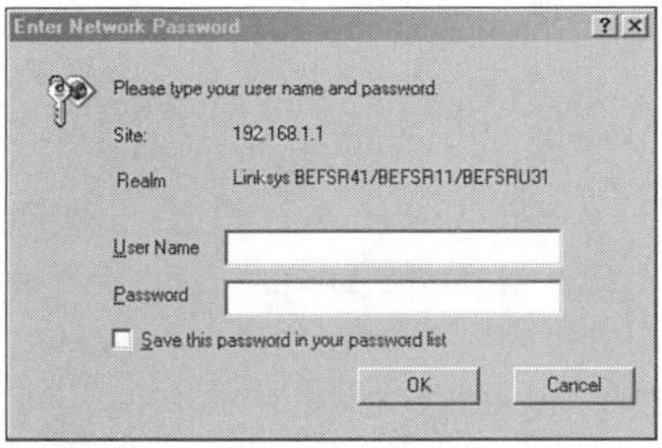

FIGURE 12.10

The Linksys router login window.

After you have logged in correctly to the router, you are shown the main setup page for the router. This is the configuration page for the router, and it handles the authentication information and Internet settings required by the ISP, as shown in Figure 12.11.

The ISP determines most of this part of the configuration, so consulting with your ISP connection information is a good idea.

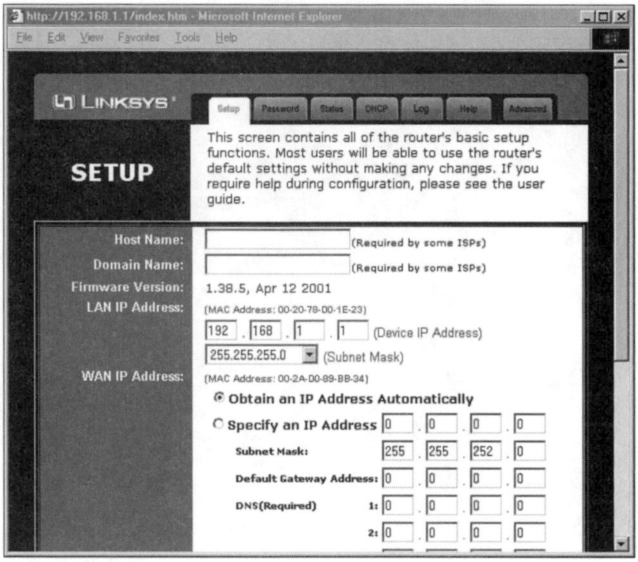

FIGURE 12.11
The Linksys Setup page.

First, the type of authentication the ISP requires must be known. If the ISP requires a certain host name and domain name, as in the case of @Home cable service, you can configure the router to return these names, by defining them in the Host and Domain name text boxes located at the top of the Setup page. If the ISP requires a login into the service, as some DSL providers do, you can provide login information that the router can use to login to the service, as shown in Figure 12.12. Finally, in case the ISP performs MAC address filtering, where only known registered MAC addresses are permitted to access the Internet, there are two solutions: You can either copy down the MAC address provided by the WAN port of the router and provide this MAC address to the ISP for access registration, or you can take the existing MAC address of the computer that has already been given access to the Internet, assuming it was previously registered, and make the router clone that MAC address. When the router accesses the Internet, it then masquerades as the cloned MAC address. This can be done by selecting the Advanced Tab, and selecting MAC Addr. Clone, as shown in Figure 12.13.

In addition to the authentication configuration, the router must be configured properly for the Internet. This mainly involves defining whether the router obtains an IP address (dynamic IP), or is assigned a permanent IP address (static IP). All this information can be defined on the Setup page under WAN IP Address.

After all this information is set, select Apply and you will have Internet access.

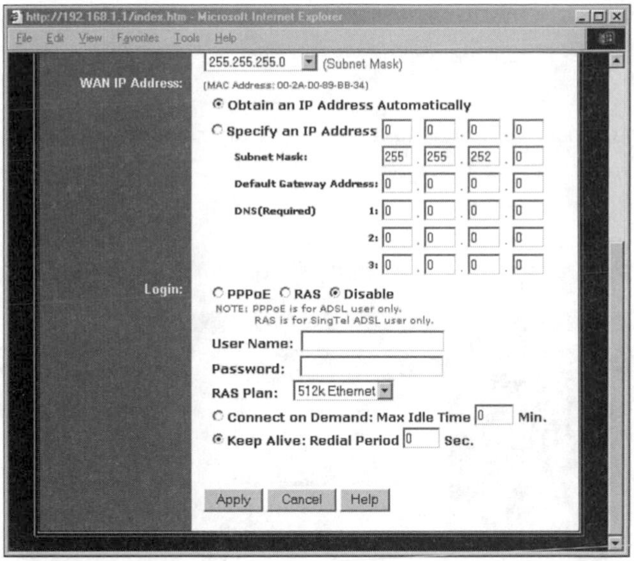

FIGURE 12.12

The Main Linksys setup page.

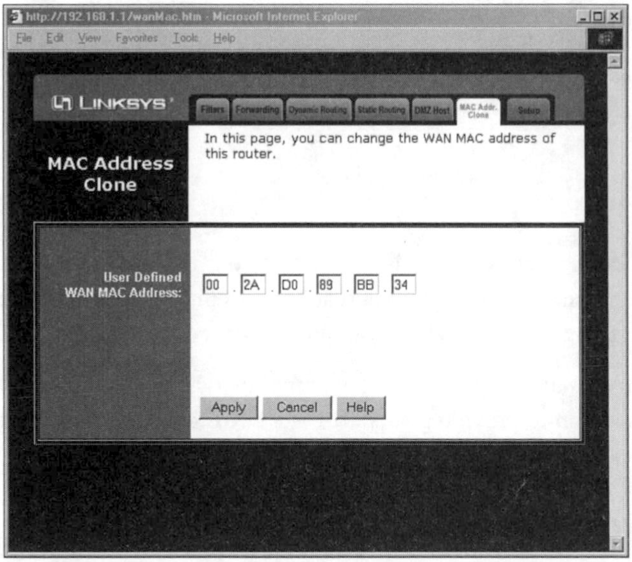

FIGURE 12.13

The MAC Address Clone page.

Most routers, including the Linksys, provide many diagnostic tools such as status screens and log files. These help in configuring the router, and enable you to check the running state and security of the firewall.

One action that you should definitely do immediately after configuration is to change the password that provides access to the router (see Figure 12.14). You do not want users to be able to gain access to your firewall and misconfigure it.

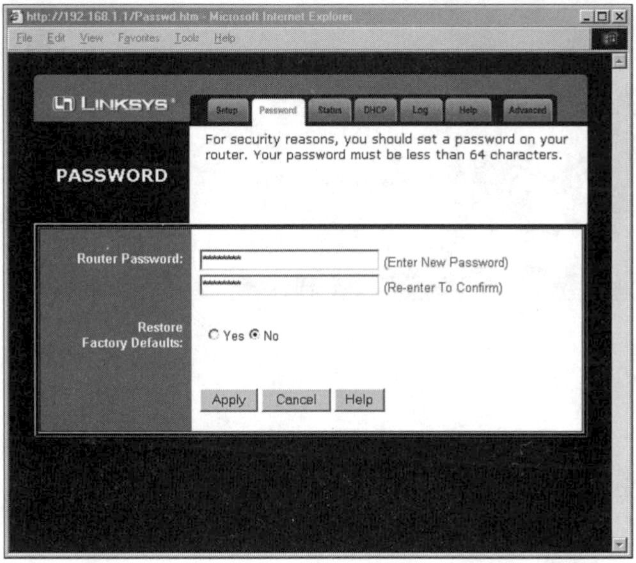

FIGURE 12.14
Changing your password.

After the router is configured, you should verify that your network can still access the Internet. You can either use a connected computer and attempt to ping the outside Internet, or attempt to access the Internet using a Web browser from an internal computer.

Most broadband routers also have advanced features such as port forwarding and dynamic and static routing, in addition to providing support for a DMZ host. All these features are well documented in the user manuals for the respective devices.

What a Broadband Router Protects

Most hardware broadband routers provide security based on mechanisms provided by *Network Address Translation*, or NAT. NAT translates an IP address from one network to a different IP address on another network. This permits a broadband router to share a single Internet IP address by translating it to many private IP addresses in an internal network. When a packet enters and leaves a router, it must be translated to and from its Internet IP address and the internal IP address that represents the internal computer. The mapping from Internet IP address to the internal IP addresses is contained in a table managed by the router. During this translation, data packets can be authenticated, filtered and logged.

In addition, because the nature of NAT never exposes the internal IP addresses to the outside world, a connection can be initiated from an internal computer to an outside Internet host, but not vice versa. Because the Internet host would only know the IP address of the firewall router, it would not be able to connect to the internal computers behind the firewall. A basic NAT firewall can be viewed as a one-way street, starting from the internal computers and continuing out to the Internet. This provides an added security benefit, as outside hosts cannot access internal network computers.

Additional protection is provided by the fact that NAT firewalls do not usually use the same network protocols as computers. Hence a TCP/IP attack using a weakness found in the protocol itself will not affect a NAT router that uses a different network protocol.

In the more expensive broadband routers, such as the NetGear FR314 or the SonicWall SOHO2, *stateful packet inspection* is performed. This occurs in the NAT firewall while packets are being translated. The firewall in this case actually keeps track of the states the connections out to the Internet are in, and in some cases, enables Internet hosts to access internal computers. An example of this would be an internal computer making a request for a file located on a FTP server. The firewall knows the state of the request, and enables the FTP to connect with the internal computer to transfer the file. Additionally, the firewall is able to prevent malicious activities, such as distributed denial of service attacks, because it is be able to observe activities occurring on its open Internet connections and close connections when needed. The more expensive routers also provide VPN support, antivirus support, and content filtering.

Broadband routers are mainly marketed and used for cable and DSL broadband connections; however, the same hardware can be adapted for dialup or ISDN connections. If security and/or Internet sharing are needed, a router can provide a simple method to provide both, even though the connection to the Internet might be slow compared to cable or DSL. NetGear markets both a 56K and ISDN version of their Internet Gateway router, and the SMC Barricade can be connected to a 56K modem using its serial interface.

Summary

In this chapter, the discussion begins with the various hardware broadband routers and firewalls suited for the home and small office environment. This is followed by a description of how to set up a broadband router and the security mechanisms a hardware firewall can provide. This chapter explains the steps required to set up a Linksys BEFSR41 EtherFast Cable/DSL Router. The next chapter takes our discussion into the benefits and risks of telecommuting.

The Benefits and Risks of Telecommuting

 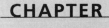
IN THIS CHAPTER

In This Chapter

The advent of the Internet and, more recently, broadband connections that provide convenient high-speed Internet access from the home, have enabled a new form of working: telecommuting. The basic idea of telecommuting is that by using telecommunications and Internet technology, an organization can provide limited or complete access to its information systems to employees working from home or the road.

There are clear benefits to telecommuting for many individuals and the organizations that employ them. However, these benefits bring risks with them, both for the end users who are telecommuting as well as the organizations that enable their workers to work in this manner.

The Advantages of Telecommuting

Telecommuting has several obvious advantages. In fact, many organizations now allow at least some of their employees to telecommute at least some of the time. Recent statistics suggest that as many as 58% of employees work from home after normal work hours, another 16% work from home on an occasional basis and 1% of workers work from home full time. These numbers appear set to only increase.

For organizations, the advantages of telecommuting can include:

- Reducing office space requirements that can reduce costs and solve office overcrowding problems.
- Leveraging employee time better by allowing empolyees to work while traveling.
- Improving employee morale by allowing them to work in the environments they prefer (at least some of the time).

Employees permitted to telecommute gain obvious benefits:

- Reducing the time spent commuting to work (if they telecommute from home).
- Scheduling their work when they are most productive.
- Increasing quality time with their families (this is a highly personal issue; some people feel working at home means they work more and spend less time with their families).
- Choosing the environment in which they want to work, instead of working in the environment dictated by their organization's offices.

These are not the only benefits of telecommuting; companies and employees have cataloged numerous other benefits when telecommuting is used appropriately for the right employees.

This isn't to say there aren't large organizational issues with telecommuting, such as the need for organizations to ensure that employees are working when they are being paid, ensuring work gets done and handling inter-employee rivalry about who is allowed to telecommute and who isn't. Organizations also need to provide the necessary hardware, software and support staff for a telecommuting program to succeed.

Still, the benefits are significant enough that since the late 1990s telecommuting is now an accepted business practice in many industries in North America.

How Telecommuting Works

Conceptually, telecommuting is simple: Any arrangement in which an employee works from outside the office and uses telecommunications or the Internet to enable that work process can be considered telecommuting.

There are varying degrees of integration with an organization's internal information systems for telecommuting employees. This ranges from limited access (an employee might only be able to access their e-mail), to moderate access (an employee can access their e-mail and maybe a corporate intranet Web site), to full access (an employee dials into the corporate network or uses virtual private networking) to work as if they are still in the office.

TIP
Virtual private networking is a way to connect to two networks across the Internet in a secure fashion. Virtual private networking is discussed in detail in the next chapter.

It is important to realize that the security issues surrounding these models increase as more access is granted to the corporate network.

At the high end, when users dial in or use virtual private networking to connect to the corporate network, their PC becomes a full member of the corporate network. In terms of their capability to perform work-related information systems tasks, there is no effective difference between being in the office or at home.

Figure 13.1 illustrates how a telecommuter can effectively become part of the corporate network.

13

THE BENEFITS AND RISKS OF TELECOMMUTING

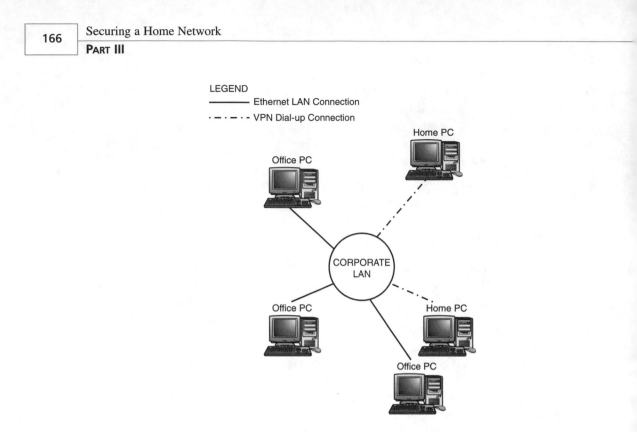

LEGEND
———— Ethernet LAN Connection
· — · — · · VPN Dial-up Connection

FIGURE 13.1

Using virtual private networking with dial-up connections to extend a corporate network to include telecommuters.

This type of full-scale connectivity has great advantages, allowing you the full flexibility you need to get work done from outside the office. However, this presents serious risks, because corporate security concerns now extend to the end user. The remainder of this chapter outlines these risks and highlights the areas of concern that are the responsibility of the telecommuter working from home or the road.

Risks of Telecommuting and Possible Solutions

When telecommuting is used to provide full access to the corporate network by employees from remote locations, serious security risks come into play. These risks range from the simple human risk to the more technical risks:

- Is the employee's remote PC physically secure?
- Is the network the employee is using to access the corporate network secure?
- Is the communication channel the employee using secure?

Any one of these risks causes potential security holes that could be outside the control of the corporate information systems departments.

In fact, there have been numerous high-profile security breaches that might be attributed to security holes created through telecommuting. For instance, an attack on Microsoft in the Fall of 2000 in which source code for future products was compromised might have, in part, been attributable to employees accessing the corporate network from home.

Is the Telecommuter's PC Physically Secure?

Organizations can do a lot to ensure that the PCs on their site are physically secure. This can prevent unauthorized users from walking up to the PCs and attempting to use them to gain access to the corporate network; it can also prevent the theft of the computers and the data they contain. In addition, it is possible to ensure that the necessary backup precautions are taken to ensure that data is secure should a system be physically damaged.

When a telecommuter's remote PC is introduced into the mix, this physical security is harder to maintain. Several problems arise:

- The physical location of the PC might not be secure. For instance, family members or visitors might have access to the PC in someone's home, or the telecommuter might leave the PC in their hotel room when they go out for the day. These are not controlled, secure environments the way a corporate office can be.
- The user might be in a public space where others can observe them typing their user-name or password.
- Telecommuters will not typically back up their computers. The result is that any work-related data stored on their PCs cannot be restored if the PC is stolen or damaged.

As a telecommuter, you should take basic precautions you might not have thought about when your personal PC was used only for personal use:

- Make sure you never leave your PC unattended in an unsecure location.
- Make regular backups of your data. Chapter 24, "Backup Strategies," provides guidelines for creating a robust backup plan.

Is the Telecommuter's Network Secure?

This is a crucial question: By enabling a telecommuter's PC to connect to the corporate network, an organization is placing a certain level of implicit trust in the network where the telecommuter's PC is being used. After the telecommuter's PC is connected to the corporate network through another network and the Internet, several problems arise:

- Is the network the telecommuter is using safe from outside attack? If an attacker compromised the network, they in turn might compromise the telecommuter's PC, and through that the corporate network.

- Is the network trustworthy? If a telecommuter is working from home, it is safe to say you can trust the users of that network. However, in a public context such as a convention center or a hotel with high-speed Internet access, nothing is known about the other individuals using or maintaining that network. How can one be sure that someone isn't intentionally trying to eavesdrop on connections originating from that network?

As an organization, several things can be done, such as limiting the networks from which users can connect to the corporate network, or assisting users in securing their home networks.

As a telecommuter working from home, you should strive to implement the maximum security of your home network as outlined in this book. Basically, if you wouldn't feel comfortable with your level of home security for your private, personal data, then you can be pretty sure you don't have a sufficient security environment for your company's critical work.

Is the Telecommuter's PC Secure?

This question is different from the physical security of a PC. Here, a corporate information systems manager needs to consider questions such as:

- Does the user's PC use a secure operating system? Windows 98 isn't secure; Windows 2000 can be made secure, as can Linux.

- Does the user's PC use strong passwords? Weak passwords are those that are easy to guess or crack.

- Does the user's PC have effective virus protection? If not, then there is a good chance a telecommuter can infect an organization's network with a virus.

As a telecommuter you want to ensure the following:

- Use a secure operating system if possible; if you can run Windows 2000 or XP at home instead of 98 or Me, do it. Windows 98 and Me do not enforce security; you can use a Windows 98 or Me PC without any username and password. The login dialog box you see after a Windows 98 or Me system starts does not prevent use of the machine, but rather is meant to identify users so they can use their personal profile and desktop settings.

- Make sure you use *strong passwords*. Strong passwords are those that combine letters, numbers and punctuation and are not based on words from the dictionary.

- Make sure you use the latest virus software and keep it regularly updated as outlined in Chapter 9, "Vaccinating Your Computer Against Viruses."

There are other things you should do to help ensure your security. You can keep any truly sensitive files you use, including those from work, encrypted on your PC. Encryption is discussed in Chapter 19, "Encryption." Similarly, make sure you routinely monitor the security of your home computer that you use for telecommuting as outlined in Chapter 20, "Testing Your Security by Attacking Yourself," Chapter 21, "Managing Your Logs," and Chapter 23, "Maintaining Your Protection."

Is the Communications Channel Secure?

This is, perhaps, the most important security issue when telecommuting is used. No matter how much you do to keep your computer and network secure, if the connection to your corporate network is itself insecure, then all the other security issues are irrelevant.

Insecure communications permit an attacker to monitor all the communication between your PC and your organization's network. This means that passwords and usernames can be seen, data in files can be captured and information will be revealed to attackers, which they can then use when attempting to attack the corporate network.

For this reason, you should discuss the security of the communication channel with the information systems staff in your organization. Specifically, consider the following:

- If you connect to the organization's network through the Internet while telecommuting, discuss the possibility of using virtual private networking, covered in Chapter 14, "Using Virtual Private Networks."
- If you dial-up to the corporate network, ask about dial-back security, in which you dial in to the network and log in and the network disconnects and calls your computer back. This enables you to limit your connections to specific locations and if someone attempts to dial in and authenticate as you from the wrong location, they will not be able to gain access to the corporate network.

Summary

If you work for an organization where you might have the opportunity to telecommute, you need to be aware of the security issues this involves. If you aren't careful as a telecommuter, you will expose your organization's computers to unnecessary security risk. In this chapter you learned about these issues and steps you can take to minimize them.

The next chapter introduces a subject mentioned several times in this chapter: virtual private networking. VPN's enable you to use the public Internet to create private connections between two computers or two networks using an encrypted communication channel. When two networks establish a VPN connection, it is as if the two networks had a dedicated physical line connecting them; in theory no one can monitor the traffic between the networks or break into the channel.

Using Virtual Private Networks

 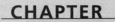

14

IN THIS CHAPTER

In This Chapter

In this chapter we will look at how Virtual Private Networks (VPNs) are used. We will discuss how they work and the uses for a Virtual Private Network. However, we will not discuss how to set up a VPN in detail, as this is beyond the scope and difficulty of this book. Nevertheless, we expect that people might need to set up a Virtual Private Network between their home and their place of work, so at the end of this chapter, we will discuss what is involved in deploying a VPN and what you need to know to get started.

What Is a Virtual Private Network?

In basic terms, a Virtual Private Network, commonly referred to as a VPN, is a private network of computers that communicates over a public network infrastructure. This is unlike a private network, where all the computers communicate over a physically private network. A VPN uses Internet tunneling and security mechanisms to provide the privacy and security needed to transport data privately and securely across the public Internet.

Tunneling is a method that allows data to be transported securely between two computers over a public network. Because the Internet is a public network, tunneling is required to provide a secure path for the exchange of data. Tunneling protects your data from being sniffed and eavesdropped upon during transport over the public infrastructure.

Virtual Private Networks have the following components:

- Data encryption—Locking data in to a form that is not comprehensible unless unencrypted with a key.
- Authentication—The process of verifying something's identification. The process verifies that the supplied identification truly belongs to the presenter of the credentials. The presenter can be a person, some data or a thing.
- Private network topology—The pictorial description of a network. A network topology allows you to view how a network is laid out as well as its components. For a VPN, the network topology consists of what public links and components the private network uses.

The combination of these three components allows a Virtual Private Network to function and provide secure data transmission over the Internet.

A VPN functions by encrypting all data before it is transported in a network tunnel, and decrypting it as it arrives at the end of the tunnel. Encryption prevents intruders from eavesdropping and stealing the data.

When data arrives at its destination; the data must be authenticated to verify that the data was not tampered with during transport or sent by an illegitimate sender. Authentication guards against intruders spoofing the identities of the network users.

Because a VPN uses the Internet, the public network links used by the VPN can become potential targets of intruders and eavesdroppers. A VPN must always protect the topology of its private network. If intruders were able to determine a VPN's topology, it would allow them to easily set up and eavesdrop on the private network.

> **NOTE**
>
> In addition to the three VPN components, VPNs are commonly coupled with firewalls at either side of the network tunnel. The firewalls provide access control to the tunnel and sometimes help the VPN function.

How Virtual Private Networks Are Used

There are two primary uses for a Virtual Private Network:

- A remote user connects to their business or office LAN; this is referred to as a client-server VPN.
- Two physically remote offices connect their LANs together; this is called a server-to-server VPN.

Client-Server Virtual Private Network

There are a number ways a company can provide internal LAN access to its employees. One popular method involves providing a dial-up modem pool for employees to connect to the LAN. This is a quite secure solution because the access to the modem pool is controlled, and the phone lines are controlled by the telephone company.

A Client-Server VPN would be an alternative method to provide employees internal LAN access. As shown in Figure 14.1, a remote user would connect to the company's internal LAN using the Internet. As for required infrastructure, the company would need to install a VPN server and provide each of the employees a VPN client.

14

USING VIRTUAL
PRIVATE
NETWORKS

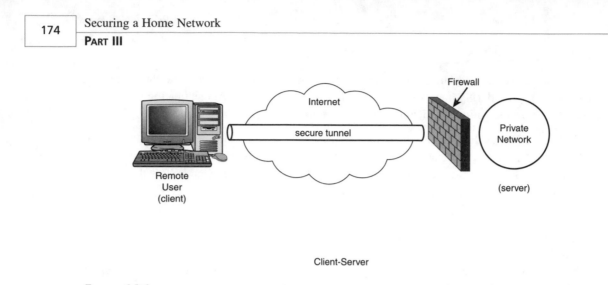

Client-Server

FIGURE 14.1

A client-server VPN.

However, a client-server VPN implementation provides a number of benefits. First, by using a VPN, the company does not need to maintain a modem pool. This saves on hardware costs and telephone line charges, and requires less maintenance as modem technology changes. In addition, a VPN provides the user with a potentially higher bandwidth connection. A modem pool implementation would limit the connection to the speed of the modem connection; however, a VPN connection would only be limited to the remote user's Internet connection, the company's Internet connection, or the current speed of the overall Internet. Lastly, a VPN implementation would only require the user to have an Internet connection. It would not matter whether the user was using a broadband connection or a dial-up connection.

Conversely, there are a few drawbacks to a client-server VPN solution. First, security is a major issue. A VPN transports data over a public infrastructure, which is easily accessible by intruders. Second, the connection to the company's internal LAN becomes coupled with the health of the Internet; if the Internet has problems, access to the internal LAN is affected. And finally, a VPN requires added hardware, software and in some cases added network bandwidth.

Server-to-Server VPN

One method to connect two remote offices is to lease or own private data lines between the two offices. This allows a company to connect two offices securely and provide guaranteed network bandwidth between the two sites. However, the costs of renting or owning private data lines are very high.

A Server-to-Server Virtual Private Network provides an alternative method to enable two remote offices to connect together securely using the existing public Internet infrastructure. As shown in Figure 14.2, two remote offices are connected using the public Internet. This provides a financial benefit because a company can obtain the same capabilities of a private network created using privately owned or leased data lines at a much lower cost by using a public infra-structure. However, a VPN does not guarantee the same network performance as a leased line, nor does it provide the same level of security as a private line and results in more maintenance because the multiple network connection must be managed.

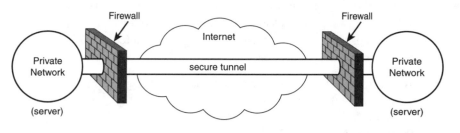

FIGURE 14.2
A server-to-server VPN.

How to Set Up a Virtual Private Network

The complete setup and deployment of a Virtual Private Network is beyond the scope of this book. However, many readers of this book might work for companies or be associated with corporations that provide a Virtual Private Network to connect to their private and internal LANs.

In this section, we will discuss the possible implementations of a VPN including software and hardware, and discuss the protocols used in Virtual Private Networks.

> **NOTE**
>
> It must be noted that the business or corporation providing the VPN access usually conducts the deployment of the Virtual Private Network tools. This is mainly because many VPNs use proprietary software and hardware or require specific configuration of the software.

14

USING VIRTUAL
PRIVATE
NETWORKS

Software and Hardware Virtual Private Networks

Similarly to firewalls, there are three types of Virtual Private Network implementations:

- Standalone software VPN
- Firewall software VPN
- Hardware VPN

Standalone software Virtual Private Networks are not coupled with a firewall, and hence provide the advantage that a VPN can connect two LANs that use different firewall technologies. In addition, standalone software VPNs do not tunnel all data traffic, as in the case of a router, but only the data that is to be transported in the VPN.

Firewall software Virtual Private Networks employ the security mechanisms provided in a firewall. The advantage of firewall based VPNs is that security is unified; the LAN and VPN are protected in all levels of the system, from the operating system interface to all network connections and applications that use the network.

Hardware Virtual Private Networks are in actuality just encrypting routers. They are limited in configuration, but provide the best performance.

Virtual Private Network Protocols

There are a number of protocols that are currently being used to create Virtual Private Networks and the secure tunneling required for such a network. In this section, we will briefly discuss a number of the more popular protocols.

- Point-to-Point Tunneling Protocol (PPTP) is a standard proposed by Microsoft and other companies, and is based on an extension of the Internet's Point-to-Point protocol (PPP). PPTP protocol does not specify an encryption scheme for the transportation of data, but is left to the implementation. This has led to some problems because security experts have criticized the encryption scheme used in Microsoft's implementation of the protocol. An advantage of PPTP is that PPP is integral to all of Microsoft's newer operating systems. Hence, all newer Microsoft operating systems are PPTP and VPN capable.

- IPSec stands for Internet Protocol Security and is a developing standard for secure communications over the Internet. IPSec provides two security services: an Authentication Header (AH) that provides authentication of data, and Encapsulating Security Payload (ESP) that provides both authentication and encryption of data. IPSec is becoming the preferred VPN protocol.

- Layer Two Tunnel Protocol is a combination of Microsoft's PPTP and Cisco System's Layer-2 Forwarding (L2F) protocol. L2F enables remote users to connect and authenticate to private networks using public Internet service providers (ISP) .

Installing the Window's VPN Connection

In this section we will describe how to create a VPN connection in Windows 98 or Me and Windows 2000.

Windows 98 or Me VPN Connection

For Windows 98 or Me, you must first enable the Virtual Private Network component in Windows. From the Start menu, select, Settings, Control Panel and Add/Remove Programs. Select the Windows Setup tab and select the Communications component as shown in Figure 14.3.

FIGURE 14.3

Select the Communications component in Windows Setup.

Select Details for the Communications component. In the Communications dialog box, as shown in Figure 14.4, select Virtual Private Networking.

FIGURE 14.4

Select Virtual Private Networking from the Communications Dialog box.

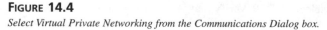

14

USING VIRTUAL PRIVATE NETWORKS

The installation of this component will require the computer to be restarted and in some cases require the Windows installation disk.

After the computer has restarted, select the Dial-up Networking Wizard and create a new connection. Under the name for the computer you are dialing, enter the name you would like to call this VPN connection. Our example uses VPN as the name, as shown in Figure 14.5. Select the device as Microsoft VPN Adapter.

FIGURE 14.5

Name the VPN connection and select the Microsoft VPN Adapter.

As shown in Figure 14.6, in the next dialog box, enter the hostname or IP address of the VPN server you would like to connect to.

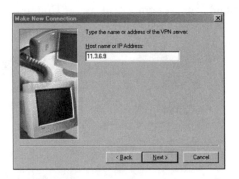

FIGURE 14.6

Enter the hostname or IP address of the VPN server.

As shown in Figure 14.7, after the VPN connection is created, an icon is created in the Dial-up Networking dialog box. Right-click on the VPN icon and select Properties.

Under Allowed Network Protocols, select TCP/IP. Verify that your settings are the same as those shown in Figure 14.8.

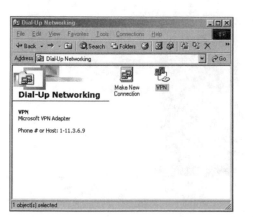

FIGURE 14.7
The newly created VPN icon.

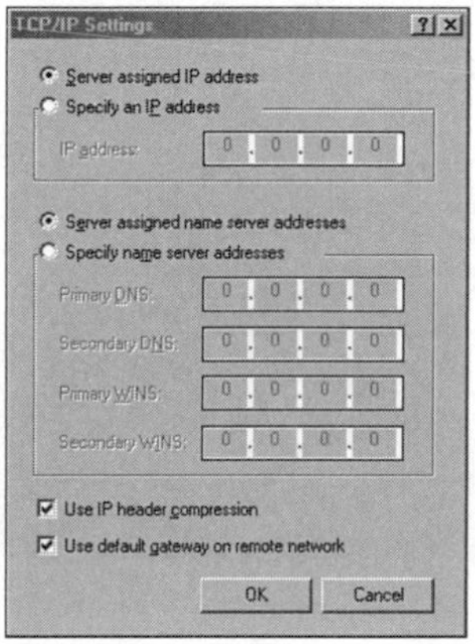

FIGURE 14.8
TCP/IP settings for the VPN connection.

Your VPN connection is now created and ready for use.

Windows 2000 VPN Connection

The VPN installation process for Windows 2000 is similar to that of Windows 98 and Me.

First you need to select the Network Connection Wizard as shown in Figure 14.9.

In the Network Connection Type dialog box, you must select Connect to a Private Network Through the Internet as shown in Figure 14.10.

14

USING VIRTUAL PRIVATE NETWORKS

FIGURE 14.9

Windows 2000 Network Connection Wizard.

FIGURE 14.10

Select Connect to a Private Network Through the Internet in the Network Connection Type dialog box.

In the Destination Address dialog box, as shown in Figure 14.11, enter the hostname or IP address of the VPN server you would like to connect to.

As shown in Figure 14.12, select the availability of the VPN connection for other users on this computer.

Finally, assign a name to this VPN connection, as shown in Figure 14.13.

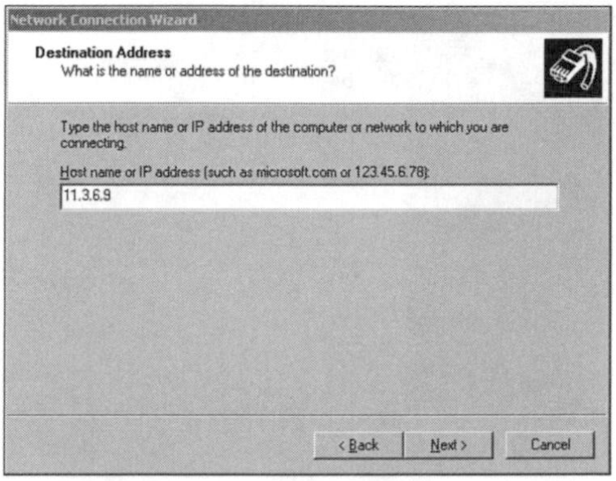

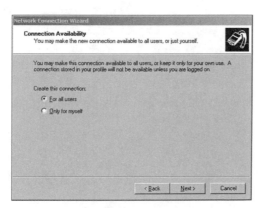

FIGURE 14.11

Destination Address: the hostname or IP address you would like to connect to.

FIGURE 14.12

Select the availability of this VPN connection for other users of this computer.

Your VPN connection is now set up and ready for use. But similarly to Windows 98 and Me, you can right-click on your new VPN connection icon and select Properties.

In your VPN Properties dialog box, you can configure your network, security, and other options. Shown in Figure 14.14 are the options for VPN security configuration.

14

USING VIRTUAL
PRIVATE
NETWORKS

FIGURE 14.13
Enter a name for this VPN connection.

FIGURE 14.14
Security options for your VPN connection.

Summary

In this chapter, we discussed what a Virtual Private Network (VPN) is, what a VPN is used for, and how VPNs are set up. VPNs provide private networking over the public Internet. This provides cost savings and added connectivity benefits, however it also increases potential security intrusions and chances of connectivity loss.

In the next chapter, our discussion delves into how to provide Internet services securely.

Providing Internet Services

IN THIS CHAPTER

In This Chapter

Most home Internet users will not need to offer Internet services from their home. However, some users do find themselves faced with this need. For instance, if you run a home office or small office, there might be compelling reasons why you want to directly offer Internet services such as a Web site running on a computer in your office or a small FTP server that allows users to download or upload files to you directly across the Internet.

In order to do this, you will need to allow some incoming Internet connections to enter your computer or LAN, and this, inherently, is a security risk that normal home users can avoid with a good firewall strategy.

Still, if you do have to offer these sorts of services, you can do it in ways that minimize the risk to the rest of your network and computers. This chapter outlines three basic strategies to offer Internet services in a secure fashion:

- Limit incoming ports
- Isolate the service
- Use a DMZ

The Risks of Internet Services

So far in this book, you have been presented with security strategies such as using personal firewall software, proxy servers, or broadband gateways, which are designed to restrict your systems to allow only outgoing access and no incoming access. Of course, if you plan to offer Internet services such as a Web server, FTP server, or mail server on your home network, by definition you need some incoming access. Otherwise, users on the Internet would not be able to access the services you were offering.

Of course, therein lies the risk: By offering limited incoming access to your network for these services, you are creating a tunnel through which an attacker can attempt to gain unauthorized access to your computers. For this reason, you need to take care when setting up your network to allow limited access to Internet services you are offering.

Typically, you will be offering access to Web or FTP services on your network. Although these can generally be implemented in a secure fashion, you need to be aware of the risks involved.

Web Server Risks

Web servers such as Personal Web Server, which comes with Windows 98 and Me and Internet Information Server, which comes with Windows NT 4 and Windows 2000, have a history of security bugs that have since been patched. Of course, there is no reason to assume that there aren't still outstanding unidentified security holes that might one day be leveraged by crackers intent on attacking Web servers on the Internet. Among the types of bugs that have been discovered are

- Attackers can expose the content of a file by composing URLs in a specific manner. This can expose the actual code of scripts on your Web server to attackers, which in turn can allow them to study your own code for any security weaknesses it might contain.

- Attackers can run operating system commands on the Web server by constructing specially designed requests to the Web server. This can allow an attacker almost unlimited access to the resources on your Web server and, potentially, your entire network.

- Attackers could create denial of service attacks by forcing the Web server to spend large amounts of time and resources processing specific types of invalid requests.

- Attackers could gain unauthorized access to the content of a database running on a Web server if they know the name of the database. This can potentially expose sensitive information in your databases to prying eyes or even allow attackers to change that information without your knowing it.

Although these security holes all have patches available from Microsoft to fix them, they are just a small example of the numerous security holes that have been exposed in Web servers.

In addition, the following security risks inherent in Web servers are not the result of bugs but are part of the design of Web servers:

- Web servers are effectively allowing Web users to access some files on the Web server computer. Normally, Web servers only allow access to files from a specific, limited directory. But, if you misconfigure your Web server, it might allow access to more files than you realize.

- Web servers can be used to provide interactive Web applications such as those written in Perl, Java, or Visual Basic. If the applications running in these languages are poorly written, they might contain security holes that can be used by an attacker. This is not the fault of the Web server but of poorly written code you make available on your Web server. If you plan to use CGI-BIN programming or any other Web application platform such as Active Server Pages or ColdFusion, you need to understand its own security limitations and ensure that your applications don't expose your Web server to unnecessary vulnerability.

Still, these risks do not mean that you shouldn't offer Web services from your network. If you have a motivated reason to do so, you should take precautionary steps to minimize the risk. After all, the only completely safe computer is one disconnected from the Internet, locked in a vault, and sunk to the bottom of the ocean. Instead, you should take advantage of the benefits of collaborating with others, which running your own Web server might offer you, while also taking the following basic precautions at the same time:

- Follow the security guidance in this chapter and the rest of this book.
- Keep your Web server up-to-date with the latest security patches.
- Pay attention to interactive applications you build, or deploy, for your Web site and make sure that no blatant bugs exist in your code.

Risks of FTP Servers

FTP servers are not as common for home and small office users as Web servers might be, but they provide a convenient way to share files with others. Using an FTP server, you can make selected files available to the general public or selected users and can provide a mechanism for others to upload files to you. Windows 98 and Me do not include FTP server software, but Internet Information Server in Windows NT and 2000 provides FTP capabilities. In addition, numerous options for FTP servers that you can download for Windows 98 or Windows Me are as follows:

- War FTP: This popular FTP server for Windows is available freely from `http://www.jgaa.com/`.
- Serv-U: This FTP server offers an easy-to-use interface for the low price of $39.95. You can download a trial version from `http://www.rhinosoft.com/`.
- Cerebus FTP Server: This free FTP server attempts to minimize the use of system resources and can be downloaded from `http://www.greenepa.net/~averett/cerberus.htm`.

Numerous other FTP servers for Windows can be found at `http://downloads.cnet.com/`.

Given the great variety of FTP servers available for Windows, it is not easy to identify specific security bugs that plague these products. However, certain basic principles of FTP server design expose you to risk. In particular, FTP servers make files available on the Internet. A misconfigured FTP server can allow any user on the Internet to download files from your PC that you don't want to make available. Even worse, the two-way nature of FTP could allow a user on the Internet to upload files or even overwrite existing files on the FTP server computer.

As with Web servers, if you take care to configure your FTP server correctly and implement a sound security plan, the benefits of providing FTP services might outweigh the risks for your particular needs.

Limit Incoming Ports

The basic principle of securely offering Internet services from your home network is to limit as strictly as possible the incoming connections that users on the Internet can make. Given this principle, you should only allow incoming access on the ports you need to use for this type of access. Some users make the mistake of configuring their firewalls to allow any incoming connection when they decide to allow Internet services, and by doing so not only make the desired service accessible but also expose all other services running on the Internet to attack from the Internet.

Consider an example: You want to offer Web services from your PC to the Internet. However, you also use Windows file sharing on your local network to share files and print. In offering Web services to the Internet, you don't want to allow users on the Internet to attempt to access files and printers on the Internet using Windows file sharing.

If you simply open up incoming access to your network, this is exactly what happens: Users on the Internet are free to attempt to establish Windows file sharing connections to computers on your network.

Instead, you want to allow incoming access only on port 80 because this is the default port used by Web servers.

The basic rule you need to follow, then, is only allow incoming connections on ports needed by services you want to be accessible from the Internet. Never just open up all incoming access to your network because you want to offer one or two services to the Internet.

Most firewalls available for home networks make this process simple. Consider the following example: You want to make a Web server on a machine on your network available to the Internet. The Web server is running on the host with the IP address 10.10.10.10 on your network, and you are using a Linksys Etherfast Cable/DSL Router.

In this situation, you can allow incoming access only to port 80 on the 10.10.10.10 machine as follows:

1. Access the Linksys administration tool using your Web browser. After logging in, you should see the Setup page of the administration tool as illustrated in Figure 15.1.

2. Click on the Advanced tab. The administration tool displays the advanced section of the tool as illustrated in Figure 15.2.

3. Click on the Forwarding tab. The administration tool will display the Forwarding page as illustrated in Figure 15.3.

4. Find the first empty line on the page. An empty line will have 0 in both of the Service Port Range fields and 0 as the last digit of the IP address.

5. Enter 80 in both of the Service Port Range fields on the first empty line.

6. Select TCP from the protocol drop-down list on the first empty line.

7. Enter 10 as the last digit of the IP address on the first empty line. The result should look like Figure 15.4.

8. Click on the Apply button.

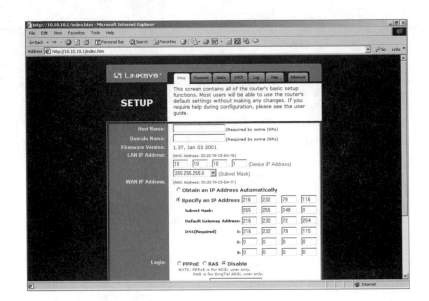

FIGURE 15.1
The Setup page of the Linksys administration tool.

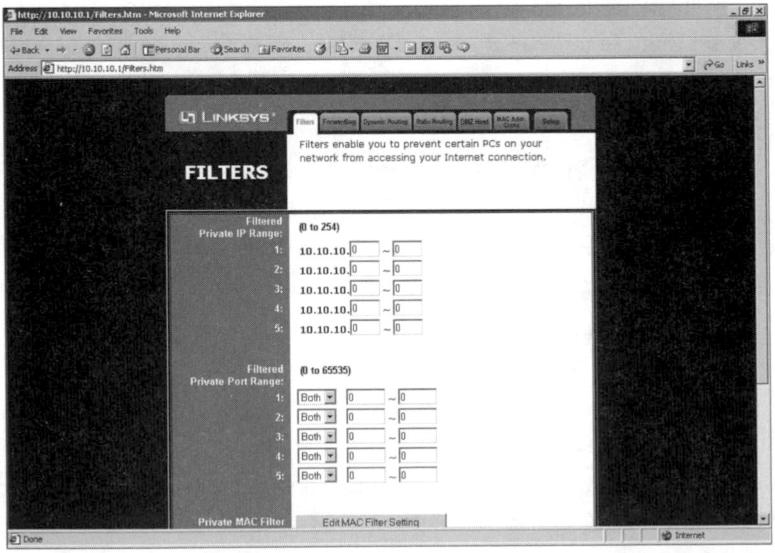

FIGURE 15.2
The advanced section of the Linksys administration tool.

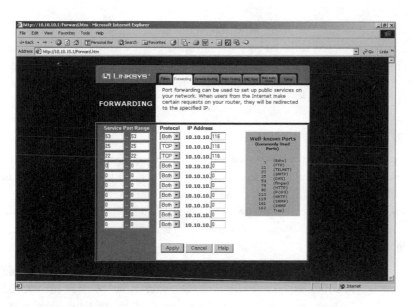

FIGURE 15.3

The Forwarding page of the Linksys administration tool.

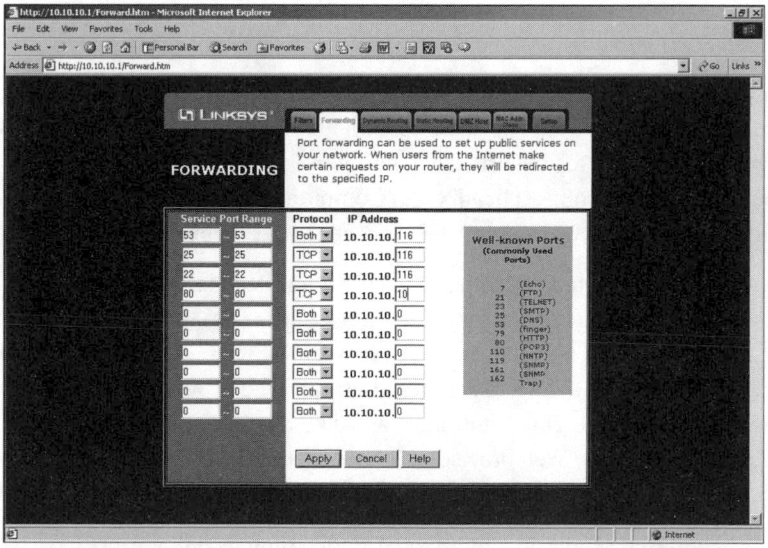

FIGURE 15.4

Allowing incoming Web access to the host 10.10.10.10 on the internal network.

The end result will be that any attempts to connect to port 80 on the router will be allowed and will be redirected to the 10.10.10.10 host that is acting as a Web server on your network. The basic principles of setting this up should work with any standard home broadband gateway even if the specifics of how to configure the router to allow an incoming Web connection might be different.

Use Non-standard Ports

Taking things further, you can consider using a non-standard port for your Internet service as a way of making it harder for attackers to identify the potential vulnerability on your network. Attackers will commonly perform port scans of hosts on the Internet in an attempt to find open ports that might expose vulnerabilities on a computer. In some cases, they might quickly scan known ports for popular services such as the Web, FTP, and e-mail in a quick attempt to find known vulnerabilities.

Of course, it is possible (and done by many would-be attackers), to perform an exhaustive scan looking for any service running on any port on a computer. However, this can take a long time, and a casual scan of a long series of hosts on the Internet might not actually attempt to scan all ports on all hosts.

For this reason, running a service on a non-standard port can make it just slightly harder for someone to attack you through the Web services you are offering; a casual attacker could miss the port.

With most Web services such as FTP or Web, it is easy to configure the server to work on a non-standard port and the service will work just fine on the new port. Typically, you will want to choose a port above 1024 for your non-standard port. You should consult a list of commonly-used ports such as that shown in Appendix C, "Common TCP Services and Ports," or a comprehensive list such as the one at http://www.stengel.net/tcpports.htm.

There is one thing you need to keep in mind. Using a non-standard port places some extra requirements on users wanting to use your Internet services. Using the Web as an example, Web servers typically run on port 80, and Web browser software knows this. Therefore, when you use the URL http://www.some.domain/, the Web browser connects to the server www.some.domain on port 80. This is the same as when the user types the URL http://www.some.domain:80/; the Web browser assumes that the user has explicitly specified port 80 in the URL when no port is specified.

But, if you run your Web server on a nonstandard port, such as 8888, users have to know this in order to access your server. Using the URL http://www.some.domain/ will fail to access your server because it is not running on port 80. Instead, users have to use the URL http://www.some.domain:8888/.

The question of whether it's suitable to your needs depends on why you are running a Web server. If you are running a highly public Web site that you want people to easily find and use, using a nonstandard port is problematic because most Internet users are not familiar with the idea of including port numbers in their URLs. If, on the other hand, you are running a Web server to share a Web site with a small group of friends or colleagues, it is reasonable to share a URL including a port number with them.

Restricting Access by IP Address

If you are running a Web site, FTP server, or other Internet service designed for use by specific individuals only, you might be able to restrict access to the service even further based on knowing where the user will be accessing the Web site from.

If you know which computer each user will be using, you can determine the IP addresses of all those computers and allow access to the service in question only from those computers.

Using the Web as an example again, imagine a Web site that you want your relatives to have access to. You know that those relatives will be accessing the site from one of two machines: 1.2.3.4 or 2.3.4.5. In this case, you can take two possible steps to restrict access to the service.

Some Web servers, such as Internet Information Server and Apache, provide the capability to restrict access based on the IP address. If you restrict access to the IP addresses 1.2.3.4 and 2.3.4.5, other users will be able to connect to the server, but will be denied access to any files on the server. This can greatly reduce the chance of attackers using the Web server as a point of attack.

Of course, this is not a perfect solution: Users from other IP addresses connect to the Web server and the Web server checks their IP addresses before denying access to the requested file. This means that it is possible to exploit potential security bugs in Web servers that ignore the authentication mechanisms of the Web server.

In order to address this, some gateways and routers provide an extra level of protection: Filtering incoming access on the basis of the IP address where the connection is originating. In this case, the firewall will not allow a connection to even reach the Web server if it comes from an invalid IP address. Typically, however, home Internet gateways such as the Linksys Etherfast Cable/DSL router do not provide this capability: Allowing an incoming connection on a specific port is an all-or-nothing proposition.

However, some higher-end routers aimed at the small office and corporate markets provide this capability. Routers that use Stateful Packet Inspection such as the SonicWALL SOHO2 from SonicWall (http://www.sonicwall.com/) generally offer this capability but tend to be higher-priced. The SonicWALL, for instance, retails for about $450.

Ideally, if you plan to use IP address restrictions, you want to enforce the restrictions both on the server in question as well as at the firewall. If your Internet gateway or firewall cannot perform IP address filtering on incoming connections, at the very least implement it on the server providing the Internet service.

Isolate Services

When you do decide to offer services on the Internet, you should take steps to isolate that service as much as possible from other services and computers in your house or office. Two main ways to do this that are not mutually exclusive are as follows:

- Use a separate machine
- Use a restricted user

Use a Separate Machine

It makes sense that if you run a Web service such as a Web server on a machine dedicated to that task, you reduce the risk that should an attacker compromise the Web server, he will be able to compromise other data and services as well. The basic concept is that if you have the resources available, each major service such as Web services, FTP services, or mail services should run on its own dedicated machine, and the only data stored on that machine should be data associated with the service running on the system.

In that way, a Web server would run on a dedicated computer and only Web site files would be stored on the computer. If an attacker found a way to compromise your Web server, only the data made available on that Web server could be compromised.

Isolate the Machine on the Network

Having said that you should use a separate machine, you might need to take extra actions to ensure that if, for instance, a dedicated Web server is compromised, no other computer on your LAN is in danger. The danger lies in the fact that although the Web service might run on a dedicated separate computer, that computer will still be connected to your LAN and it might be possible for an attacker who has gained access to the Web server to then launch attacks against other machines on your network.

To prevent this, you need to take steps to isolate the machine as much as possible on your network. Using a Web server as an example, this includes doing the following:

- Make sure that the Web server does not belong to the same Windows workstation or domain as other machines on your network. This will prevent that machine from having file sharing or printing access to other machines on the network.
- Use different usernames and passwords on the Web server than on other machines on the network. This is especially true of any administrator passwords.

- If you run services such as FTP servers or mail servers on other machines on the network for internal use (as opposed to use from the Internet), try to restrict access to these by IP address and then deny access from the Web server.

Use a Restricted User

If you can't run your Internet services on a dedicated machine, you need to take steps to limit access of the service's process to resources on the computer it is running on.

Consider the situation in which a Web server is running on the personal computer you use for your daily work. You want users to be able to access your Web site files through the Web server, but if the server is compromised, you want them to have minimal access to your sensitive work files.

The way to do this is to run the Web server software as a special user with restricted access. All programs on a computer run as a specific user. Normally, when you log in and run applications, the programs you launch run as you, and their capability to access files and resources on the computer is based on your account's permissions to do so. However, some software might run as other users. This is particularly true of applications that start at boot time and run in the background: This includes software that provides Internet services such as Web server software. These applications can be designated to run as any specific user in operating systems such as Windows NT, 2000, or Linux. In this way, you can restrict access to resources by restricting the rights of that user to access resources on the system.

> **NOTE**
>
> You need to be running a true multiuser operating system to run background services as specific users. Windows 98 and Windows Me are not true multiuser systems, and, accordingly, you can't control the user a process runs as: All processes run as the same user (including applications you run while working) and have equal permissions to access files and resources on the computer.

It is normal practice to run services, such as Web servers, as special users created just for that process. These user accounts are typically highly restricted, having permission only to access files needed to provide access to a Web site. In most cases, the result is that if a service such as Web server is compromised, the attacker's access to the system is limited to the permissions of the user under which the Web server software is running.

By way of example, Internet Information Server typically creates a special guest user who it runs as. This account is called IUSR_COMPUTERNAME, where COMPUTERNAME is the name of the computer on which the Web server software is running. Then, the IUSR_COMPUTERNAME user must have permission to access files that are part of the Web site and will have limited or no access to any other files on the system.

Allowing Controlled Access with a Demilitarized Zone

In Chapter 10, "Overview of Firewalls," you were introduced to the idea of a demilitarized zone or *DMZ*, which is one or more machines on a pseudo-internal network. Your internal network allows no incoming access from the Internet or the DMZ. The DMZ allows limited incoming access from the Internet. The DMZ can then be used for public servers such as Web servers and mail servers. If an attacker succeeds in compromising systems in the DMZ, he still cannot compromise systems on the internal network.

Some higher-end gateways and firewalls provide the capability to create a DMZ network. This includes units such as the SonicWALL SOHO2 mentioned earlier in this chapter. If your router or gateway devices can create a DMZ, you can use this DMZ to run dedicated computers for your Internet services and still keep your internal network as secure as it was before you started offering the Internet services. This is the technique typically used in corporate installations in which security is critical.

DMZs and Home Broadband Routers

Be careful when using the term DMZ. Most home broadband routers, including those from LinkSys, D-Link, 3-Com, and Netgear, use this term in an incorrect and misleading way. They use DMZ to mean a single machine on your internal network to which you allow unlimited incoming access while all other machines on the network have limited, controlled incoming access. This is not a real DMZ because it doesn't create a separate, pseudo-internal network and simply exposes one host on your internal LAN. The reason home network gateways provide this facility is for some network games that require open access between two systems.

Unfortunately, this is not a true DMZ, and if you use this DMZ feature to provide access to a machine offering Internet services, not only do you expose all ports on that machine, but also that machine becomes a potential source of attack against your entire network. The DMZ feature of home Internet gateways should be used with great caution.

Summary

This chapter has discussed how to go about offering Internet services in a secure fashion. Most home readers will not need to offer Internet services, and this chapter will really only help inform them about the issues others face. But, if you do plan to offer Web, FTP, or other services from your network, you need to carefully consider the suggestions made in this chapter, including using a DMZ, using a restricted user, restricting by IP address, and isolating processes to secure those services sufficiently so that they do not expose your data and resources unnecessarily.

In the next chapter you enter into a new section of the book: "Privacy and Data Security." The first chapter in this section deals with the question of human issues in security such as how people should choose passwords, deciding what information to provide to Web sites on the Internet, and the physical security of your computer systems. Other chapters in the section address cookies, anonymous surfing, and encryption.

Privacy and Data Security

PART
IV

IN THIS PART

Human Issues in Security

IN THIS CHAPTER

In This Chapter

Keeping your computers and yourself secure on the Internet means much more than simply using the right virus software and firewall or Internet gateway. There is a whole human side to security in which you need to consider behavior—your own as well as that of others—and how that impacts your security when using the Internet.

Submitting Information to a Web Site

When you use the World Wide Web, there will be many instances in which you will be asked to submit personal information such as your name, address, and phone number or even your social security number and credit card number to a Web site. You should take great care in this regard and only submit the information, and the minimum of information, when you can feel safe doing so.

The danger here lies in several areas:

- If you provide contact information to a Web site, that site can turn around and sell your information to others for use in unsolicited mass e-mail–based promotions or targeted mail campaigns. Your phone number could also lead to unsolicited telemarketing calls.

- If you provide contact information to an unknown Web site, you have no guarantee of how that information will be used: When someone knows your home address and phone number, you could be targeted for different types of scams and physical attacks such as break-ins.

- Beware of identity theft: With your name and social security number, it is possible for someone to assume your identity. This can affect your credit rating, threaten your job and future, or lead to serious problems with the law. Never give out your social security number on the Internet unless there is a valid reason for it (for instance, a government agency requests it or you are applying for a job) and then only when you can verify who is receiving the information.

In the end, the danger of the Web and the Internet is the uncertainty of where your personal information goes when you submit a form or send an e-mail. After all, it is impossible to be certain if the place where your form is being submitted is really the recipient you intend to receive the information. For instance, it is possible for illegitimate individuals or organizations to pose as major organizations on the Internet or to misdirect a form if they have sufficient skill.

For these reasons, you should take some basic precautions:

- Maintain an alternative e-mail address
- Provide minimal information
- Provide personal information by alternative means

Maintain an Alternative E-mail Address

To protect yourself from unsolicited e-mail and keep your primary e-mail account for personal and business use only as you determine is appropriate, you should consider opening a free e-mail account with a provider such as HotMail (`www.hotmail.com`) or Yahoo! Mail (`mail.yahoo.com`). By doing this, you can ensure that the e-mail address you distribute to unknown parties on the Internet is one that you don't have to read, don't really care about, and can cancel without adversely affecting your work and personal communication.

Then, whenever you need to provide an e-mail address in a Web form, you can use this alternative e-mail address.

You might want to consider an anti-spam e-mail service such as SpamMotel (`www.spammotel.com`). With SpamMotel, you can create a special e-mail address for each Web form you submit and keep a note of when and who received that address. Then, any e-mails sent to one of these special addresses is forwarded back to you with the note about the when and how you originally used that address. If you find out that one of your special addresses is used for spam, you can block messages sent to that particular address. You can also respond to incoming messages to these addresses and your true identity will be removed by SpamMotel before the message is sent to the recipient.

The end result is a system for completely hiding your identity and tracking which form submissions led to spam. It also adds a level of inconvenience because you must generate these custom e-mail addresses from SpamMotel for each form you submit on the Web.

Taking things a step further, some privacy advocates on the Internet suggest that you use false e-mail addresses, deliberately altering your address so that it is invalid or use one of many anti-spam e-mail addresses when filling out Web forms or posting to online discussions or newsgroups. These techniques allow you to prevent spam and can actually serve to hide your identity. However, there is a problem: Some sites to which you will need to provide your address will need to be able to send e-mails back to you, but they also might sell your address to spammers. In this case, if you use one of these techniques, the legitimate e-mails as well as the spam messages will be blocked.

Provide Minimal Information

The importance of keeping tight control over what personal information you reveal and when is crucial. The more information you provide, the more likely it is that it will be abused and potentially used for criminal purposes such as identity theft. For this reason, consider the following limitations on the distribution of information:

- If a Web site asks you to create profiles to use the site, consider not creating the profile or not using the site. Unless you get some genuine benefit from creating a profile, don't provide the profile information to the Web site.

- If you need to provide personal information to a site, consider limiting that information to only what the site needs to provide you with the service you need. First, only provide information in the mandatory fields and not the optional fields, if possible. Second, minimize the information provided: If an address is required by the Web site, does it really need your complete address?

Never provide a credit card number or social security number to a Web site unless there is a valid and verifiable reason for the site to request the information. Credit card numbers can be stolen and abused and end up costing you money or compromising your credit rating. When you must provide a credit card number, make sure that you know the Web site to which you are providing it and have read their security policies with respect to credit cards and credit card theft. Your social security number is particularly sensitive: Although your credit card company can help you in some cases of theft or abuse of your number, if your social security number is in the hands of the wrong party, identity theft can occur and have devastating consequences.

> **NOTE**
>
> Some advocates of privacy on the Internet would suggest that if you must provide personal information to a Web site to gain service from it, you should falsify the information using phone numbers such as 123-456-7890, e-mail addresses such as a@b.c, and false names such as First for the first name and Last for the last name. Of course, this can protect your identity while still allowing access to services that require the creation of profiles or providing personal information. However, there are cases in which this might be considered fraud. You need to be sure that there are no legal ramifications to falsifying your identity before creating such a false identity on a Web site.

Provide Personal Information by Alternative Means

With some sites, it might be more prudent to provide personal information, such as a credit card number, by alternative means. For instance, on many e-commerce sites, you can place your order online but then provide your credit card number by fax or telephone. The advantages of this are three-fold:

- Your credit card number is not transmitted on the Internet.
- You can verify the phone number you are calling against directory assistance to be sure that you are calling the correct organization.
- You can ask additional questions on the phone before providing your card number (that is, if you are not faxing).

Secure Web Connections

When you do need to provide personal information on the World Wide Web or the Internet in general, it is important to be aware of when your connections are secure.

Secure connections, such as the Secure Sockets Layer connections used by Web browsers and servers, encrypt your data while it is in transit from your computer to the destination server and, in theory, only the destination server should be able to unencrypt the data.

> **TIP**
>
> Encryption and related ideas are discussed in detail in Chapter 19, "Encryption."

Secure connections of this sort are important to maintaining your privacy and security when engaged in transactions on the Internet. Because it is relatively easy for eavesdroppers on the Internet to view the contents of any packet of information that passes them on the Internet, without encryption there would be no method of transmitting sensitive data that could be considered even remotely secure.

This doesn't mean that SSL-style encryption used on the Internet is foolproof; with enough computing power, time, patience, and skill, an attacker intent on compromising SSL-encrypted data could do so. However, SSL is enough of a deterrent that it effectively prevents this type of eavesdropping. This means that the real security concerns you need to address are those affecting information when it is stored on your computer or on the server maintained by a given Web site or company.

Having said all this, there are a few things to keep in mind when using the Internet.

First, when submitting sensitive personal information such as a credit card number or your social security number in a Web form, make sure that the connection is secure; there are two main ways to do this:

- The address in the address bar of your Web browser shows `https://` at the start instead of `http://`. For example, the Web address in Figure 16.1 indicates a secure Web connection.

Figure 16.1
Secure Web connections have `https://` addresses.

- The browser shows a closed padlock when viewing the current page.

  🔒   Internet Explorer

  🔒   Netscape 6

To ensure that you have a secure Web connection, both of these should be present when viewing the form you are about to submit. However, this is actually not sufficient to ensure the security of data your are about to submit. This is because of the way in which Web communication occurs. On the World Wide Web, data moves around in short, finite-length connections. Each connection works as follows:

1. Your browser contacts a Web server, requests a Web page, and provides any form data it might be submitting.

2. The server finds the Web page and returns it to your browser.

3. The connection is closed.

4. Your browser displays the page.

This means that when your browser is displaying a page such as a Web form and the two security indicators are present, all you know is that the page currently being viewed was retrieved by the browser across a secure Web connection. This doesn't mean that when you actually submit a form the new connection this creates will be secure. This all depends on whether the form you are currently viewing has been designed to submit its data using a secure Web connection.

Of course, it is the general practice of any reliable e-commerce site to make sure that forms are both retrieved and submitted across secure Web connections. Still, without a site explicitly indicating this on the form you are about to submit, you can't actually be positive that this is the case, and you normally would have no way to know this before submitting the form.

Fortunately, you do have one option if you are uncertain whether your data will be submitted using a secure Web connection: Look at the HTML code of the form you are viewing and check for yourself. This is actually easier than it sounds.

First, you need to display the HTML source code for the page you are currently viewing. The way you do this depends on which browser you are using:

- In Internet Explorer 5.5, select Source from the View menu. Internet Explorer will display the source code of the current document being displayed in Internet Explorer in Notepad. An example of the source code for a form is illustrated in Figure 16.2.

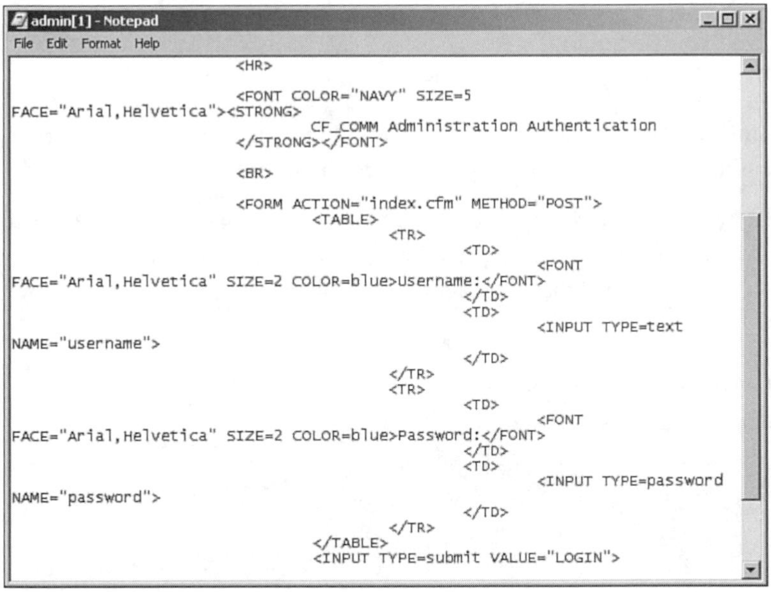

```
admin[1] - Notepad
File Edit Format Help
                              <HR>

                              <FONT COLOR="NAVY" SIZE=5
FACE="Arial,Helvetica"><STRONG>
                                        CF_COMM Administration Authentication
                              </STRONG></FONT>

                              <BR>

                              <FORM ACTION="index.cfm" METHOD="POST">
                                        <TABLE>
                                                  <TR>
                                                            <TD>
                                                                      <FONT
FACE="Arial,Helvetica" SIZE=2 COLOR=blue>Username:</FONT>
                                                            </TD>
                                                            <TD>
                                                                      <INPUT TYPE=text
NAME="username">
                                                            </TD>
                                                  </TR>
                                                  <TR>
                                                            <TD>
                                                                      <FONT
FACE="Arial,Helvetica" SIZE=2 COLOR=blue>Password:</FONT>
                                                            </TD>
                                                            <TD>
                                                                      <INPUT TYPE=password
NAME="password">
                                                            </TD>
                                                  </TR>
                                        </TABLE>
                                        <INPUT TYPE=submit VALUE="LOGIN">
```

FIGURE 16.2
Internet Explorer displays HTML source code in Notepad.

- In Netscape 6, select Page Source from the View menu. Netscape will display the source code of the current document being displayed in Netscape in a special window. An example of the source code for a form is illustrated in Figure 16.3.

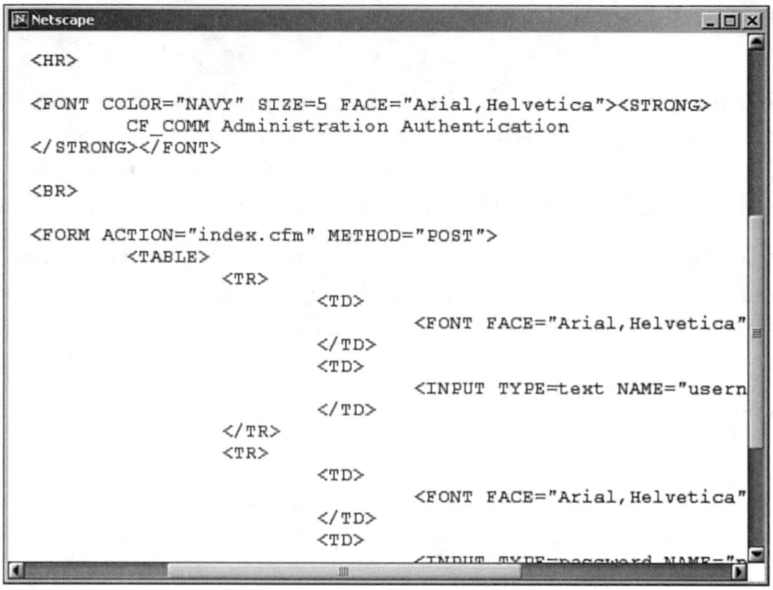

```
<HR>

<FONT COLOR="NAVY" SIZE=5 FACE="Arial,Helvetica"><STRONG>
        CF_COMM Administration Authentication
</STRONG></FONT>

<BR>

<FORM ACTION="index.cfm" METHOD="POST">
        <TABLE>
                <TR>
                        <TD>
                                <FONT FACE="Arial,Helvetica"
                        </TD>
                        <TD>
                                <INPUT TYPE=text NAME="usern
                        </TD>
                </TR>
                <TR>
                        <TD>
                                <FONT FACE="Arial,Helvetica"
                        </TD>
                        <TD>
                                <INPUT TYPE=password NAME="p
```

FIGURE 16.3

Netscape displays HTML source code in a special window.

When the source code is displayed, you need to find the place in the code where the target of your form submission is specified. This will be specified in the FORM tag.

As you might be aware, HTML consists of a lot of tags that take the form *<TAGNAME>*, *<TAGNAME options>*, or *</TAGNAME>* interspersed with text that will be displayed in the browser. In this case, you are looking for the FORM tag, which probably takes one of the following forms:

- <FORM METHOD="POST" TARGET="*some URL*" ...>
- <FORM METHOD="GET" TARGET="*some URL*" ...>
- <FORM TARGET="*some URL*" METHOD="POST"...>
- <FORM TARGET="*some URL*" METHOD="GET"...>

> **TIP**
>
> HTML tags are not case sensitive. Some Web developers use lowercase as in `<form target="`*`some URL`*`" ...>`, whereas others will use uppercase as previously outlined. In other cases, Web developers might appear to randomly mix upper- and lowercase styles as in `<form TARGET="`*`some URL`*`" ...>`.

The important point here is the URL specified in the part of the tag that looks like `TARGET="`*`some URL`*`"`. Depending on this URL, you can determine whether the form will submit using a secure Web connection. The following rules will allow you to determine this for yourself:

- If the URL is a complete URL of the form `http://some.host/some/file.html`, the form will not submit across a secure link. (The key here is the `http://` part of the URL.)

- If the URL is a complete URL of the form `https://some.host/some/file.html`, the form will submit across a secure link. (The key here is the `https://` part of the URL.)

- If the URL is a partial URL (that is, doesn't start with `http://` or `https://` but is either a filename or a path and filename such as `/some/path/and/file.html` or `../path/to/file.html`), the form will submit over the same type of connection that was used to retrieve the form itself. If the form you are submitting was obtained over a secure connection, it will be submitted using a secure connection.

> **NOTE**
>
> Just remember, no matter how secure the Web connection you use to send personal information to a Web site is, you are still trusting the Web site or the company receiving the information to keep your data safe and not misuse or abuse it!

One-Time Transactions

An interesting new e-commerce development is the idea of one-time credit card numbers for e-commerce transactions. The basic idea behind this approach to credit card security is that each time you want to make a credit card payment online, your credit card company will provide you with a unique, one-time-use number that you provide to a vendor instead of your credit card number. When the vendor processes the credit card transaction, your credit card company will charge your card and the number will become invalid so that it cannot be reused even if it is stolen.

One of the biggest dangers in conducting e-commerce transactions with your credit card is not that the transaction itself will be spied on or that the vendor you provide the card to will mis-charge you, but rather that the number will be later stolen from the vendor's computer data-bases by an attacker and then used to execute false charges on your card. For instance, many recent Internet security scares have centered on the theft of credit card numbers from less-than-secure company computer systems.

In fact, more than one million credit card numbers have been stolen from Web sites in the year ending March 2001. Sometimes, the theft of these card numbers is used to execute fraudulent charges, but other times stranger things happen. In one incident in 1999, an attacker stole 300,000 card numbers from an e-commerce site and then demanded a ransom to prevent the exposure of those numbers. When the ransom was not paid, thousands of numbers were released publicly on the Internet. A similar extortion incident happened recently with 25,000 card numbers being revealed after being stolen from a site that provides credit card processing services to online merchants.

All-in-all, online credit card theft poses a significant risk even if some credit card companies would like to argue that online credit card fraud is no more prevalent than in off-line transac-tions. The one-time transaction scheme described previously is designed to address just these sorts of problems.

American Express is an excellent example of one-time credit card transactions. Their Private Payments scheme allows card holders to generate limited life transaction numbers to use when making online purchases instead of providing their card numbers. The service is made avail-able free of charge, which makes it accessible to all card holders. Software for private pay-ments can be downloaded for Windows users, or numbers can be generated online through the American Express Web site. Information about Private Payments can be found at `http://www26.americanexpress.com/privatepayments/info_page.jsp`.

American Express is not the only credit card company to offer single-use numbers for e-commerce. Discover offers deskshop, which allows the creation of single-use numbers each time you make an Internet purchase. Using custom software, you can generate a number and fill in a vendor's Web form often with only a few clicks and the deskshop software can store and maintain profiles to make e-commerce shopping quicker and easier. Details of the Discover one-time transaction scheme can be found at `https://discoverdeskshop.card2.novusnet.com/discover/service/app_Home.htm`.

Physical Security

One area of security most people overlook when thinking of computer and Internet security is the area of physical security. You can have the best firewall with a well-designed security configuration, implement a robust back-up plan, and take extra precautions when submitting personal information on the Internet, but if you ignore physical security, it is possible all your hard work to secure your computer on the Internet might be meaningless.

Consider a simple example: You run a small home business and want to keep your business records secure. Using a combination of an Internet gateway firewall and good anti-virus software, you decide you are as secure from attack on the Internet as you can be.

However, you overlook the obvious: When clients are visiting your office, they have ample opportunity to walk up to any one of a number of unused computers and access any data on the local network. This is because computers are located in tucked away corners where they can be used unobserved and are often left logged in for extended periods of time with no supervision.

In this scenario, someone intent on compromising your corporate data only needs to pose as a potential customer to gain access to your computers and your data. All your efforts to implement an effective Internet security strategy have not served to effectively secure your computers or network.

It is important, therefore, to also consider the physical security of your network. Pay attention to the following key issues:

- Are your computers kept in secured locations, or is it easy for unauthorized users to walk up to your computers and use them?

- If your computers are not in secure locations, do you leave them logged in but unattended? You should never do this if you can't be sure of the security of the location.

- Do you perform regular backups of your data? If not, you risk loss of your data not because of an attacker but because of hardware failure or a natural disaster. Consider implementing a backup strategy as outlined in Chapter 24, "Backup Strategies."

- Can you trust all the authorized users on your network? If not, you need to find a way to audit their activities on an occasional and, if possible, random basis. This way, you can assure yourself that authorized users are not abusing their access to your computers and data.

Of course, in the home context, most of these issues are not likely to be of concern. But, in a small office setting, they could easily become important security considerations.

Summary

This chapter reviews many approaches to security that do not rely on firewalls, proxies, or network hardware. Instead, you learned about how you can govern your behavior and the behavior of others to help ensure your privacy and security. This includes prudently selecting passwords and paying attention to when and where you provide personal information on the Internet.

Taking privacy concerns one step further, the next chapter addresses Internet cookies. Internet cookies, a mechanism to allow Web sites to track your usage and behavior, are the subject of a lot of controversy in the privacy arena: Many privacy advocates argue that they are evil, whereas many Web sites argue that they are completely harmless. The next chapter will introduce you to cookies, how they work and their benefits and dangers. You will also learn how to control cookies on your system if you decide they aren't for you.

Cookies

IN THIS CHAPTER

In This Chapter

To understand how to maintain your privacy on the Internet, it is necessary to understand what is threatening your privacy and how you can preserve your privacy. This chapter provides an overview of the Internet cookie.

In this chapter you will learn about the following topics:

What Is a Cookie?

An Internet cookie, also known as a magic cookie, is simply a text file that is placed on your computer's hard drive by a Web site when you visit that site. As such, it cannot be used to transmit a virus or destroy files on your machine. However, a cookie can be stored on your machine for an indefinite period of time, thus causing privacy issues. Figure 17.1 is an example of a cookie file opened in Notepad, which is a text editor.

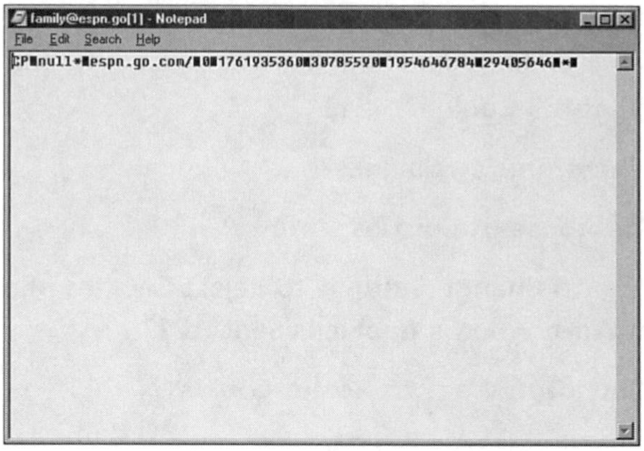

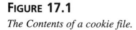

FIGURE 17.1
The Contents of a cookie file.

Although a cookie can contain private or confidential information, in theory only the server that set the cookie can access it on your computer. The purpose of a cookie is to store user information or options so the Web site can retrieve that information when you return to it.

Cookies can be used to make your Internet surfing experience more convenient by remembering the following:

- Personal information such as username and password
- The number of times you have visited a Web site
- Which products you have placed in your shopping cart and what you have purchased from a given Web site in the past
- Site preferences such as which items to display and the colors used to display them

What Information Is Stored in a Cookie?

A cookie contains as much information as the sending Web site deems necessary, and the contents of the cookie can be encrypted. Generally, only the server that set the cookie knows the name and value of it.

However, there is a limit or "cap" to the number of cookies that can be stored on your machine and to the size of a cookie file. Netscape enables a maximum of 300 cookies to be set on your machine and deletes the least used cookies when space is needed for new cookies. In addition, Netscape enables a maximum of 20 cookies from a server or domain. Internet Explorer saves cookies to a folder, so the folder size can be set, but the default size is 2% of your hard drive. The maximum size of a cookie file is 4KB.

A cookie must contain at least two parameters, its name and its value, but it might contain up to six parameters:

- Name of cookie
- Value of cookie
- Expiration date of cookie
- Path (URL) the cookie is valid within
- Domain the cookie is valid within (extension of path for multiple servers within a domain)
- Secure connection flag (if set to TRUE, the cookie will only be used under secure server conditions such as SSL)

NOTE

A cookie can only contain personal information that you have revealed to a Web site. Therefore, privacy is ultimately the user's responsibility.

The Lifetime of a Cookie: Persistent Versus Session

There are two types of cookies: persistent and session. They are determined by their lifetime. A *persistent* cookie remains on your hard drive for a specified period of time after you visit a Web site. The expiration date of a persistent cookie is set by a Web site, and will remain on your hard drive until that date. Persistent cookies can be set to last on your machine for only a few days or months, or can be set to remain on your machine for years or even decades. An example of the use of a persistent cookie is when a Web site assigns you an anonymous code (stored in a cookie) so that the Web site operator can keep track of you and other returning users. For example, if you visit Travelocity's Web site (www.travelocity.com), log in (or create a new account), and check the box next to 'Remember my log-in name' you will have a persistent cookie sent to your machine. The purpose of this persistent cookie is to remember you the next time you visit the Travelocity Web site from the same computer.

On the other hand, a *session* cookie is one that expires when you log out or close your browser, or shortly thereafter. Session cookies can be used by Web sites to keep track of items in your virtual shopping cart, or to prevent users from repeatedly taking part in polls during a session.

An example of a session cookie can be seen when taking part in an online poll, such as at ESPN's Web site (www.espn.go.com). The first time you visit this Web site you will find a poll to vote in, but further visits to the Web site from the same computer (in the same browser session) will not allow you to take part in their poll. Instead, the Web site will display results from the current day's poll.

Where Are My Cookies?

Cookies are stored in different locations on your computer, depending on the browser. To view the contents of a cookie, open it using a text editor, such as Notepad. Netscape Navigator and *Internet Explorer (MSIE)* store cookies in different locations.

Where Netscape Navigator Stores Cookies

Netscape Navigator places cookies into a file named cookies.txt, located in the Netscape folder (the default path is c:\Program Files\Netscape\Navigator on Windows-based PCs.

Where Internet Explorer Stores Cookies

Depending on your version of Internet Explorer, cookies are stored in different locations on your computer. With Explorer 3.x, cookies are stored in the folder `c:\windows\cookies`. Explorer 4.x stores cookies in the folder `c:\windows\Temporary Internet Files`.

> **NOTE**
>
> Cookies are stored in the same format regardless of which version of Internet Explorer is used.

Cookies are first stored in RAM while the browser is active. After the browser is closed, it saves the cookies to the appropriate file or folder. Each time the browser is opened, it retrieves the cookies from their location on the hard drive.

> **NOTE**
>
> On Mac machines running Internet Explorer, cookies are stored in a file named MagicCookie.

You can delete cookies on your system just as you would delete any file on your computer, but you must first quit the browser. Deleting cookies while your browser is still open will cause them to be re-saved onto your hard drive once you close the browser.

> **CAUTION**
>
> If you delete the cookies from your hard drive, you will have to re-enter any required information when you visit a Web site again.

> **TIP**
>
> Here's an alternative to deleting the file cookies.txt (Netscape) or the entire contents of the cookies folder (MSIE): Delete only the cookies associated with Web sites you don't intend to visit regularly, or view the contents of your cookies and delete the cookies whose contents give away more information than you are comfortable with. You can do this by opening the file(s) in a text editor such as Notepad.

The Abuse of Cookies

The problem with cookies is not what they do to your computer, but what they can store and transmit to the server that they originated from. Many Web sites use cookies merely to avoid re-entry of usernames and passwords, or to load user preferences. But there is the potential to abuse this simple, yet powerful, tool.

Some Web sites, namely advertising and tracking Web sites such as DoubleClick Network, use cookies to monitor a user's surfing habits. In many cases, data about the sites you have visited, when you have viewed a banner advertisement and other sites you visit from the advertiser's site are gathered and sold to marketers and advertisers.

> **NOTE**
>
> Cookies are transmitted from a Server to a Client and back as an HTTP header. To understand how a cookie works, you need to understand how HTTP works. If you want to find the specifications for the HTTP header, check out the following link: http://www.cis.ohio-state.edu/htbin/rfc/rfc2109.html.

Why Do I Have Cookies from Sites I've Never Visited?

This is a very controversial subject. When you visit a Web site that subscribes to an advertisement service, such as the DoubleClick Network, the site looks on your machine for any DoubleClick cookies. If any of these cookies are found on your machine, that cookie file, along with the information contained in it, is sent to the DoubleClick Network. They then take the information that has been gathered about you (from the original Web site and other Web sites who subscribe to this advertisement service), send back relevant advertisements, and possibly more cookies. If you did not have any of these cookies, you will receive an advertisement that is not intentionally geared toward you, and then you will receive a cookie from the advertisement service.

The problem with all this is that it is done without your knowledge or consent, and there is no knowing what is done with your personal information after it is collected.

> **TIP**
>
> You can find out more about this topic, try a cookie demo, and find out about software that can prevent this by visiting www.privacy.net.

How to Change Settings to Reject Cookies or to Warn when a Cookie Is Sent

Depending on the browser and version, a user has several choices for dealing with how cookies are handled when a Web site attempts to send a cookie to her computer. The browser can be set to reject all cookies, to warn when a cookie is being sent, or to accept all cookies. Recent versions of Netscape Navigator and Internet Explorer also allow users to create pre-set lists of the Web sites they want to allow, or reject, cookies from.

TIP
If you set your browser to prompt you when a cookie is sent, you will see a pop-up every time a cookie is sent. Some sites send multiple cookies per session, so this can get tiresome after a while.

CAUTION
If you reject a cookie from a Web site, the Web site might repeatedly look for the cookie on your machine and might even try to replace it.

Changing Cookie Settings on Netscape Navigator 3.0 and Internet Explorer 3.0

With Netscape Navigator 3.0 and Internet Explorer 3.0 (MSIE), the user is only able to set the browser to Alert Before Accepting Cookies. By setting this feature, a user will be prompted each time a cookie is sent. Select Cancel to reject the cookie and OK to accept the cookie.

To set Netscape Navigator 3.0 to alert before accepting cookies, use the following steps:

1. Click on the Options menu so that Navigator will display it.
2. Select Network Preferences from the Options menu. Navigator will display the Network Preferences dialog box.
3. Click on the Protocols tab from the Preferences dialog box. Navigator will display the Protocols menu as illustrated in Figure 17.2.
4. Click the box next to Accepting a Cookie from the Show an Alert Before menu.
5. Click the OK button.

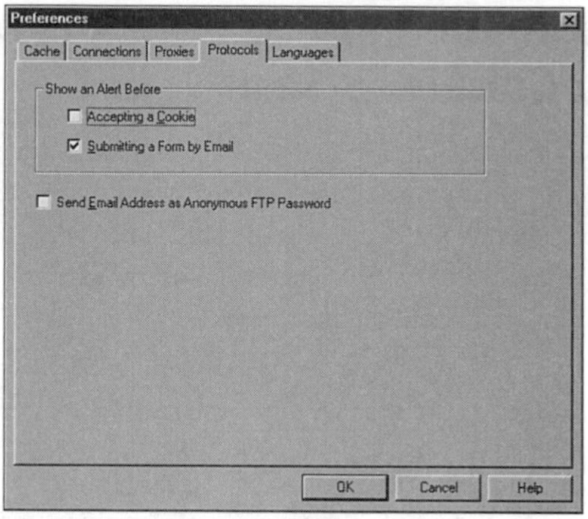

FIGURE 17.2

The Protocols tab in Netscape Communicator 3.0.

To set Internet Explorer 3.0 to alert before accepting cookies, perform the following steps:

1. Click on the View menu, and Internet Explorer will display it.

2. Select Internet Options from the View menu. Internet Explorer will display the Internet Options dialog box.

3. Click on the Advanced tab from the Internet Options dialog box. Internet Explorer will display the Advanced menu.

4. Click the box next to Accepting a Cookie from the Show an Alert Before menu.

5. Click the OK button.

Changing Cookie Settings on Netscape Communicator 4.xx and Internet Explorer 4.0

Netscape Communicator 4.xx and Internet Explorer 4.0 have more advanced options that allow the user to set the browser to accept no cookies, some cookies (from a pre-set user-defined list), or all cookies. Both browsers also have the ability to alert before accepting cookies (from version 3.0).

To set Netscape Communicator 4.xx to alert before accepting cookies, use the following steps:

1. Click on the Edit menu, and Netscape Communicator will display it.

2. Select Preferences from the Edit menu. Communicator will display the Preferences dialog box, as shown in Figure 17.3.

3. Click on the Advanced category from the Preferences dialog box. Netscape Communicator will display the Advanced category menu, as illustrated in Figure 17.4.

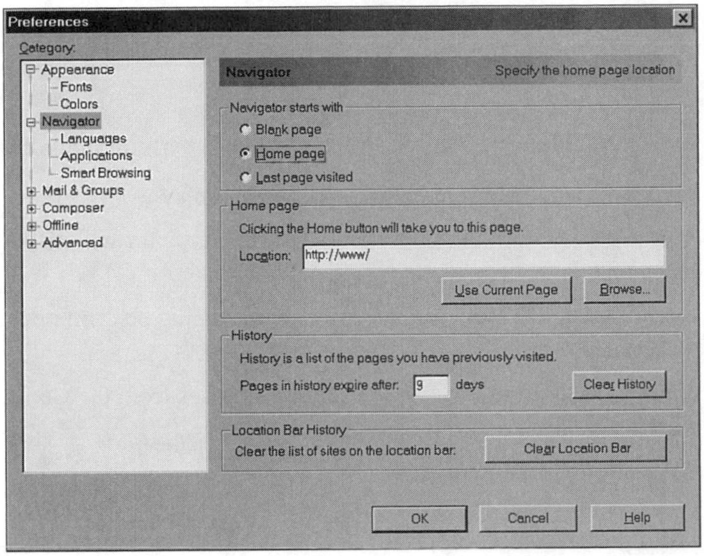

17

FIGURE 17.3

The Preferences dialog box, using Netscape Communicator 4.xx.

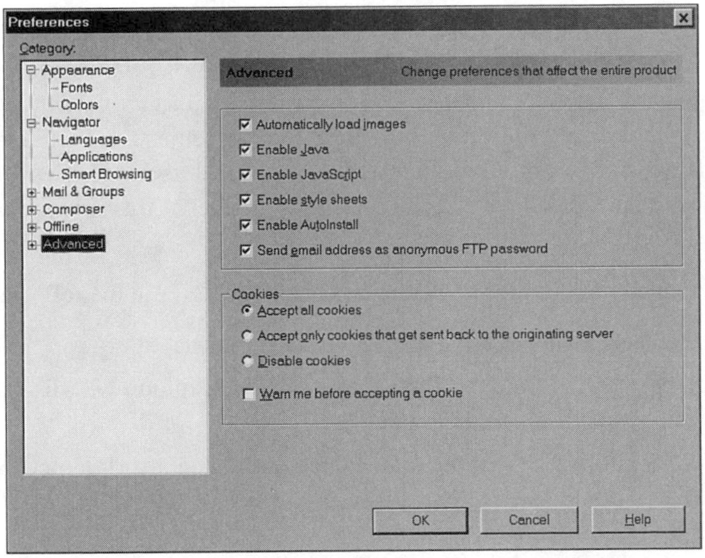

FIGURE 17.4

The Advanced category, displayed in the Preferences dialog box in Netscape Communicator 4.xx.

4. Click the Warn Me Before Accepting a Cookie box from the Advanced menu, under the Cookies option. To reject cookies, select the Disable Cookies preference.

5. Click the OK button.

To set Internet Explorer 4.0 to alert before accepting cookies, perform the following steps:

1. Click on the View menu, and Internet Explorer will display it.

2. Select Internet Options from the View menu. Internet Explorer will display the Internet Options dialog box.

3. Click on the Advanced tab from the Internet Options dialog box. Internet Explorer will display the Advanced menu.

4. Click the circle next to Prompt Before Accepting Cookies from the Cookies section of the Advanced menu.

5. Click the OK button.

> **NOTE**
>
> To disable all cookies in Netscape Navigator 4.0 or Internet Explorer 4.0, click Disable instead of Prompt in step 4.

Changing Cookie Settings on Internet Explorer 5.x

There are significant differences between Internet Explorer 4.0 and 5.x. With Internet Explorer 5.x, the user has the ability to pre-set four different security settings and can add Web sites to each group: Internet sites, local intranet sites, trusted sites and restricted sites. You have the power to place sites into these four groups based on your level of trust or fear toward the Web site.

To set Internet Explorer 5.x to prompt before accepting cookies, use the following steps:

1. Click on the Tools menu, and Internet Explorer will display it.

2. Select Internet Options from the Tools menu. Internet Explorer will display the Internet Options dialog box, as shown in Figure 17.5.

3. Click on the Security tab from the Internet Options dialog box. Internet Explorer will display the Security menu, as illustrated in Figure 17.6.

> **NOTE**
>
> The Internet icon from the Web content zone box is already highlighted. The Security level for this zone is displayed in the lower half of the window.

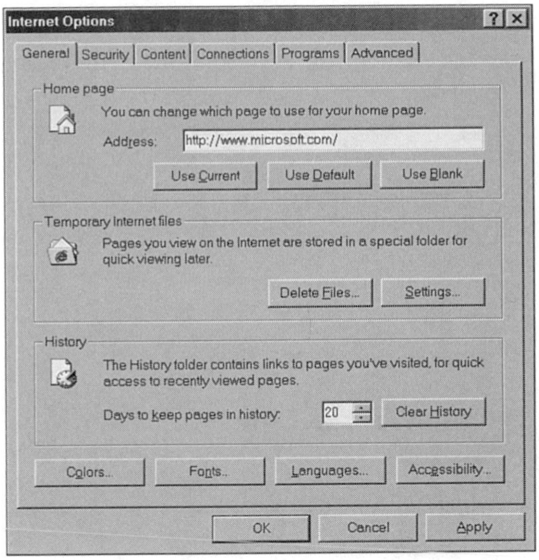

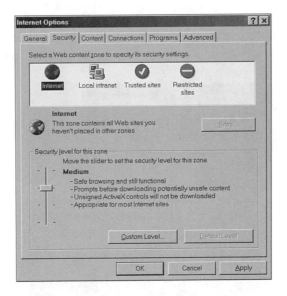

FIGURE 17.5

The Internet Options dialog box.

FIGURE 17.6

The Security tab, accessed in the Internet Options dialog box.

4. Click the Custom Level button to display the Security Settings window. Figure 17.7 illustrates the Security Settings window displayed in Internet Explorer.

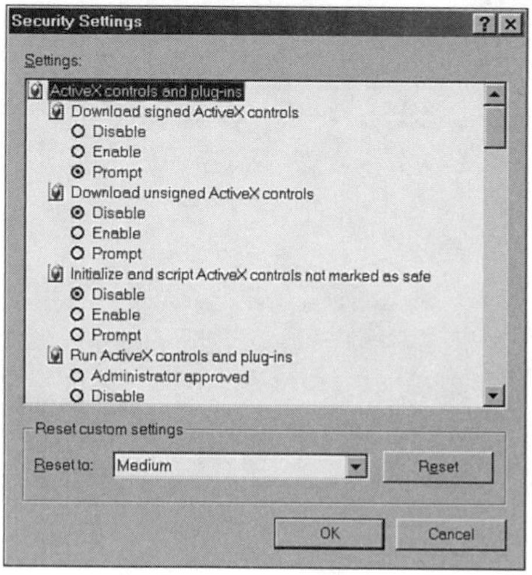

FIGURE 17.7

The Security Settings window.

5. Scroll down to the Cookies section from the Security Settings window. As shown in Figure 17.8, Internet Explorer will display the cookie-handling options.

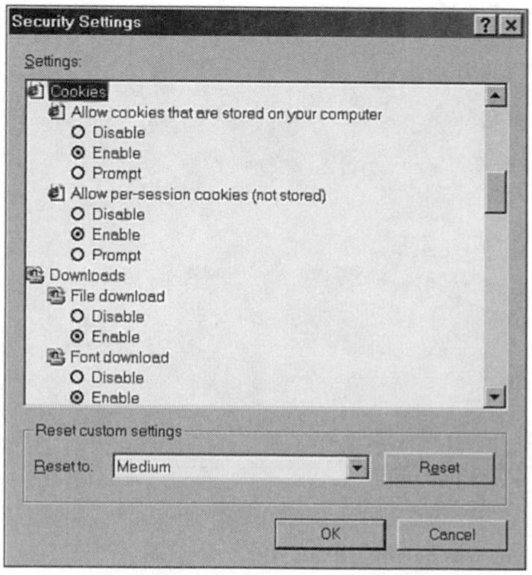

FIGURE 17.8

The Cookies section of the Security Settings window.

6. Set both the Allow Cookies that Are Stored on Your Computer and the Allow Per-session Cookies options to Prompt. To reject cookies, select Disable instead of Prompt.

7. Click the OK button.

NOTE

Internet Explorer will prompt you every time a Web site attempts to send a cookie to your machine.

Changing Cookie Settings on Netscape 6.xx

Netscape 6.xx has several advantages over Netscape Communicator 4.xx. In addition to the cookie features of Netscape Communicator 4.xx, which allow you to specify how the browser should handle cookies, Netscape 6.xx has enhanced cookie management options that allow you to view stored cookies, remove cookies from your machine, and manage cookies site-by-site.

To set Netscape 6.xx to alert before accepting cookies, perform the following steps:

1. Click on the Edit menu, and Netscape will display it.

2. Select Preferences from the Edit menu. Netscape will display the Preferences dialog box, as shown in Figure 17.9.

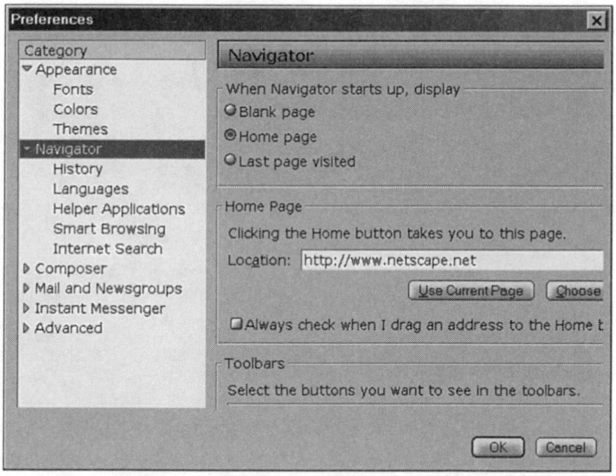

FIGURE 17.9

The Preferences dialog box, using Netscape 6.xx.

3. Double-click the Advanced category from the Preferences dialog box. Netscape will display the Advanced category menu, as illustrated in Figure 17.10.

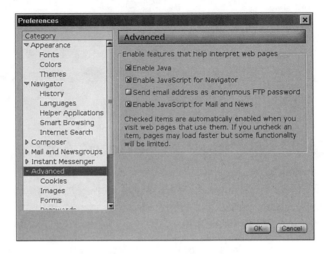

FIGURE 17.10

The Advanced category, displayed in the Preferences dialog box in Netscape 6.xx.

4. Click the Cookies subcategory to display the cookie options. As shown in Figure 17.11, Netscape will display the cookie options.

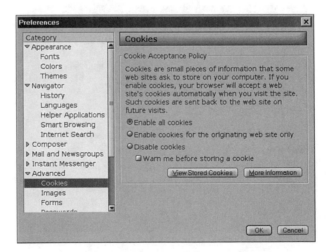

FIGURE 17.11

The Cookies subcategory of the Advanced category, in Netscape 6.xx.

5. Click the Warn Me Before Storing a Cookie box from the Advanced menu, under the Cookies option. To reject cookies, click the Disable Cookies button.

6. Click the OK button.

When Do I Want to Accept Cookies?

The answer to this question is not as straightforward as you might think. The correct answer to this question depends on the person. Although rejecting cookies probably won't diminish your Web surfing experience, there are times when it is necessary to accept a cookie. You would be unable to shop online, enter online contests, or take part in online polls without accepting cookies. The easiest way to find out how it would affect you is through trial and error. In most cases, Web sites will warn against rejecting cookies, but rejecting the cookies shouldn't prevent you from viewing the site. However, there is the possibility that you might not be able to view the site. But it isn't difficult to change your browser settings to accept a Web site's cookies if you feel you are missing out on the full experience. Some would argue that it is safer to reject a cookie than to accept it, but this is why browsers allow you to set this feature. Ultimately, the decision is yours to make.

NOTE

Many secure Web sites require you to accept cookies in order to view the contents of their Web site.

Cookie Software

Two separate privacy issues regarding cookies are as follows:

- Web sites are able to track your personal information and movements on the Internet by retrieving cookies from your hard drive.

- Anyone can determine the Web sites you have visited by viewing the contents of your cookies.txt file (Netscape Navigator), cookies folder (MSIE), or cache memory on your computer.

The following section lists software that will allow you to maintain your privacy by managing your cookies and controlling the flow of information to and from your machine.

NOTE

Visit www.privacy.net for additional privacy resources and Cookie software.

Cookie Software for Windows-Based PCs

Following are some useful cookie managing programs for Windows-based PCs that will control the flow of cookies and ensure that others aren't able to examine your cookies in an attempt to monitor your Internet surfing habits.

Cookie Crusher 2.6

Cookie Crusher 2.6, from The Limit Software (www.thelimitsoft.com), is an excellent cookie manager. This software allows you to see the issuing site, the expiration date, and the ID of the cookies stored on your hard drive, as well as allowing you to set filters for accepting or rejecting cookies issued by Web sites. In addition to the usual features of a cookie manager, Cookie Crusher 2.6 has the added feature of indicating the intended purpose of a cookie when you first encounter it.

Cookie Pal

Cookie Pal, by Kookaburra Software (www.kburra.com), is another excellent cookie manager. Cookie Pal also allows you to see the issuing site, the expiration date, and the ID of the cookies stored on your hard drive, as well as allowing you to set filters for accepting or rejecting cookies issued by Web sites. In addition, using Cookie Pal's Session tab (version 1.6), you are able to see all the cookies handled during the current browsing session.

Cookie Sweeper

Cookie Sweeper (www.cookiesweeper.com) is an online program that allows you to view the cookies on your hard drive. Cookie Sweeper also allows you to categorize, search, and delete cookies from your machine. In addition, you can create a custom list. Using this custom list, Cookie Sweeper will search for offending cookies (cookies that contain private data such as your name, address, passwords, and so on) and delete them.

CookieMaster

ZDNet's CookieMaster version 2.0a (http://www.zdnet.com/downloads/stories/info/0,,000CKP,.html) is a great cookie monitor. CookieMaster allows you to log cookie and browser events, as well as delete existing cookies from your hard drive.

Window Washer

Webroot's Window Washer (www.webroot.com) automatically cleans up your browser's cache, cookies, history, recent document list, and more. This software works with Internet Explorer, Netscape Navigator, and AOL browsers.

NSClean

NSClean, from Privacy Software Corporation (www.nsclean.com), is a multi-purpose privacy tool for use with Netscape Navigator. NSClean allows you to edit and delete cookies, warn of or refuse cookies, remove traces of information from your hard drive, and prevent unauthorized access to and from your machine.

IEClean

Privacy Software Corporation's IEClean (www.nsclean.com) is a multi-purpose privacy tool for use with Internet Explorer. IEClean allows you to edit and delete cookies, warn of or refuse cookies, remove traces of information from your hard drive, and prevent unauthorized access to and from your machine.

Cookie Software for Macs

The following list of cookie managing programs for Macs will ensure that cookies are not placed onto, or taken from, your machine without your knowledge. In addition, these programs will also ensure that others cannot view the cookies on your computer.

MacWasher

Webroot's MacWasher (www.webroot.com) automatically cleans up your browser's cache, cookies, history, recent document list, and more. This software works with Internet Explorer, Netscape Navigator, and AOL browsers.

Cookie Dog

Cookie Dog version 1.0.4 (http://mac.tucows.com/preview/132404.html), is a shareware cookie manager application for use with Internet Explorer. Cookie Dog allows you to view the contents of every cookie and delete all or selected portions of cookies. In addition, Cookie Dog can automatically delete unwanted cookies.

Other Possible Solutions to Cookies

There are several alternative methods of dealing with cookies. It is possible to fool the browser and the Web site, so that cookies accepted by your browser won't be placed onto your machine when you terminate the program. Other alternative methods (specific to the Netscape Navigator and Internet Explorer browsers, as well as Macintosh machines) are discussed in the following sections.

For Netscape Navigator

A possible solution is to delete the file cookies.txt, replace it with a new file of the same name, and then write-protect the file. By doing this, the Web site will not be allowed to alter the cookies.txt file. When this is done, the file size will be zero, so it is easy to tell if a cookie finds a way to get onto your machine by checking the file size.

A second solution for Netscape Navigator is to delete the contents of the files cookies.txt and netscape.hst. Then set the file attributes for these two files to System, Hidden and Read-only. You might have trouble with some sites using this method, but it is easy to undo.

A third solution is to delete the cookies.txt file and replace it with a cookies folder. This should stop cookies from writing to your hard drive because the cookies are expecting a file to write to. When they encounter a folder, the cookies cannot write to it.

For Internet Explorer

Internet Explorer does not use a single cookie file. Instead, cookies are placed into the cookie folder as separate cookie files. To stop specific Web sites (such as the DoubleClick Network) from sending cookies, open the cookie file associated with the Web site you want to stop in a text editor and corrupt the data by editing it. Then lock the file. The Web site will recognize that a cookie file exists, so it won't place a new one onto your machine. However, the information contained within the cookie will be of little or no use to the Web site.

Mac Specific

A solution for Mac machines is similar to that of the third Netscape Navigator solution. However, Macs do not have a file named cookies.txt; instead the file is called MagicCookie. Delete this file, and then create a folder with the same name. This should stop cookies from writing to your hard drive because cookies are expecting a file to write to. When they encounter a folder, the cookies cannot write to it.

Summary

In this chapter you learned about cookies, how they are used by Web sites to track your movements and gather information about you, why you need to be wary of advertising services, and how to prevent cookies from being sent to your machine. The next chapter further explores the themes of privacy and data security on the Internet. You will learn how to surf the Web anonymously using anonymous browsers and how to send e-mails anonymously using remailers.

Anonymous Surfing

IN THIS CHAPTER

In This Chapter

Many users of the Internet feel they are anonymous, traversing the worldwide network as unseen prowlers in the dark of night. The reality is that this is far from the truth. There are several ways that you can be tracked on the Internet; you are far from anonymous when you use the Internet. In order to protect yourself online, it is vital to learn how to explore the Internet without giving away your identity, and to know what measures are needed to ensure your privacy. This chapter is devoted to understanding how to surf the Web and use e-mail anonymously.

What Is Anonymous Surfing?

To use the Internet in anything resembling an anonymous fashion means that you need to pay attention to the two main mediums you use on the Internet: the Web and e-mail.

Anonymous surfing refers to using the Internet to browse Web Sites, and send and receive e-mail, without being tracked—without having your identity captured by Web sites, marketing and research firms, or hackers. In order to understand how to prevent this from happening, it is important to learn how you are spotted and tracked on the Internet.

How Am I Spotted On the Internet?

There are several pieces of information that you give away unknowingly when you are connected to the Internet, whether you are browsing Web sites or sending and receiving e-mails. As such, anyone can track you using the following pieces of information:

- Cookies stored on your machine or in an open browser, such as Internet Explorer 5.5 (MSIE) or Netscape 6
- IP address of your machine, assigned to you by your Internet service provider (ISP)
- E-mail address, contained in messages you send and receive over the Internet

Tracking Your Web Usage with Cookies

Cookies are text files that are sent to your browser by Web sites when you visit them. After you finish a session, the browser will store the persistent cookies to your hard drive, and delete the session cookies. This topic is covered in detail in the Chapter 17, "Cookies."

The cookies that are stored on your machine can be used by Web sites to gather personal information on you, your Internet movements, and your online purchasing habits.

We All Have Unique Addresses on the Internet

Your IP address is the Internet Protocol address assigned to your machine or network by your Internet Service Provider. This can be thought of as a mailing address for your computer, and works much like your home address. This topic is covered in detail in Chapter 3, "How the Internet Works."

Any computer that you make contact with over the Internet, whether you are simply browsing a Web site, sending/receiving e-mail, or using a chat room, automatically receives your IP address. This IP address is needed so that the machine communicating with your machine knows where to send responses.

Unfortunately, after your IP address is captured, it is not difficult to determine your true identity by using a combination of tracing tools. Your IP address can be used to determine who your service provider is and the approximate physical location (region) of your machine. But only a small amount of additional work is required to gather more information about you, using your IP address, e-mail address, and cookies on your machine.

> **NOTE**
>
> For more information on IP addresses, read "The IP Address: Your Internet Identity," on the Internet at: `http://consumer.net/IPpaper.asp`.

Your E-mail Address: How It Can Be Used to Track You

Your e-mail address is sent out on the Internet every time you send an e-mail. Although this statement seems obvious and harmless, what you need to understand is that any information placed on the Internet is visible to anyone who knows what to look for and where to look for it.

Many people believe that when they write, send and receive e-mails, the messages are sealed up inside an envelope and are unreadable to anyone other than the intended receiver. This is far from the truth, unless you encrypt your messages. E-mail can be thought of as being similar to a postcard: The message contained in an e-mail can be accessed by anyone who wants to intercept it, as long as the e-mail message crosses their path on the way to the intended receiver.

After your e-mail address is known, it isn't very difficult to do a search over the Internet to determine your identity—especially if you've filled out forms over the Internet at non-secure sites or given out your personal information to Web sites.

Browsing the Web Anonymously

When you surf the Internet, you might not be aware that anyone with a little knowledge of how the Internet works can track you, and piece together bits of information about you, until you are no longer simply an anonymous traveler on the Information Highway. If you plan on using a typical browser to surf the Internet, such as Microsoft's Internet Explorer, you should understand that everything you do is public. Nowadays, there are many downfalls of using a public browser when you are on the Internet:

- Your activities and the Web sites you visit can be tracked
- The contents of your hard drive can be searched and altered remotely
- Your identity can be stolen and used without your knowledge

The best way to prevent these and other unwanted activities from happening to you is by browsing the Web anonymously. Anonymous Browsers are designed to hide your actions and your identity from the Internet.

Anonymous Browsers

Anonymous browsers can protect your identity when you surf the Web so that you can remain anonymous while online. While some anonymous browsers are only available for a fee, many offer free or trial versions with less power, or a time delay, that are also effective in maintaining your privacy and anonymity online.

How Anonymous Browsers Work

Some anonymous browsers work as a middleman: They get instructions from you on where to go on the Internet, go there, retrieve the Web page, then return it to you without any knowledge of your existence to the Web site you are viewing; while other anonymous browsers simply prevent your name, IP address and other revealing information from being sent to Web sites.

Web Browsing Tools

The following list of tools will maintain your privacy while browsing the Internet:

Anonymizer (www.anonymizer.com) is a Web-based anonymous browser that works with your existing Internet browser. It includes cookie encryption and URL encryption. A free trial is offered on the Web site, and the monthly cost is $5. A Web page displayed with Anonymizer is illustrated in Figure 18.1.

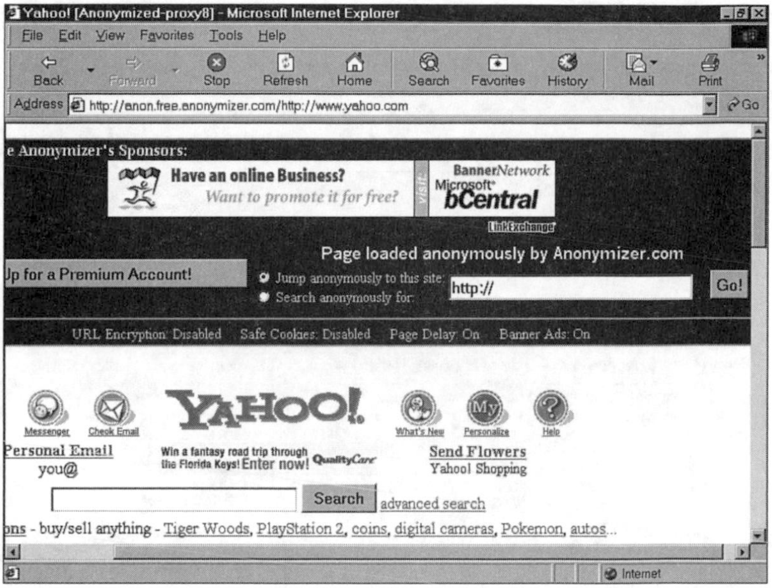

FIGURE 18.1

The Yahoo! Web site is displayed using Anonymizer.

Freedom (www.zeroknowledge.com) is a free package of features and services. It includes a firewall, form filler, cookie manager, ad manager, and keyword alert. There is also a premium version for $49.95 per year that includes e-mail encryption and anonymous browsing.

IDsecure (www.idzap.com) is an anonymous browser service. A free version is available, but does not protect your anonymity from your ISP. However, the paid service, which costs $50 per year, includes URL hiding and supports password protected sites.

SafeWeb (www.safeweb.com) is a free anonymous Web browser service that works with your existing browser. SafeWeb fetches Web pages for you and encrypts all information sent between their servers and your computer. Figure 18.2 illustrates a Web page displayed using SafeWeb.

18

ANONYMOUS
SURFING

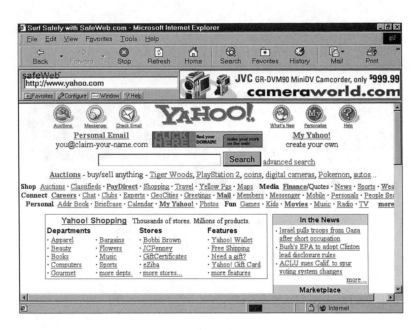

FIGURE 18.2
The Yahoo! Web site is displayed using SafeWeb.

Using E-mail Anonymously

Although many people don't recognize the need for privacy when using their e-mail, there are many reasons why someone would want to be anonymous when using e-mail:

- Sending and/or receiving sensitive information
- Concern about companies or the government tracking your actions
- Not wanting to be put in an awkward or bad position because of your controversial or negative opinions
- Not wanting your ISP, or your employer, to view or store your confidential e-mails
- Exercising your right to privacy
- Not wanting to receive spam e-mails

In order to prevent people from gathering information on you through e-mail, you can use *anonymous remailers*. Anonymous remailers are programs you can use to send and receive e-mail without having to use your actual name, and which don't include information such as your IP address.

Anonymous Remailers

Anonymous remailers can be used to hide your identity when using e-mail. You can think of anonymous remailers as being similar to a post office box. Although many require you to fill out a registration form or pay a user fee, they enable you to control your privacy and restrict others from gaining knowledge about you without your consent, or from stealing information about you.

How Do Remailers Work?

Generally, a remailer will take your e-mail and strip away the header, which includes your name and address, replace it with a false header and then send it to the intended recipient. You are then notified that your e-mail has been delivered. When you receive a response from someone, the header from their e-mail is also removed and replaced with a dummy header. Essentially, the remailer works to protect the anonymity of all its users.

Pseudo-Anonymous Remailer Versus True Anonymous Remailer

There is a distinction between remailers that are truly anonymous and those that are mostly anonymous. With a pseudo-anonymous remailer, such as Microsoft's Hotmail (`www.hotmail.com`) or Yahoo! Mail (`http://mail.yahoo.com/`), your identity might appear to be anonymous, but the Operator of the service knows your real name and real e-mail address (unless you falsify this information) as well as the IP address of the computer you sent the e-mail from. In addition, the Operator might be forced to give out that information if they get a court order, which is rare but does occur.

A truly anonymous remailer, such as The Freedom Remailer (`http://freedom.gmsociety.org/`), is completely secure and private. Remailers such as this require you to download software that encrypts the message and then sends it to its destination through a series of remailer sites, where the message has instructions for the remailer to move the message to its next stop.

> **NOTE**
>
> For further information on anonymous remailers, visit the following Web address:
> `http://www.obscura.com/~loki/remailer/remailer-essay.html`.

Although truly anonymous remailers provide a higher degree of security and anonymity, they tend to be confusing to the average user. Pseudo-anonymous remailers are generally much more user-friendly, yet they don't provide the same level of security. As a result, it is better to use the appropriate remailer for the task at hand. If you are sending an e-mail that requires protection or anonymity, you are better off using the true remailer; but if you are just being cautious, most pseudo-anonymous remailers are adequate, as long as you don't give out private information when you sign up.

E-mail Tools

There are a number of tools and services you can use to maintain your e-mail privacy on the Internet:

PrivacyX (www.privacyx.com) is a free e-mail system that uses anonymous digital certificates. This system uses strong encryption, digital signatures for authentication, and is anonymous.

HushMail (www.hushmail.com) is a secure Web-based e-mail system that uses a key management encryption system to maintain your privacy and the content of your e-mail. There is a free version, and an upgrade version that costs $60 per year.

ZixMail (www.zixit.com) is a secure add-on to your existing e-mail system. It uses strong encryption and has a time-stamped certified receipt to verify its delivery. It can be used to send secure e-mails to anyone, and costs $24 per year.

Microsoft's Hotmail (www.hotmail.com) is a free pseudo-anonymous, Web-based e-mail provider. Although the security of this system is not as effective as the others, it is user-friendly, and can be accessed from any computer connected to the Internet.

Summary

This chapter taught you the basic principles and techniques for maintaining your privacy and anonymity online. You can choose to browse the Web anonymously with tools such as Anonymizer or generate pseudo-anonymous e-mails with tools such as HotMail. The decision about what degree of anonymity and privacy you require is a personal one, but the tools are available to maintain whatever level of privacy you desire.

The next chapter deals with encryption. You will learn about the different types of encryption and how encryption works. Encryption allows you to encode data in such a way that it is hard, if not nearly impossible, for eavesdroppers to decode the content. Encryption is widely used on the Internet for secure e-mail transactions as well as keeping Web-based e-commerce secure.

Encryption

IN THIS CHAPTER

In This Chapter

Privacy and security are very important in the information age, and the transparent nature of the Internet has created the need for encryption. Encryption is essential to maintaining your privacy and ensuring the authenticity and accuracy of the information you send and receive over the Internet. This chapter focuses on what encryption is, why it is needed, and how to use it.

What Is Encryption?

Encryption is the alteration of text (usually an e-mail message) into coded form that can only be translated by the intended recipient (and in some cases the sender). Although the idea of encrypting computer messages might be relatively new, encryption has been used for thousands of years by governments and the military. In ancient Rome, Julius Caesar used to send encoded messages using the "shift by three" method. What that means is that every letter in the message was shifted three such that every A was represented by the letter D, every B was represented by the letter E, and so on. Although that method of encryption was adequate for its time, such a simple method could easily be decoded nowadays, especially with the use of a computer. Therefore, more advanced methods had to be created.

But before we can discuss encryption further, it is important to understand several terms:

- Cryptography: The science of altering messages to make their content secret.
- Cryptographer: Someone who uses (or practices) cryptography.
- Cryptanalysis: The science of *cracking* or breaking encoded text; determining the correct content of a message that is intended for someone else.
- Cryptanalyst: Someone who uses cryptanalysis.
- Encryption: The process of encoding a message in order to make its contents unknown.
- Decryption: The process of decoding a message in order to make it understandable.
- Plain text: The message (or data) in its original form.
- Cipher text: The message after it has been encrypted.
- Key: Used to create encrypted messages, and to decrypt coded messages. Only the correct key will decode an encrypted message.

Why Do I Need Encryption?

Encryption is necessary for transmitting (or storing) a message, or data, without revealing its contents to anyone (and everyone) who wants to see it. The Internet is not a private and hidden place. In fact, when you send an e-mail to someone, it passes through several networks on its way to the destination. As a result, someone with a little know-how could easily intercept your message and do whatever he wanted to it (store it, distribute it, alter it, and so on). E-mails are as private as a postcard, which isn't a problem if you are merely corresponding with a friend; but if you are transmitting sensitive information, the thought of having it land in the wrong hands (such as a competitor in the business market) is frightening. This is why encryption is necessary. Encryption allows you to send something to another computer without having the entire world get a readable copy.

Encryption Basics

Numerous encryption algorithms are in use today, but most encryption is based on one of two classes: symmetric keys versus asymmetric keys. In addition, encryption is also categorized based on its key length.

Asymmetric Keys Versus Symmetric Keys

The *symmetric* key encryption system uses only one key for encryption and decryption, whereas an *asymmetric* key encryption system makes use of a public and private key. The public key is one that you would give to anyone who wants to send you encrypted messages, and your private key is what you would use to decrypt that message. Although both systems have advantages (as well as drawbacks), it is up to you to decide what value your data has to you, how much it would affect you if that data was captured by someone else, how likely it is that someone would find that information of use, and how much (money, system resources, time, and so on) you are willing to spend to ensure that your data is protected? Only then can you determine which system is better suited for your needs. But in the real-world, most encryption systems use a mix of both asymmetric and symmetric keys to ensure the highest level of security while using the least amount of system resources.

> **TIP**
>
> For a graphical explanation of how key encryption works, check out the following link: http://www.pajhome.org.uk/crypt/rsa/intro.html

19

ENCRYPTION

Advantages of Asymmetric Keys

Several advantages to using asymmetric keys are

- Key management: Because you have a private key and a public key, it is easier to send and receive encrypted messages. By posting your public key on the Internet (with a Key Server such as VeriSign), anyone can send you encrypted messages from anywhere in the world by simply looking up your name on that server. With symmetric keys, you are required to find some secure way of giving your key information to a second party; depending on your level of paranoia (and need for data security), this could require a face-to-face meeting, which isn't always feasible.

- Security: This system makes use of highly complicated algorithms. As a result, this system is more secure than the symmetric key system (when using the same bit size for encryption). What that means is that 128-bit asymmetric encryption is stronger, and would take longer to crack, than 128-bit symmetric encryption.

Advantages of Symmetric Keys

Several advantages to using symmetric keys are as follows:

- Complexity: Even though the symmetric key system is of lower complexity, this does not mean that it is not secure. For example, if I were to send you an encrypted message that contained only slightly important data (such as my date of birth), it would take less time for the data to be encrypted on my machine and decrypted on your machine.

- Real-time use: The advantages of using a faster algorithm are that it can be used for real-time solutions such as securing digital phone lines. But, the asymmetric encryption method could not be used to secure cellular phone communications as effectively because the complexity of the algorithm would result in delays during the conversation.

- Resources: Because of the less complex algorithm, this method requires less computer resources (such as CPU speed), so it is more cost-effective.

Encryption Algorithms

Many different encryption algorithms are currently available. The following lists some of the more well-known and used algorithms:

RSA

The RSA asymmetric encryption algorithm is named after its creators, Rivest, Shamir, and Adleman. This encryption algorithm is used in public key cryptography. RSA makes use of incredibly large prime numbers to protect the integrity of data.

DES

The DES symmetric encryption algorithm, Data Encryption Standard, was turned into a standard by the United States *National Institute of Standards and Technology (NIST)*, and is widely used in the financial industry. DES uses a 56-bit key, so it is still safe for use against attack, except by governments or large corporations.

IDEA

The International Data Encryption Algorithm, developed in Zurich, Switzerland, uses 128-bit key encryption. It is highly used and considered to be one of the better publicly known algorithms.

DSS

The Digital Signature Standard, used by the United States government, is only used for digital signatures. Digital signatures are used to verify the authenticity of an e-mail, and the identity of the sender.

Key Length

Key length refers to the size of the key used to encrypt the data. This is a good measure of the complexity for breaking an encryption algorithm, but it is not the only measure. Some algorithms are more effective than others, despite using fewer bits in the encryption key. Keys are measured using binary digits or bits.

TIP

For more information on binary digits, visit the following Web site: http://www.howstuffworks.com/bytes.htm

---

Basically, a 40-bit number is 2 to the power of 40, or 1,099,511,627,776 (just over 1 trillion). A 56-bit number is 2 to the power of 56, or 72,057,594,037,927,936. A 128-bit number is 2 to the 128th power, or a little over 340,000,000,000,000,000,000,000,000,000,000,000,000. The addition of each binary bit doubles the size of the binary number, so consider a 512-bit number. A 512-bit number would be slightly larger than 10,000,000,000,000,000,000,000, 000,000,000,000,000,000,000,000,000,000,000,000,000,000,000,000,000,000,000,000, 000,000,000,000,000,000,000,000,000,000,000,000,000,000,000,000,000,000,000,000,000 (that's a one with 154 zeros). It is because of the massiveness of encryption key numbers that we don't have to worry too much about them being broken—at least not in the very near future.

NOTE

For every binary digit added, the size of the binary number doubles. This means that for every bit you add, the number of possible key values doubles.

How to Use Encryption

Chances are that you've already encountered encryption in some form when browsing the Internet—without even realizing it. Microsoft Internet Explorer and Netscape Communicator both use encryption for secure links, called *SSL (Secure Sockets Layer)*, which is an Internet security protocol to transmit sensitive information. Or, maybe you've heard of *TSL (Transport Layer Security)*, which is the more general security protocol that SSL is part of. You can tell whether you are using a secure link by checking the following:

- If the URL, or Web address, starts with `https` instead of just `http` (note the 'S' at the end), you are using a secure link.
- If there is a small padlock icon located in the bottom right corner of your Web browser (on the status bar), you are using a secure link.

Cryptography Plug-ins

Several programs can be downloaded from the Internet and installed to give you the ability to encrypt e-mails. Disappearing Email (`http://www.disappearing.com/`) and SigabaSecure (`http://www.sigaba.com/`) are two programs that can immediately improve the integrity of your messages because they use 128-bit encryption. Both programs are free and integrate into your mail program as plug-ins. In addition, both of these plug-ins use automatic key distribution and management, which makes the program easier to use.

The Pretty Good Privacy Encryption Tool

Pretty Good Privacy (PGP) is a very useful encryption tool that can be used on its own or integrated into your current e-mail program. PGP is based on the RSA encryption algorithm, which relies on the fact that incredibly large prime numbers are difficult for a computer to factor. This section gives step-by-step installation instructions, as well as list Web sites where the latest versions are available for free download.

With PGP, you can distribute your public key easily because it appears as a block of text. You can distribute your public key in the following ways:

- Make your public key available on a public key server, such as VeriSign (`www.verisign.com`) or Network Associates Inc. (`www.nai.com`).
- Export your public key to another program or copy it into a text file.
- Send your public key out to others in the body of an e-mail message.

PGP can be downloaded free from the following Web sites:

```
http://www.pgp.com/products/freeware/default.asp
```

```
http://web.mit.edu/network/pgp-form.html
```

Installing PGP onto a Windows-based PC

After you have downloaded PGP, you must open the installation program, PGPfreeware installer, in order to install the software onto your computer. To install PGPfreeware 7.0.3 onto a Windows-based PC running Windows 98, follow these instructions:

1. After you open the installation program, the PGPfreeware— Installer Welcome window will appear, as illustrated in Figure 19.1. Click the Next button to continue with the installation.

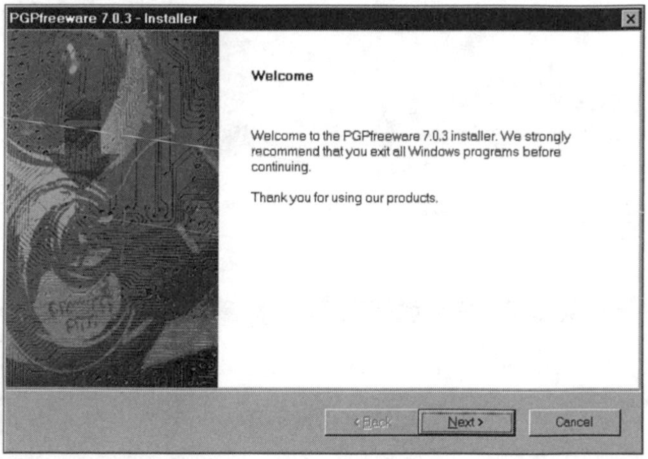

FIGURE 19.1

The PGPfreeware—Installer Welcome window.

2. As demonstrated in Figure 19.2, the License Agreement window will appear. Click the Yes button to accept the license agreement and continue with the installation.

3. The next screen is the Read Me window, as shown in Figure 19.3. Click Next to continue.

4. As shown in Figure 19.4, the User Type window will appear. If you do not already have a PGP keyring, click No, I'm a New User, and then click Next. If you already have a PGP keyring, simply click Next to continue.

5. The next screen is the Install Directory window, as illustrated in Figure 19.5. The Default Destination Folder is C:\...\Network Associates\PGP for Windows 98. If this is where you want to store the PGP program, click Next. Otherwise, click the Browse button, select the folder where you would like to store PGP, and then click Next to continue.

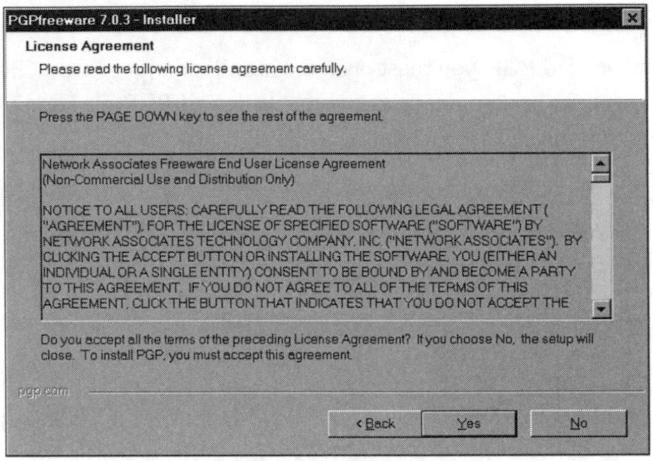

FIGURE 19.2

The PGPfreeware License Agreement.

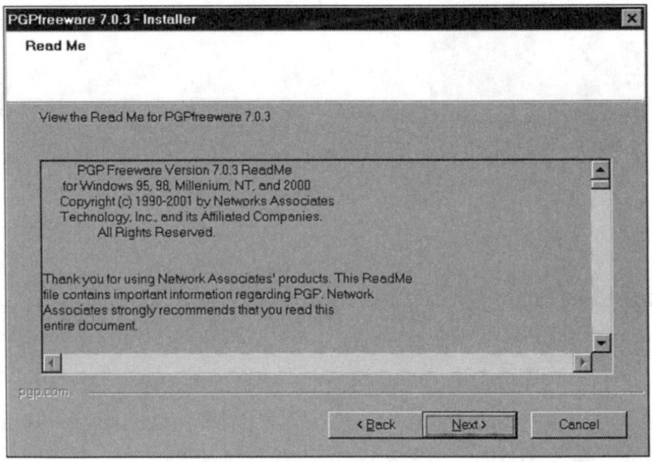

FIGURE 19.3

The PGPfreeware—Read Me window.

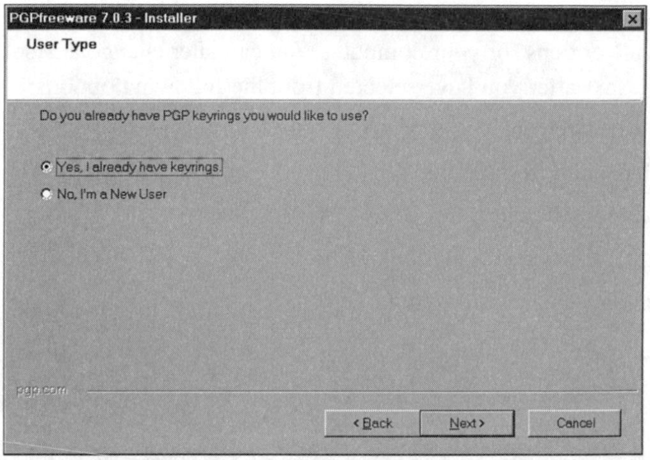

FIGURE 19.4

The User Type window (keyrings).

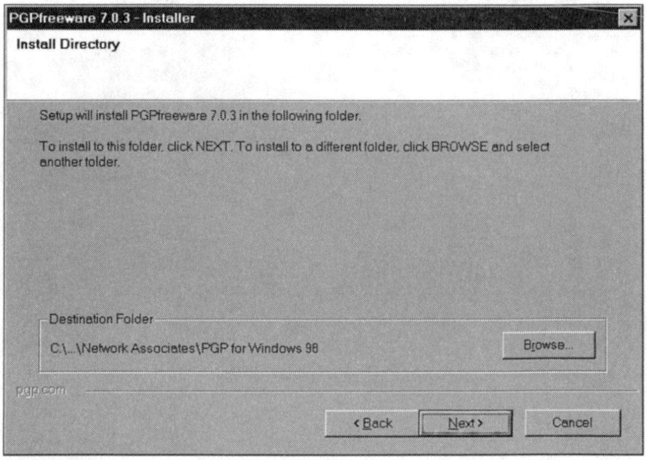

FIGURE 19.5

The Install Directory window.

19

ENCRYPTION

6. As demonstrated in Figure 19.6, the Select Components window requires that you choose the appropriate options for your computer. You can later change any selections you have made. Click Next after you have selected from the following options:

- PGP Key Management
- PGPnet Personal Firewall/IDS/VPN
- PGP Plugin for Microsoft Outlook
- PGP Plugin for Microsoft Outlook Express
- PGP Plugin for Qualcomm Eudora
- PGP Plugin for ICQ
- PGP Documentation

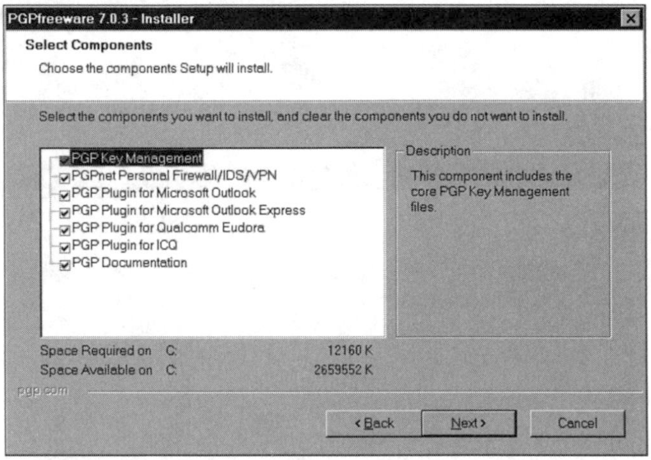

FIGURE 19.6
The Select Components window.

7. The Start Copying Files screen will appear, as illustrated in Figure 19.7. Review your settings, and then click Next to continue.

8. The next screen is a PGP advertisement window (Do you know what you're missing?), as shown in Figure 19.8. Click Next to continue, and you will see the Setup Status bar.

9. The next window is the PGP Set Adapter window, as demonstrated in Figure 19.9. This window will only appear if you selected PGPnet Personal Firewall/IDS/VPN in step 6 of the installation. Select the network adapter(s) you want secured/unsecured, and then click OK to continue.

10. As shown in Figure 19.10, the PGP Key Generation Wizard Welcome window will appear. Click Next to continue.

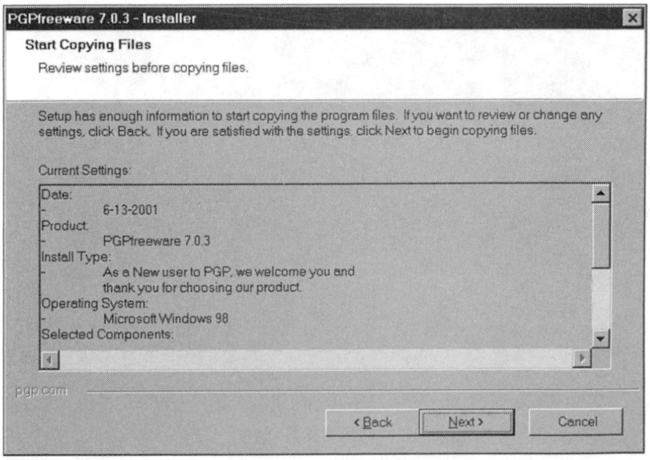

FIGURE 19.7

The Start Copying Files window (review settings).

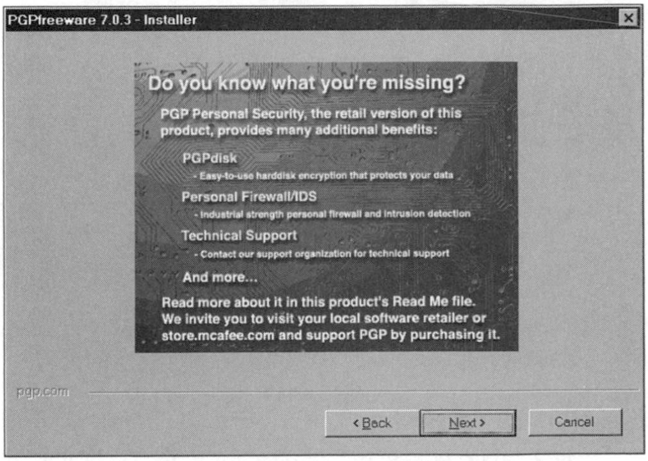

FIGURE 19.8

The PGP advertisement window.

11. Figure 19.11 illustrates the Name and Email Assignment screen. Enter the name and e-mail address that you want to associate with the Key you are generating. Click Next to continue with Key generation after you have completed entering your name and e-mail address.

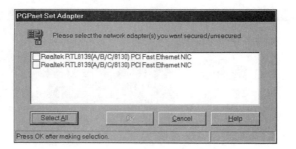

FIGURE 19.9

The PGPnet Set Adapter window.

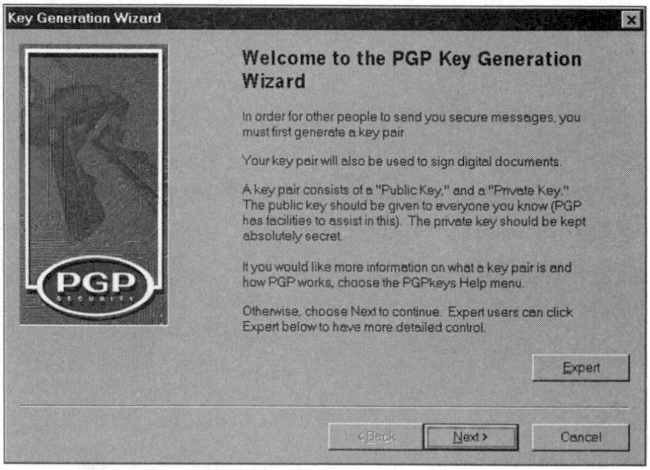

FIGURE 19.10

The PGP Key Generation Wizard Welcome window.

12. The next screen is the Passphrase Assignment window, as shown in Figure 19.12. Enter a passphrase in the appropriate box, and then repeat it in the confirmation box. A passphrase is a long password that is eight characters long or more, usually a sentence or phrase. Click Next to continue.

13. The Key Generation Progress bar will appear, as illustrated in Figure 19.13. Click Next to continue when the bar is completely solid.

14. The next screen is the Completing the PGP Key Generation Wizard window, as shown in Figure 19.14. Click Finish to continue.

15. As illustrated in Figure 19.15, you will see the PGP Install Wizard Complete window. Click Finish to restart your machine, or uncheck the box to restart later.

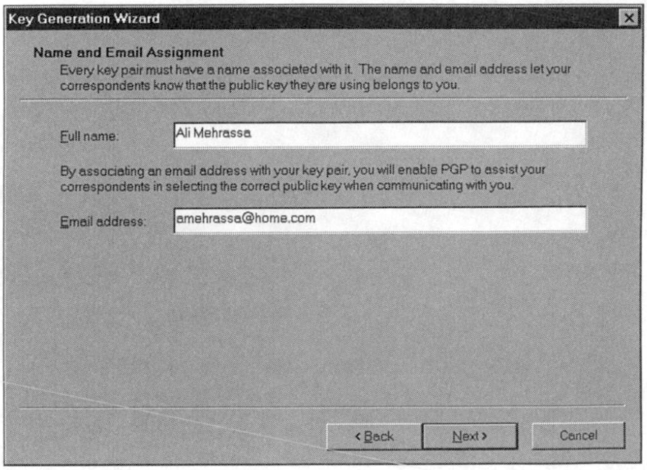

FIGURE 19.11

The Name and Email Assignment screen.

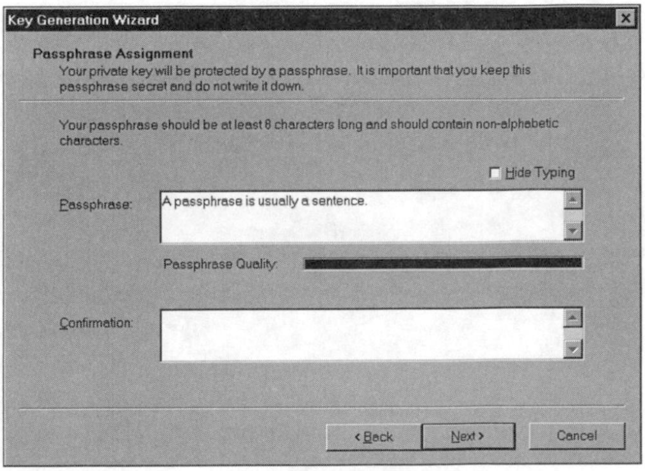

FIGURE 19.12

The Passphrase Assignment window.

19

ENCRYPTION

CAUTION

You must restart your computer before changes will take affect. If you choose not to restart in step 15, make sure to manually restart before using PGP.

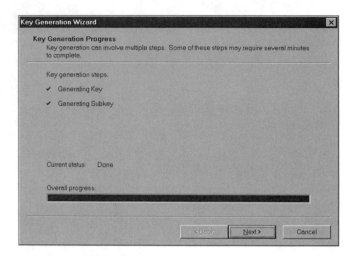

FIGURE 19.13

The Key Generation Progress bar.

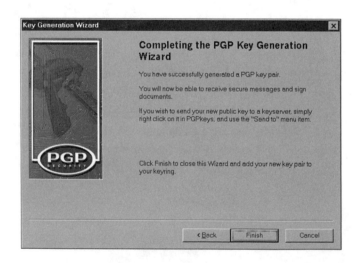

FIGURE 19.14

The Completing the PGP Key Generation Wizard window.

TIP

After PGP has been installed, you can Modify, Repair or Remove this program by re-opening the installer program.

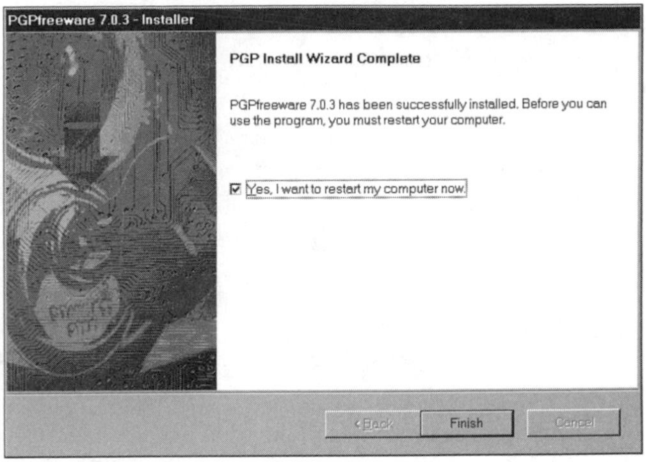

FIGURE 19.15
The PGP Install Wizard Complete window.

Using PGP

PGP can be used from within many of the popular e-mail programs, such as Qualcomm's Eudora and Microsoft's Outlook and Outlook Express. But PGP can also be used from within Web browsers. In addition, the PGP Toolbar even allows PGP to be used from within programs that aren't designed for integration. For detailed information on how to use PGP, refer to the Documentation that is automatically installed onto your machine with the PGPfreeware.

> **TIP**
>
> You can view the documentation for PGPfreeware on the Internet at the following
> ftp site: `ftp://ftp.pgpi.org/pub/pgp/7.0/docs/english/PGPWinUsersGuide.pdf`.

Before you can use PGP, you must create a new key pair. This step was included in the step-by-step installation instructions. You can create a new key pair by opening the PGPKeys program and following the PGP Key Generation Wizard (steps 10-15 of PGP installation), accessed from the PGP menu, which is located within the Programs menu. The Programs menu is accessed from the Start menu.

Some of the following tasks can be performed without the use of an e-mail program, by using Windows Explorer and the right mouse button (shortcut menu), or by selecting the PGPtray from the system tray located in the bottom right hand corner (Start bar). Listed in the following are some of the more common tasks that can be performed with PGP:

19

ENCRYPTION

- Secure your e-mails with encryption: Select the file or e-mail you want to encrypt from Windows Explorer, right-click to activate the shortcut menu, and then select Encrypt (or encrypt and sign) from the PGP menu.

- Clean files from your machine: You can permanently delete files from your machine by selecting the files from Windows Explorer (or from the desktop) and by right-clicking to activate the shortcut menu. From the shortcut menu, select Wipe from the PGP shortcut menu, and click OK when prompted to confirm.

- Decrypting coded messages (with an e-mail program that supports the PGP Plugin): If the encrypted file is not automatically decrypted when you open it, click the Decrypt/Verify button from the PGP menu located in your e-mail program. Enter your passphrase and click OK.

- Decrypting coded messages (with an e-mail program that doesn't support the PGP Plugin): Open the e-mail from within the e-mail program. Then activate the PGPtray, select Current Window submenu, and then select Decrypt/Verify. Enter your passphrase and click OK.

Summary

In this chapter, you learned about the need for encryption as a means of protecting your data. In addition, this chapter deals with some of the basics of encryption and introduced tools that can be used to protect the data you store on your computer or transmit over the Internet. In the next chapter, you will learn useful techniques for testing the security of your home computer or network: by attacking yourself, you can determine the weaknesses in your security settings and configuration.

Testing and Recovery

PART
V

IN THIS PART

20 Testing Your Security by Attacking Yourself   255

21 Managing Your Logs   267

22 Recovering from a Disaster   283

23 Maintaining Your Protection   291

24 Backup Strategies   303

Testing Your Security by Attacking Yourself

IN THIS CHAPTER

In This Chapter

Now that you have a security plan in place, you need to verify the integrity of the plan. One aspect of this is ensuring that your firewall or proxy is effectively denying access to your home computer or network, and that no unwanted services within your network are answering requests from the Internet.

You can do this by scanning your ports, the basic technique used by attackers to identify weaknesses in security on the Internet. This chapter provides the justification for attacking yourself with port scanning, and then discusses various online services and software packages you can use to attack yourself.

Why Attack Yourself?

When Internet crackers want to attack a computer or network on the Internet, one of the first steps they take is to run a *port scan*. A port scan attempts to identify TCP/IP ports on which they can make connections to the computer or network, and to identify the services answering those requests. At the very best, these port scans will only reveal the ports you have configured your firewall and computers to grant incoming connections to, but at worst they might reveal ports and services that you did not realize were accessible from the Internet, and that pose serious security risks.

For this reason, it is wise to periodically run port scans against your home network yourself. These scans will provide you the same information that an attacker would gain from a port scan, and enable you to identify weaknesses in your security configuration.

Basic Principles of Self Attacks

Attacking yourself with a port scan is not a complicated procedure, but it can be time consuming, depending on the depth of attack. The key principle is that you cannot port scan your own network from within your network. This means you cannot test your home Internet security effectively from within your home; the port scan must originate from elsewhere on the Internet.

Having said that, you need to consider the following when running port scans against yourself:

- Should I run a limited or comprehensive scan?
- How frequently should I scan my network?
- What should I watch for in scan reports?

Limited Versus Comprehensive Scans

Potentially, there are more than 65,000 ports that could be answering requests on your home network. Typically, most software uses a small set of known ports and not the entire 65,000, but a malicious Trojan horse or other application might use any arbitrary port for its purposes.

However, scanning all ports for all potential vulnerabilities is time consuming, and can even cause the system being scanned to stop working altogether, or possibly cause congestion on the system's Internet connection. Some comprehensive scans take as long as five hours to complete.

As an alternative, it is not uncommon to test for common, well-known vulnerabilities by scanning a limited set of ports. This can be done frequently without affecting system performance or causing the scanned system to cease functioning.

For this reason, you need to consider when you want to perform which type of scan. For instance, after configuring your security system, you would be well-advised to conduct a comprehensive scan to ensure that the system is as secure as planned. Then, you can perform regular limited scans to ensure all major vulnerabilities are secure.

Subsequently, if you change your security configuration, install major new software that can expose your system, or think a Trojan horse has infected your system, you can use a comprehensive scan to double-check things.

Scanning Frequency

The question of how often to scan is tied to your needs and how you use your computers. If you never change the security settings of your network, and rarely download and install new software, you might be able to scan infrequently, maybe once per month or less, especially if you are conscientious about keeping your antivirus software up-to-date, monitoring security alerts, and taking corrective action when possible.

The more you change your system or security settings, or the less often your antivirus software is updated, the more often you should consider scanning for security vulnerabilities.

Another point to consider is that if you offer services to the Internet from your computer, you should consider more frequent scanning. As new types of vulnerabilities come to light, port scanning services will add these vulnerabilities to the ones they test for on each scan.

Red Flags in Scan Reports

When you run a scan, there are certain red flags you should watch for in the reports that are generated. Depending on the service or software you use, the nature of these reports will vary, but generally they will tell you the following:

20

TESTING BY
ATTACKING
YOURSELF

- Any ports that are accessible from the Internet
- The services running on the accessible ports
- Any known security vulnerabilities with the services that are accessible

In this information, you need to pay attention to several key points:

- If a port you hadn't intended to be accessible is accessible, you need to check your firewall settings to determine the reason why.
- If a service you hadn't intended to be accessible is available, you need to check both your firewall settings and the system running the service to determine why the service is running. Sometimes, a running service you weren't aware of is actually a Trojan horse running for malicious reasons.
- If any of the security vulnerabilities are flagged in the report as urgent or high risk, you should take any action suggested in the report. Typically, this might include updating software to newer versions, or tightening up the security policies in your firewall.
- If you see security vulnerabilities that potentially offer root or administrative access to your computers, provide access to data on your computer, or permit attackers to corrupt data on your system, you should take immediate action to eliminate the vulnerability. Typically, these reports will offer advice about how to eliminate any vulnerabilities they find.

Online Port Scanning Services

There are two approaches to running a port scan on your own computer. The first is to use software designed for port scanning, as described later in the section "Port Scanning Software." However, running port scanning software yourself requires access to another system from which to run the scan, and can require advanced networking knowledge to complete successfully.

Because of this, numerous port scanning services are available on the Internet, and this section discusses them. They offer a wide variety of scans, ranging from a basic limited scan for no cost, to complete, comprehensive scans that can cost as much as $100 per scan.

ShieldsUP!

Steve Gibson is famous on the Internet as a vocal security expert, exposing many of the security vulnerabilities on the Internet. He offers several free security services on his Web site, http://grc.com/.

His ShieldsUP! service provides a free port scanning service that scans common ports and looks for well-known security vulnerabilities on your system. Although by no means a comprehensive scanner, it does come with excellent documentation about port scanning, security risks on the Internet, and provides detailed advice about what you can do if you find yourself exposed.

Because the service is free, fast, and informative, it is a good starting place for running a quick check of your security.

LeakTest

Port scanners such as ShieldsUP! are designed to test your security against unwanted incoming connections. However, security is a two-way street: You want to be sure that unwanted outgoing connections are also disallowed. Good personal firewall software or proxy servers, for instance, will prevent unauthorized outgoing connections from occurring.

Protection against unauthorized outgoing connections is more important than it sounds. At first, you might think this is unimportant because you are initiating outgoing connections. However, a Trojan horse can install software running in the background on your computer that will initiate outgoing connections to provide information about you, your data, or even access to your system to the author or distributor of the Trojan horse.

For this reason, you need protection against unauthorized outgoing connections. Steve Gibson has written a free piece of software called LeakTest that can be used to test whether you are adequately protected against unauthorized outgoing connections. You can download LeakTest from http://grc.com/lt/leaktest.htm.

You download LeakTest as a Windows executable file that you can execute immediately after downloading. The interface of LeakTest is simple. It will display a Ready to Test window, as illustrated in Figure 20.1.

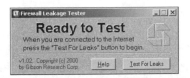

FIGURE 20.1

The LeakTest Ready to Test window.

To test your system for leaks, simply click on the Test for Leaks button. If your firewall asks whether LeakTest should be permitted any type of access to the Internet, deny the access. LeakTest will complete its test and display a report window like the one in Figure 20.2.

If the report indicates that LeakTest was unable to connect, that is the first good sign: It means LeakTest failed to make an unauthorized connection to the Internet. If the report is that your firewall was penetrated, then you need to revise the configuration of your firewall to ensure that it will deny unauthorized outgoing access to the Internet.

20

TESTING BY
ATTACKING
YOURSELF

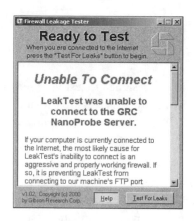

FIGURE 20.2
The LeakTest report window.

To fully test things, LeakTest recommends that after successfully denying access to LeakTest, you should exit from LeakTest, restart it, and retry the test, but this time if your firewall asks whether you want to enable LeakTest to access the Internet, allow the access to happen. This time, the report will be that the firewall was penetrated. Keep in mind, of course, that the first test denying access to the network is the critical one, and this latter test simply reinforces your control over the behavior of your firewall with respect to unauthorized connections to the Internet.

Security Space

Security Space (`http://www.securityspace.com/sspace/`)is a Canadian service offering a wide variety of security scans, ranging from a basic free scan to a range of commercial scans. At the low-end, the Security Space offers the No Risk Audit. This free service runs 662 vulnerability tests and scans more than 1,500 ports at the time of writing. However, it does not report specific results, but instead gives you a general sense of your security status. As illustrated in Figure 20.3, the audit reports a number of vulnerabilities found in four categories (high risk, medium risk, low risk, and general alerts), and then rates your security on a percentage scale.

> **NOTE**
>
> An important distinction needs to be noted here: Scanning ports simply determines whether the port can be accessed or not; testing for a vulnerability checks for known security bugs and problems with the services that answer connections on the accessible ports. The combination of port scanning and vulnerability scanning improves the value of the scan.

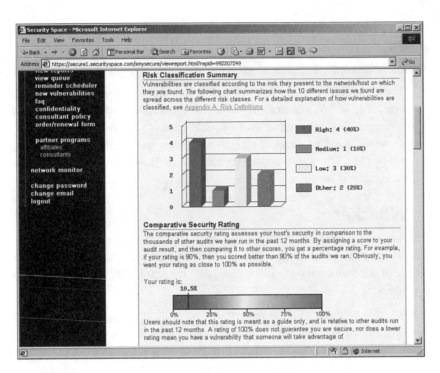

FIGURE 20.3

The Security Space No Risk Audit report.

However, the No Risk Audit provides no specifics about the types of vulnerabilities. To obtain information about the actual security vulnerabilities found during the scan, you will need to use one of the following three commercial audits:

- Desktop Audit: Performs 209 vulnerability tests common in DOS and Windows and scans 1,500 ports. The reports that are generated offer detailed information about the vulnerabilities that are found. A Desktop Audit costs Can$15 (Canadian dollars) for one month of unlimited scanning.

- Standard Audit: Performs the same 662 vulnerability tests and 1,500 port scans as the No Risk Audit, but offers detailed information about the vulnerabilities that are found. The cost of a Standard Audit ranges from Can$49 for a one-time scan to an annual subscription permitting unlimited scans for a year for Can$799.

- Advanced Audit: Performs the same 662 vulnerability tests as the Standard Audit and No Risk Audit, but scans all possible (65,535) ports. The report includes detailed information about the vulnerabilities that are found. The cost of an Advanced Audit ranges from Can$99 for a one-time scan, to an annual subscription for unlimited scans for a year for Can$1599.

In addition to the four scans already described, two other free scanning services are offered by Security Space:

- Basic Audit: Performs a scan of 1,500 ports and offers a detailed report of the results.
- Single Test: Enables you to perform a scan for any single vulnerability from Security Space's database of 662 vulnerability tests (the same tests used in the No Risk, Standard and Advanced audits). Theoretically, you could manually perform each of the 662 vulnerability scans using the Single Test scan 662 times, then run the Basic Audit and the end result would be the same as the Standard Audit. The difference would be the amount of time and effort it would take to complete the scan.

Hacker Whacker

Hacker Whacker (http://www.hackerwhacker.com/) is another commercial service offering a range of commercial scanning services. There is no free base scan, but new users get to run one free test scan after which they must begin paying for scans. Hacker Whacker offers five levels of membership:

- One Scan Membership: A single scan of all 65,535 TCP ports, more than 800 common UDP ports, and Netbios security vulnerabilities that expose your Windows files to the Internet. The port scans also include testing for known vulnerabilities in the services running on those ports. A single scan membership costs $9.99.
- Home Membership: Provides unlimited scans identical to the one-time scan for a period of three months for $29.99. The Home Membership is designed for scanning a single host.
- Business Membership: Provides the same scans as a home membership, plus a Web site scanner and e-mail server scanner that tests for problems specific to Web and e-mail servers. Three months of unlimited scans costs $89.99 and permits easy scanning of all hosts on a single network.
- Network Membership: Provides the same scans as a business membership, but allows scanning of systems other than the one from which you initiate the scan, as long as the scan remains in the same network. Three months of unlimited scans costs $129.99.
- Consultant Membership: Provides the same scans as a business membership, but permits arbitrary scanning of any computer on the Internet. Three months of unlimited scans costs $299.99.

The Hacker Whacker service provides one of the least expensive ways to scan all your ports. The One Scan Membership permits you to scan all TCP ports for only $9.99.

Keep in mind that even though the network and consultant memberships allow you to theoretically scan systems you do not necessarily have access to, to scan a system which you don't have the right to scan is a violation of U.S. federal law. Any unauthorized use of a computer system is against the law, and uninvited port scans consists of unauthorized use of a computer system.

Secure Design

Secure Design offers two free online scanning services at `http://www.sdesign.com/cgi-bin/fwtest.cgi/`. These two services offer different forms of limited scanning:

- Basic Scan: Performs a quick port scan for Windows file sharing and a basic list of common TCP ports, and displays the results in your Web browser.
- Complete Scan: Performs the same scans as the Basic Scan, but on both TCP and UDP ports. The results are e-mailed to you.

Port Scanning Software

Port scanning software enables you to fully control and configure the scanning process, and do it without the per-scan costs often associated with comprehensive online scanning services. However, there are other costs associated with online scanning software, including the following:

- You need access to a remote computer on which to install and run the scanning software to scan your network. You cannot scan your network effectively from within your network.
- The leading port scanning packages are free, but are only available for Linux and Unix systems; very few port scanners are available for Windows or the MacOS, and the most popular ones are not for Windows or the MacOS.
- With port scanning software you will need to decide how to configure the software, which ports to scan, and how to scan them. The online scanning services have made most of these decisions for you, based on extensive databases of ports and vulnerabilities.

The leading port and security scanning packages are all available for Linux or Unix systems:

- SATAN (Security Administrator Tool for Analyzing Networks): SATAN was one of the first publicly available port scanners and created quite a controversy when it was released, ostensibly as a tool for protecting networks, because it also put crackers' tools within reach of everyday computer users. SATAN scans for common network security problems, offers tutorials about problems it encounters, and suggests ways to fix the problems. You need Unix or a Unix-like system to use SATAN. SATAN will not run in Windows. You can find SATAN at `http://www.fish.com/satan/`.

20

- Nessus Security Scanner: Nessus is a robust security scanning solution for Unix and Linux systems. A modular architecture enables users to develop plug-ins to add new vulnerability scans to Nessus, which provides a flexibility not available in many port scanning tools. Nessus uses a two-tier architecture with a server that conducts the scans, and a client used to manage and monitor scans. While the client is available for Windows, the server is not. Nessus takes security scanning to the utmost by not just detecting potential problems, but actually attempting to exploit the problem. If you have a security hole that can be used to crash your computer, Nessus will probably succeed in crashing your computer when it finds the hole. You can find Nessus at `http://www.nessus.org/`.

- Nmap (Network Mapper): Nmap is a popular and powerful port scanner available for most platforms, including the MacOS. Windows support is in the works but not yet available. Designed to scan entire networks, it can also be used to scan individual PCs. Nmap is available from `http://www.nmap.org/`.

This doesn't mean there aren't Windows-based port scanners that you can use. For example, there is a free Windows port scanner from Foundstone. SuperScan is a full-scale TCP port scanner for Windows that is available from `http://www.foundstone.com/rdlabs/proddesc/superscan.html`.

After downloading SuperScan, you can install it by double-clicking on the `superscan.exe` application you downloaded. This will install SuperScan and launch the software as shown in Figure 20.4.

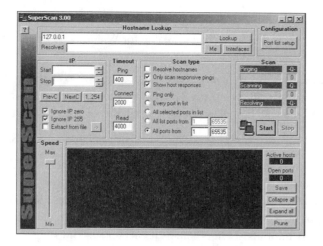

FIGURE 20.4

SuperScan port scanner for Windows.

To illustrate how to run a port scan with SuperScan, consider running a comprehensive port scan of all ports from 1 to 65,535 on a single PC with the IP address 127.0.0.1. To do this, use the following steps:

1. Enter 127.0.0.1 in the Start text field in the IP section of the SuperScan window.

2. Enter 127.0.0.1 in the Stop text field in the IP section of the SuperScan window.

3. Make sure the Show Host Reponses checkbox in the Scan Type section of the SuperScan window is selected.

4. Make sure the All Ports From radio button in the Scan Type section of the SuperScan window is selected.

5. Enter the port range from 1 to 65535 in the text fields next to the All Ports From radio button in the Scan Type section of the SuperScan window.

6. Click on the Start button.

SuperScan will begin the port scan. The Scanning entry of the Scan section of the window will turn green and show signs of activity while the scan is running. The results of the scan are shown as a tree in the blue report section across the bottom of the window under the IP address of the host being scanned. You can expand entries by clicking on the plus sign next to the entry as shown in Figure 20.5.

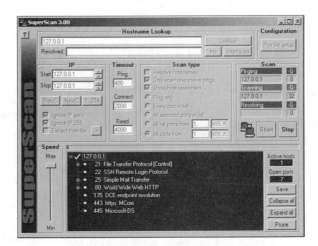

FIGURE 20.5
Scan results in SuperScan.

20

Summary

In this chapter you have learned an important technique for maintaining your security: attacking yourself with port scans. This technique enables you to see the same information attackers would see when they probe your network for security vulnerabilities and take corrective action if needed. You can attack yourself with Internet-based services or using specialized port scanning software.

The next chapter discusses another important topic for maintaining security: managing and monitoring the activity logs generated by your network software, firewall software, and Internet gateway hardware.

Managing Your Logs

IN THIS CHAPTER

In This Chapter

After you have designed your protection by implementing firewalls and other security mechanisms, you will not want to monitor proactively all the time. This would be too time-consuming. Instead, you need a way to periodically check the state of your system to make sure nothing untoward has happened and to ensure that your security is working. One mechanism for doing this is log analysis. Many programs, including personal firewall software, maintain logs of their activities, which can be used for analysis purposes.

The Role of Logs

Most programs that provide services maintain *logs* of their activities. Logs are records of actions taken by the software and, possibly, attempts by users to use the service. These records can provide invaluable insight into the unseen happenings on your computer or network.

Typically, logs are created in one of two ways:

- An application maintains its own log files. These are normally text files with each line containing a log entry.

- An application uses the Windows system logs to track its activities. Windows NT and 2000 provide system logging services in three logs: an application log for logging application activity, a system log for use by the operating system itself, and a security log to log events related to security and user authentication. These logging services do not exist in Windows 98 or Windows Me, so are typically only used by server software that runs on NT or 2000.

These logs are essential to understanding what is happening on your system, especially unseen activity taking place in the background. Log files can provide you with a lot of information, including the following:

- Warnings and alerts about misconfigured or misbehaving software

- Indications of unauthorized users using your computers

- Insight into the level and diversity of use of Internet services you provide, such as Web sites or FTP content

- Reports of attempts to violate your system's security by attackers, or attempts by viruses to infect your system

This chapter discusses general techniques for using these logs to your advantage in maintaining your security.

Log Management and Analysis Strategies

For security purposes, you need to pay attention to several types of logs:

- Logs generated by your firewall system (such as personal firewall software, which is discussed in Chapter 7, "Using Personal Firewall Software," or broadband routers, which are discussed in Chapter 12, "Using a Broadband Router"). These logs let you know what types of attacks or probing are being directed at your system.

- Logs generated by Internet services you decide to provide such as a Web server, FTP server, or mail server. These logs let you know how your Internet services are being used and whether anyone is abusing, or attempting to abuse, these services.

- Logs generated by antivirus software. These logs let you know whether you have been infected by a virus or a virus has attempted to infect your system and was successfully stopped. This can also help you track down the source of viruses.

- Logs generated by your operating system, such as user authentication logs and user activity logs. These logs let you know who is using your system and how, and enable you to identify unauthorized or questionable use of your system.

With many applications you have control over several features of the logging process:

- Verbosity of logs: This indicates how much information to actually record in the logs.

- Log rotation frequency: In order to avoid logs growing excessively large over time, some applications implement log rotation policies that delete old log files or old log entries based on policies you define. Even where log rotation features aren't provided, you can develop manual log rotation schemes.

Choosing Log Verbosity

In some advanced applications such as the Apache and Internet Information Server Web servers, as well as Windows NT and 2000 system logs, you can control the type of information that gets logged as well as the amount of information that gets recorded with each log entry. The amount of information recorded in logs is known as the log's verbosity.

Typically, applications write different types of log messages. Common types include

- Information messages: These are simple information messages about the normal operation of an application; they are the least critical messages and include those which track the starting and stopping of applications.

- Warning messages: These are cautionary messages of potential problems, but not actual errors; they usually signal a developing problem and include messages that indicate failure to perform actions that normally succeed.

- Error messages: These are messages indicating actual errors in the configuration or operation of an application; they indicate actual problems that need to be addressed, such as failure to load libraries or failures for applications to understand and use their configuration.

If your application provides the capability to control which types of log messages are recorded, this can provide a useful way to filter out extraneous information from logs. For instance, in most circumstances, after you have an application running correctly on a regular basis, information-type messages serve little purpose in regular logs. On the other hand, warning and information messages might be useful in diagnosing problems that might arise.

The decision about what to include in logs depends on several factors. First, you need to consider the amount of disk space you have available to store your logs, and how quickly the log files you need to keep will grow. You can only learn this over time by watching the pattern of how fast your log files grow. If you have a disk space problem, you need to consider which types of messages not to include in your logs.

In addition, you should consider the value of certain types of messages. An application might generate large numbers of information messages that serve little purpose or value in tracking the health of your system, but which clutter up your log files and even dominate them. In a case like this, you might have a strong argument for not logging information messages. Similarly, if an application generates large numbers of warning messages for perfectly innocuous events, perhaps because of a poorly designed logging mechanism in an application, you might need to stop logging warning messages to avoid having logs overrun with nothing but useless warning messages. Again, you can only learn this with time and familiarity with your software.

TIP

The specifics of how to choose the level of logging verbosity are very application-specific. You need to consult your software's documentation to learn how to do this.

Log Rotation

In order to make logs useful, it is common practice to rotate the logs. This has different meanings in different cases. For applications such as personal firewalls and Web server software that write log messages in their own files, log rotation usually means that a historical set of log files are kept for a fixed period of time, and before that fixed period of time, all logs are deleted.

Let's consider a concrete example to make this clear: You feel that it is useful to keep logs from your personal firewall software for one month. Before that time, log messages are too old to be of real value to you. In addition, you decide that keeping all log messages for a given week in a single file provides a convenient way to organize your logs.

Your rotation might then work like this:

1. The current week's log messages are stored in a file that might be called `firewall.log`. In addition, the logs for the last four weeks are in the files `firewall.log.1` (one week old), `firewall.log.2` (two weeks old), `firewall.log.3` (three weeks old), and finally `firewall.log.4` (four weeks old).

2. At the end of each week, logs are rotated as follows:

   A. `firewall.log.3` is moved to `firewall.log.4` (which overwrites the old `firewall.log.4`).

   B. `firewall.log.2` is moved to `firewall.log.3`.

   C. `firewall.log.1` is moved to `firewall.log.2`.

   D. `firewall.log` is moved to `firewall.log.1`.

   E. A new `firewall.log` file is created.

The end result is four historical weeks of log information, cleanly separated into four separate weekly files.

You can create a simple batch file to automate this rotation. To do this, create a text file named `rotate.bat` with a text editor such as Notepad and enter the following batch program:

```
cd c:\logfiles
move firewall.log.3 firewall.log.4
move firewall.log.2 firewall.log.3
move firewall.log.1 firewall.log.2
move firewall.log firewall.log.1
```

NOTE

This script assumes you keep your log files in the directory `c:\logfiles`. If you don't, change the first line and replace `c:\logfiles` with the directory where you store your log files.

This batch file performs the log rotation described previously except for the last step, creating a new `firewall.log` file. This file will be created automatically when the next log message is generated by your firewall software.

In order to rotate your logs, you need to run this batch file on a weekly basis:

```
C:\batch\>rotate.bat
```

On Windows NT or 2000 systems you can use the built-in scheduling tool to run this script automatically on a weekly basis. You schedule commands using the at command. For instance, to schedule this batch file to run once per week at 12:01 a.m. on Sundays, use the following command:

```
C:\>at 00:01 /every:sunday c:\batch\rotate.bat
Added a new job with job ID = 3
```

This command assumes that the batch file is stored in the directory c:\batch.

> **TIP**
>
> This scheduling capability is not available in Windows 98 or Windows Me; it is part of Windows NT and 2000. Instead, you need to use another scheduling tool, such as those at http://downloads.cnet.com/.

Some applications do not keep log messages in plain files as previously described. Instead, they are kept in a specialized database. This is the way the Windows system logs are maintained. In this case, the typical approach to log rotation is to rotate entries out of the log based on some set of policies. Examples include the following:

- Removing messages from the log when they are older than a specific number of days
- Removing the oldest message from the log when the size of the log exceeds a specific limit, and a new message needs to be written to the log

For instance, the Windows system logs use a combination of these approaches, enabling you to specify a maximum log size in addition to expiration times for log messages. You can control this with the Event Viewer in Windows NT or 2000. For example, in Windows 2000, you open the Event Viewer as follows:

1. Open the Control Panel.
2. Double-click on the Administrative Tools folder.
3. Double-click on the Event Viewer icon.

Windows 2000 will display the Event Viewer as illustrated in Figure 21.1.

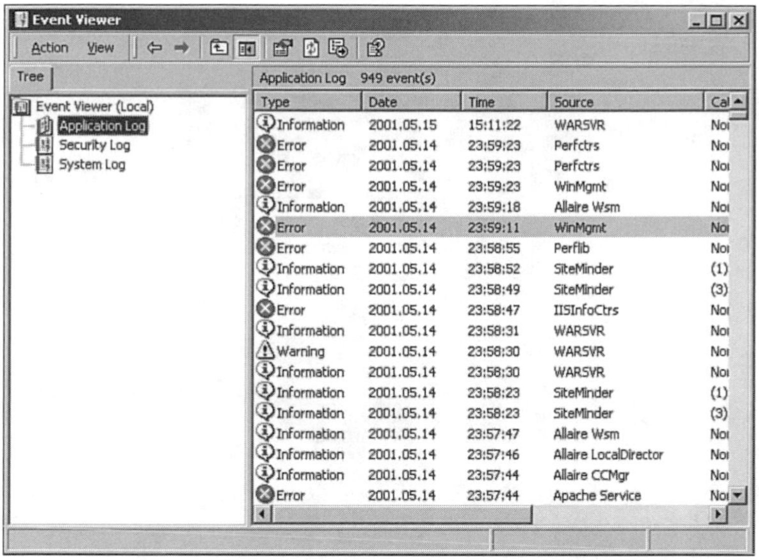

FIGURE 21.1
The Windows 2000 Event Viewer.

NOTE

In Windows NT, you can open the Event Viewer by selecting Programs, Administrative Tools, Event Viewer from the Start menu. In this chapter we are using the Windows 2000 Event Viewer for our example.

You can configure the log rotation policies for any of the Windows 2000 system logs as follows:

1. Select the log to configure in the left panel of the Event Viewer window. You can choose the application, security, or system log.

2. Select View, Filters from the menu bar of the Event Viewer. The Event Viewer will display the Log Properties dialog box for the selected log, as illustrated in Figure 21.2.

3. Click on the General tab to display the General page of the Log Properties dialog box, as illustrated in Figure 21.3.

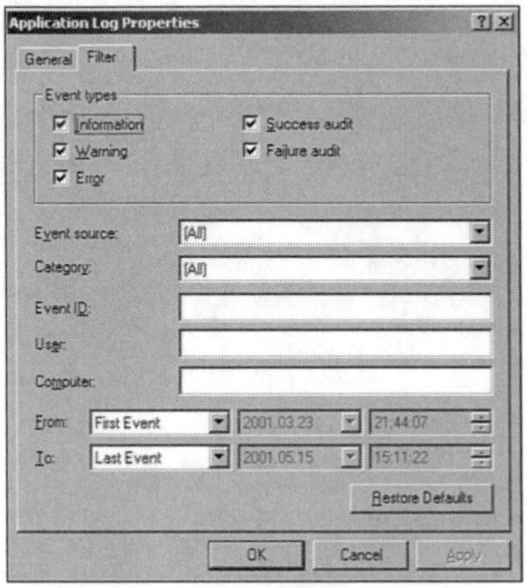

FIGURE 21.2
The Application Log Properties dialog box.

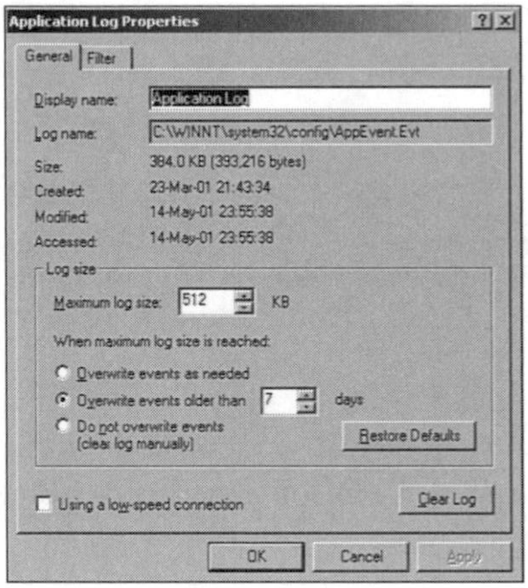

FIGURE 21.3
The General page of the Application Log Properties dialog box.

4. In the Log Size section of the General page, set the maximum size of the log in kilobytes in the Maximum Log Size text field.

5. Select additional log rotation policies by choosing one of the following radio buttons:

   • Overwrite Events as Needed: If you select this option, then only the size of the log matters, and when the log reaches the maximum size, each new log message forces the oldest message to be removed from the log.

- Overwrite Events Older than X Days: This option enables you to specify a maximum age for log messages in days. In this case the size rule applies, and if a message is still in the log after the number of days specified, it will be deleted from the log.

- Do Not Overwrite Events: This option forces all messages to remain in the log regardless of age or size of the log, and you will need to remove them from the log manually.

6. Click on the OK button to close the Log Properties dialog box.

Log Analysis Tips

The purpose of going to all this effort to choose your log verbosity and implement a rotation policy is to have useful log information available to analyze for a particular purpose. In the case of this book, we are interested in analyzing logs for the purposes of maintaining and ensuring the security of your systems and networks.

The question of what to look for in your logs is dependent on what application generated the log. For personal firewall software or a broadband router, you need to watch for the following in your logs:

- Repeated attempts to access a specific blocked port from a specific IP address. This can signal someone trying to use a specific service to gain access to your network or computer.

- Access to a series of ports in order from the same IP address. This can signal someone attempting to scan your ports, looking for points of weakness in your firewall protection and security design.

- Access to a port you have enabled, but from an IP address you are suspicious of (usually because you took note of that address in a previous log analysis). If an IP address is repeatedly connected to ports on your network but you are suspicious of the reasons for it to be doing so, it might signal someone trying to use a service you are offering, such as a Web server, to compromise your computer or network.

- A strange level of accesses to a valid service from a specific address in a short time period. This might signal an attempt at a denial-of-service attack.

If you are analyzing the logs of a specific application, the things to look for will be different but application-specific. For instance, in a Web server, you might want to look for the following:

- Repeated attempts to access non-existent HTML documents or CGI-BIN scripts from a specific IP address in a fixed period of time. This might signal a denial-of-service attack.

- A strange order or pattern to the documents being requested from a single IP address during a single session. This might signal some type of automated crawler browsing your site. Although the reason for this might be to index your site for a search engine, it can also signal an attempt to analyze the source code of your site to look for security weaknesses, especially if you use interactive code such as Java or JavaScript in your site.

- Errors indicating files not being found. This doesn't reflect a security problem, but indicates that you have bad links within your site or into your site from someone else's site.

Example: ZoneAlarm Logs

In Chapter 7, you were introduced to the ZoneAlarm personal firewall, which is freely available for download at `http://www.zonelabs.com/`. ZoneAlarm provides a logging facility that enables you to log firewall activity to a text file, in addition to the default pop-up notices you receive when using the firewall.

By default, logging is not enabled in ZoneAlarm, so you need to activate it as follows:

1. Open the ZoneAlarm window by double-clicking the ZoneAlarm icon in the Windows toolbar. The main ZoneAlarm window will be displayed as illustrated in Figure 21.4.

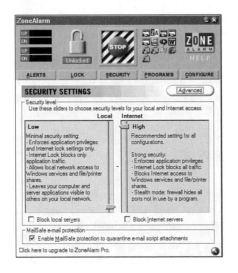

FIGURE 21.4

The ZoneAlarm window.

2. Click on the Alerts button to display the Alerts page, as illustrated in Figure 21.5.
3. Select the Log alerts to a text file checkbox in the Alert settings section of the Alerts page. ZoneAlarm will log to a standard log file location: `C:\WINNT\Internet Logs\ZALog.txt`. The size of the current log file will be displayed next to the filename.

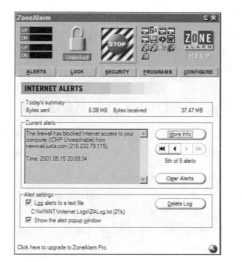

FIGURE 21.5

The Alerts page of the ZoneAlarm window.

After you activate logging, ZoneAlarm will start generating the log file. The following is an excerpt from an actual ZoneAlarm log file:

```
PE,2001/05/07,22:35:23 -7:00 GMT,RealPlayer,216.218.135.99:80,N/A
FWOUT,2001/05/07,22:44:14 -7:00 GMT,10.10.10.10:1734,10.10.10.25:139,TCP
➡(flags:S)
FWIN,2001/05/07,22:44:35 -7:00 GMT,10.10.10.25:138,10.10.10.10:138,UDP
FWIN,2001/05/07,22:45:41 -7:00 GMT,216.232.79.115:0,10.10.10.10:0,ICMP
➡(type:3/subtype:3)
FWIN,2001/05/07,23:16:50 -7:00 GMT,10.10.10.25:137,10.10.10.10:137,UDP
```

Each entry in the log file takes a single line and consists of the six fields separated by commas:

- The type of entry
- The date of the entry
- The time of the entry
- The source IP address and port of the attempt to cross the firewall
- The destination IP address and port of the attempt to cross the firewall and port
- The transportation protocol of the access attempt (which should be TCP, UDP or ICMP)

For instance, consider the following entry:

```
FWOUT,2001/05/07,22:44:14 -7:00 GMT,10.10.10.10:1734,10.10.10.25:139,TCP
➡(flags:S)
```

This entry tells us the following: that an application on the system 10.10.10.10 tried to make an outgoing connection (FWOUT stands for "firewall outgoing") to the host 10.10.10.25 on port 139 using the TCP protocol at 22:14 on 7 May 2001.

Because ZoneAlarm keeps its logs in a text file on your system, you can use the technique described in the Log Rotation section earlier in this chapter to implement a log rotation strategy for ZoneAlarm. Otherwise, the file will keep growing until you disable logging in ZoneAlarm or delete the log file.

Example: Linksys Cable/DSL Router Logs

The Linksys Etherfast series of Cable/DSL Routers can also maintain logs for your reference. The Linksys router is an example of a hardware firewall and is discussed in Chapter 12.

As a hardware device, it has limited storage space in which to write the logs, and the logs tend to be very basic and cover a short period of time, reflecting recent access attempts only. Still, these logs can be used to monitor firewall activity in a close-to-real-time mode if you suspect someone is attempting to port-scan your system or attack your network.

By default, the Etherfast series of Cable/Routers disable logging. To enable logging, use the following steps:

1. Open the administrative Web application for your router in your Web browser as illustrated in Figure 21.6. If the IP address of your router is 192.168.0.1, then open `http://192.168.0.1/` in your Web browser.

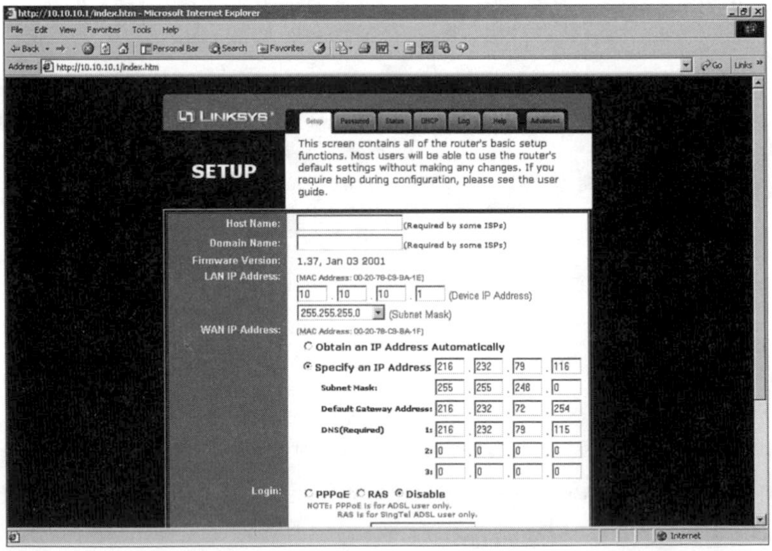

FIGURE 21.6

The LinkSys Etherfast administrative Web application.

2. Click on the Log tab to display the Log page as illustrated in Figure 21.7.

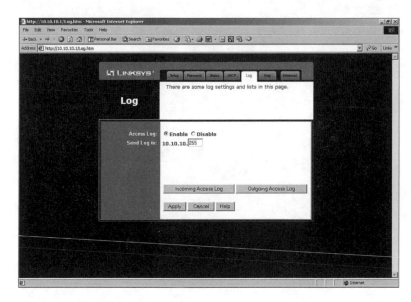

FIGURE 21.7

The Log page of the Linksys administrative tool.

3. Click on the Enable radio button to enable logging.

4. Click on the Apply button. The router will apply the settings.

When activated, you can choose to display two different logs from the Log page of the administrative Web application: an incoming access log and an outgoing access log. The format of both logs is similar. For instance, the incoming access log illustrated in Figure 21.8 shows the Incoming Log Table window that is displayed when you click on the Incoming Access Log button.

This log shows two pieces of information for each entry: the IP address from which a connection originated, and the port to which the connection was made. The Outgoing Access Log provides slightly more detail, as illustrated in Figure 21.9.

Here you can see the internal IP address of the host making the outgoing connection, the destination IP address of the connection, and the port number being used to establish the connection.

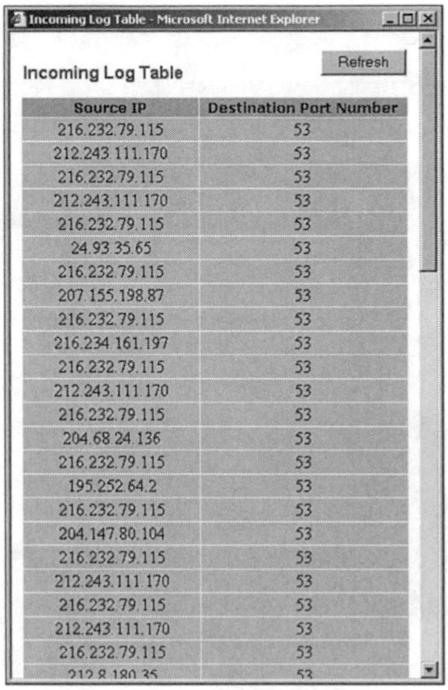

FIGURE 21.8

The Incoming Log Table window.

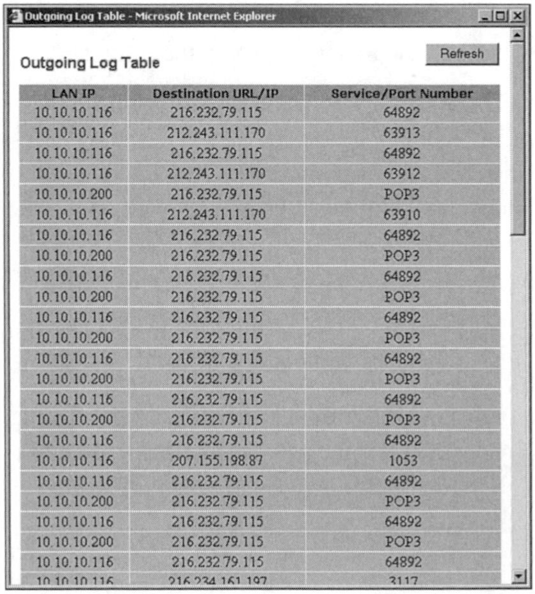

FIGURE 21.9

The Outgoing Log Table window.

Example: Norton AntiVirus

Antivirus software also keeps logs that are useful for maintaining your security. By default, Norton AntiVirus maintains an activity log. Norton AntiVirus is introduced in Chapter 9, "Vaccinating Your Computer Against Viruses."

The log generated by Norton AntiVirus reports on the results, for instance, of complete system scans and reports of infected files that were detected. You can access the log as follows:

Double-click on the Norton AntiVirus icon in the Windows toolbar. Windows will display the Norton AntiVirus window, as illustrated in Figure 21.10.

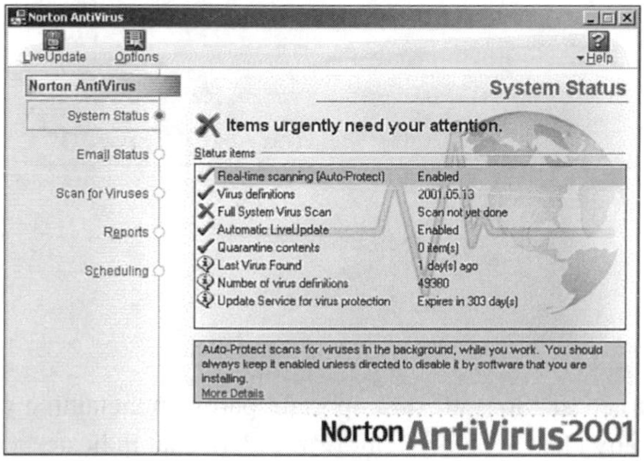

FIGURE 21.10
The Norton AntiVirus Window.

Click on the Reports menu entry to display the Reports page of the window seen in Figure 21.11.

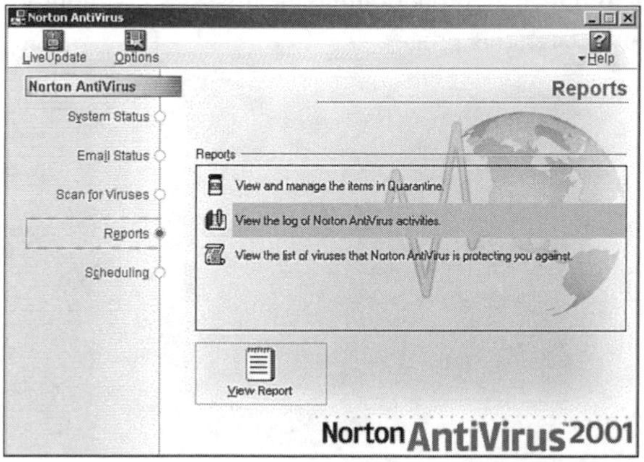

FIGURE 21.11
The Reports page of the Norton AntiVirus window.

Double-click on the View the Log of Norton AntiVirus Activities entry on the page to display the Activity Log dialog box, as illustrated in Figure 21.12.

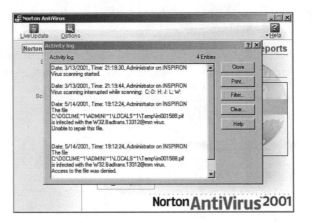

FIGURE 21.12

The Activity Log dialog box.

Summary

In this chapter you learned that logs are an important part of maintaining your security. They enable you to periodically check your system for behavior that indicates a failure in security. Most applications including firewalls and antivirus software offer logs. You need to implement a sound rotation plan for your logs and analyze them periodically.

The next chapter addresses an important security subject: what to do when your security messages fail and your system is compromised. You can't keep running a compromised system, so you need to take action to return to a functioning, clean system without losing any data. The next chapter guides you through this process.

Recovering From a Disaster

IN THIS CHAPTER

In This Chapter

If you have reason to think your system has been compromised, you have to take action: It is better to waste some time checking whether you have been compromised, than to assume you are safe and later find your data deleted or your system under the control of some remote attacker on the Internet.

This chapter outlines basic strategies for determining whether your system has been compromised and, if it has, taking steps to resolve the situation.

Get Offline

Without a doubt, the first course of action when you suspect your system has been compromised, either by a network attacker or by a Trojan horse, worm, or other virus, is to disconnect your computer from the network: Unplug any phone lines and network cables; if you have a wireless network, remove the wireless network card, or turn off your access point.

If you have a broadband Internet connection, it is probably a good idea to disconnect it from the external Internet connection as well.

This act of isolating the suspect computer from the network and the Internet achieves several goals:

- If an attacker is still trying to gain access to your computer, you will stop them in their tracks.
- If an attacker has gained access to your system, you deny them that access while the system is disconnected from the network.
- If a worm has infected your system (such as an e-mail worm like Melissa), disconnecting your computer will stop it from spreading any further.
- If a Trojan horse is active on your system, sending information to its author, you stop it by disconnecting from the network.

By isolating the suspect computer you have bought yourself some time. You can proceed with care to diagnose the problem and resolve it without the pressure of thinking your system is under constant threat from its network connection.

Have I Been Compromised?

If you think your system might have been compromised, you need to start by determining whether that is in fact the case. There are two main types of compromise:

- Compromise by an attack from the Internet
- Compromise by a virus, Trojan horse, or worm

Have I Been Attacked?

To determine whether you have been attacked, you need to look for symptoms of an attack. Some of these symptoms are obvious, while others are subtle, obscure, and easily missed. Some of the obvious signs that you have been compromised by an attacker include:

- Your system appears to be operating on its own, as if controlled by an unseen person. The unseen person is probably the attacker.

- Your system seems to run unbearably slowly at all times, even when you are not running any applications. An attacker could be using your computer to conduct resource-intensive computing tasks.

- Your passwords magically change and you can't log into your computer.

- On Windows 2000 or NT, you discover new user accounts have been created that you know for a fact did not previously exist and that you did not create.

- On Windows 2000 or NT, applications or processes appear in the Task Manager that you cannot associate with known system processes, background applications, or software you are running. These could point to applications being executed by an attacker.

- Files or directories magically disappear. The attacker could have deleted them.

- New mail messages that you have not previously read are marked as read; an attacker could be monitoring your e-mails.

Of course, not all signs are so obvious. Other, more subtle things might be occurring if you have been compromised:

- An attacker might be stealing data from your system, but not deleting data or running applications. There is no outward sign that this is occurring.

- An attacker might no longer be using your system, but the system is still in a compromised state. The attacker could return to your system at a later time, but in the meantime, it is not being abused by the attacker.

- An attacker might have placed a small program on your system that is easy to miss that steals all the passwords you type. This can even be hidden by replacing a standard system service with an altered one that performs the standard service and steals passwords. There would be no clear outward sign that the service was compromised.

Still, regardless of the obvious signs of compromise, there are a few steps you can take to check your system to see if someone has gained unauthorized access:

1. Check your logs for anomalous behavior and suspicious incoming connections, as outlined in Chapter 21, "Managing Your Logs."

2. Attack yourself as outlined in Chapter 20, "Testing Your Security by Attacking Yourself," to see whether you have a weakness and, if you do, focus on that weakness and check its logs for problems more carefully.

3. Monitor information about new threats that emerge as outlined in Chapter 23, "Maintaining Your Protection," and follow guidance for checking whether you have been compromised using any new threats that have emerged.

4. Watch load activity on your router or broadband gateway. You can pay attention to activity lights, and if they seem more active than usual or show collision lights, it is possible unauthorized use of your Internet connection is taking place that might signal a compromised system. Also, check the logs of your broadband gateway or personal firewall software for connections that were permitted and should not have been.

5. Monitor the load on your PC. If it is higher than average even though the system remains responsive, it could signal an attacker is using your system resources. Consult Chapter 23 for guidance on how to monitor system load and check running processes.

Do I Have a Virus?

Even if you have not been directly attacked from the Internet, your system might still have been compromised by a virus, Trojan horse, or worm. In this case, you can't assume that the virus hasn't corrupted your virus checker. You will want to check your system using a clean virus checker.

To do this, you need to use a rescue disk or rescue disk set that you created when you installed your virus software, as outlined in Chapter 9, "Vaccinating Your Computer Against Viruses."

Although the specifics of using these rescue disks differs across the various antivirus packages on the market, the basic principles are the same:

1. Reboot your computer from the first rescue disk.

2. If a menu is presented to let you select how to scan your computer, select the most comprehensive scan available (preferably this will include the boot sector of your hard disk and all files on the disk). Some virus packages will start scanning as soon as they boot.

3. Follow any instructions that are presented.

4. If, after completing the scan, your system is reported as clean, reboot your computer. However, if your virus scan reports the presence of any virus, Trojan horse, worm, or other malicious software, you should assume you have a compromised system and proceed accordingly as outlined in the rest of this chapter.

Also, you should remember that you need to keep your antivirus software up-to-date with the latest virus signatures. If you don't do this, the software is next to useless because it won't protect you against the new viruses that are constantly being unleashed on the Internet.

My System Won't Boot

If your system won't boot, it might not be a signal of a security breach. There are many other possible causes:

- Your disk might be corrupted due to software bugs or hardware problems.
- Your disk's cable might have come loose inside the case.
- Your computer's CPU or motherboard might be damaged.
- Your computer's BIOS might be corrupted and need to be reflashed.
- Your memory might be bad.

Still, there is a chance that an attacker has successfully compromised your system and made it unbootable.

The first step to fixing your booting problem is to reboot from an emergency repair disk that some operating systems such as Windows NT and 2000 offer to make. These disks enable you to attempt to recover a corrupted disk and use your system as outlined in the documentation for your operating system. After your system is running, proceed to follow the guidance in this chapter to check for signs of a security breach and, if necessary, take corrective action.

Failing that, you can attempt to place your hard disk in another computer as the second drive; this will allow you to recover important files as outlined in the section "Recover Your Data," after which you can proceed to rebuild your system as outlined later in this chapter.

If you can't even do that, you probably have little choice but to proceed to rebuild your system as outlined in the section "Rebuild Your System."

> **NOTE**
>
> The question of how to recover a PC that has system misconfiguration, buggy soft-ware, hardware problems, or a corrupted disk is really beyond the scope of this book, which deals with security-specific issues. You will need to consult more general pur-pose books for information on Windows or MacOS system recovery or PC hardware repair.

Recover Your Data

Before you proceed with any other recovery steps after you determine your system has been compromised, you want to attempt to recover any crucial data stored in any important files. This is not to say that you want to recover application files or system files, but if you have crucial data that is not in your last backup, you should try to save it to floppy disk, ZIP disk or other removable media. These files might include word processor documents, spreadsheets, mailbox folders, or other files you recently changed or created.

Of course, there is every chance these files have been corrupted by the compromise of your system; Nonetheless, keeping the files on hand allows you to inspect them later for attack information that can be gleaned.

The reason you want to recover files is that you generally will want to erase all the files on your hard disk and rebuild your system after a compromise occurs.

> **CAUTION**
>
> It might sound like a good idea to back up your system fully before proceeding with other recovery steps such as rebuilding your system, but this is a bad idea. If your system has actually been compromised, you will be introducing the effects of that compromise into your back up set, which will only be restored later.

Analyze Your Security

If you have been successfully attacked from the Internet, you will want to close up any holes as soon as possible. If you run a broadband Internet router, you will want to closely analyze your security settings, following the guidance in Chapter 12, "Using a Broadband Router," and try attacking yourself as outlined in Chapter 20 to verify the value of your security configuration.

If you only use personal firewall software, when you reinstall it in the next step, make sure you have the latest version and consult Chapter 7, "Using Personal Firewall Software" again to make sure your security configuration is sound.

Rebuild Your System

If your system has been compromised by an attacker or a virus that can't be cleaned, the generally accepted course of action is to rebuild your system from scratch. There is too much chance that critical system files have been corrupted and are working on behalf of the attacker or virus author performing unknown malicious tasks. For instance, it is not uncommon for attackers to replace critical system files with ones that steal passwords you type, or create open connections to your system that the attacker can use at any point in the future to gain access to your system.

For this reason, you need to perform a complete rebuild of your system. The general steps for this are as follows:

1. Boot from the installation CD-ROM for your operating system.

2. Make sure you format all your hard drives when the installation program provides this option. The installation programs for Windows 98, Me, NT, and 2000 all provide the capability to format disks as part of the installation.

3. Reinstall your operating system.

4. Reinstall any software you use from their original sources. If you have downloaded copies of software from the Internet, don't use them; they could have been corrupted. Instead, download new copies.

5. Restore your data from your backup. Backups are discussed in Chapter 24, "Backup Strategies." Make sure you only restore data files, and not application files or system files.

6. Reassess your security policies based on the guidance in this book.

7. Run a complete virus scan of your system using the latest available virus signatures. If you need to download virus signatures, don't connect the system you are rebuilding to the network. Instead, download them on another system and copy them to the system you are repairing using a floppy disk or ZIP disk.

8. Reconnect your system to the network and the Internet.

9. Test your Internet connection by accessing the World Wide Web.

10. Retest your security as outlined in Chapter 20.

TIP

It is important to remember that your backup potentially contains corrupted data and files if your system was compromised before your last backup was generated. This is why it is advisable to only restore data files, and not applications or system files. Compromised application or system files would recompromise your system. Compromised data files mean the data might be corrupted, but is unlikely to introduce new security weaknesses into your newly built system.

Summary

In this chapter you learned basic techniques to employ when you think your system has had a security breach including approaches to data recovery, system rebuilding, and checking for viruses.

Of course, the ideal circumstance is to avoid a breach altogether. The next chapter provides guidance on a range of techniques you can use to help maintain your security. These range from keeping your knowledge of security issues and your software up-to-date to proactively monitoring system load, performance, and logs.

Maintaining Your Protection

In This Chapter

At this point in the book you should have already completed or be able to set up a firewall, address physical and personal security issues, manage your cookies, and design an effective antivirus strategy. However, this is no time to rest on your laurels. The skills, knowledge, and opportunities for those intent on breaching computer security increase daily and maintaining security requires ongoing vigilance. This chapter outlines critical things you can do on an ongoing basis to maintain your newfound security.

Keep Up-To-Date About Threats

The most important thing you can do to maintain your security is to keep abreast of what's happening on the Internet with respect to security. When you see a news story on television or in the newspaper about an Internet security incident, make sure you follow it up. Find out what happened, and check any related security advisories with CERT or other information sources.

Make it a point to periodically (the more often, the better) visit at least some of these key information sources:

- `http://www.virus.com/`
- `http://www.mcafee.com/anti-virus/default.asp?`
- `http://www.symantec.com/avcenter/hoax.html`
- `http://www.cert.org/`
- `http://www.ciac.org/ciac/`
- `http://www.securityportal.com/`
- `http://csrc.ncsl.nist.gov/`
- `http://www.zdnet.com/zdhelp/filters/subfilter/0,7212,6001787,00.html`

Keep Your Software and Hardware Up-To-Date

In addition to being aware of the latest threats, you need to be diligent in updating software that is likely to pose security threats. In particular, you need to watch for updates and patches for the following types of software:

- Your operating system
- Your Internet software (browsers, media players, e-mail software, and so on.)

- Your antivirus software
- Your Internet security hardware and software

Updating Your Operating System

Perhaps the most important aspect of keeping your system secure is keeping your operating system updated. When security holes are exposed in Windows or MacOS, they create known avenues of attack for hundreds of thousands of online machines. This is why Microsoft and Apple are quick to release patches you can install to fix these problems. Make it a point to track these patches at the Web site for your operating system vendor and download any security patches that are considered vital for your system. The following are the Web sites of the major operating system vendors:

- Apple (http://www.apple.com/): MacOS 8, 9, and X
- Microsoft (http://www.microsoft.com/): Windows 98, Me, NT, 2000, and XP
- RedHat (http://www.redhat.com/): RedHat Linux 6.2, 7.0, and 7.1
- Caldera (http://www.caldera.com/): Caldera eDesktop 2.4
- SuSE (http://www.suse.com/): SuSE Linux 7.1

> **TIP**
>
> Keeping up-to-date with patches is a bit of a double-edged sword. Although it is important to install patches for critical security holes as quickly as possible, remember that patches themselves can have bugs or security holes. It isn't unheard of for patches to introduce system instability, and sometimes operating system vendors need to quickly release patches to fix the patches. For this reason, you need to weigh the threat posed by the security hole and how long the patch has been out and in use (the longer a patch has been around, the less likely it will cause your system to become unstable).

Updating Your Internet Software

After your operating system, your Internet software is the next biggest source of security bugs and holes that make you vulnerable on the Internet. For instance, many of the Microsoft Outlook e-mail viruses, such as the Melissa virus, leverage security flaws in Microsoft Outlook. As Microsoft has become aware of these holes, they have rushed to release patches for Outlook. Similarly, Web browsers such as Internet Explorer and Netscape have been known to have security bugs that can do anything from exposing your personal information to providing a Web site access to files on your hard disk.

For this reason, you should install security fixes for your Internet software as soon as they become available. If new versions promise security fixes, you should consider upgrading to the new versions as soon as the new version has proven itself to be stable and reliable.

The following are the types of software you should particularly watch for security fixes

- Web browsers (such as Microsoft Internet Explorer and Netscape Navigator)
- Mail clients (such as Microsoft Outlook and Eudora)
- Media players (such as Microsoft Media Player and Real Player)
- FTP clients (such as WS_FTP)
- Instant Messaging Clients (such as ICQ, MSN Messenger or AOL Instant Messenger)

The following Web sites will provide you with information about the latest patches and upgrades available for popular Internet Software:

- Internet Explorer: `http://www.microsoft.com/ie/`
- Netscape Navigator: `http://home.netscape.com/computing/download/index.html`
- Microsoft Outlook: `http://office.microsoft.com/`
- Eudora: `http://www.eudora.com/`
- Pegasus Mail: `http://www.pmail.com/`
- Microsoft Media Player: `http://www.microsoft.com/windows/windowsmedia/en/default.asp`
- Real Player: `http://www.real.com/`
- AOL Instant Messenger: `http://home.netscape.com/aim/index.html`
- ICQ: `http://www.icq.com/download/`
- MSN Messenger: `http://messenger.msn.ca/`

Your Antivirus Software

Because so many security risks on the Internet revolve around viruses, Trojan horses and worms, it is essential to keep your antivirus software up-to-date. For most leading antivirus packages, there are two aspects to this:

- Keeping your virus signatures updated: Virus signatures contain the definitions of viruses used by the software to check for problems. Virus signatures tend to update quickly.

- Keeping your virus engines updated: Virus engines are the actual scanning software built into your virus checker. These engines are occasionally updated, although nowhere near as frequently as signatures are updated.

The following Web sites provide the latest information about virus updates for popular antivirus software:

- Norton AntiVirus: `http://www.symantec.com/avcenter/index.html`

- McAfee VirusScan: `http://www.avertlabs.com/`

- F-Secure Anti-Virus: `http://www.f-secure.com/virus-info/`

- PC-cillin: `http://www.trend.com/pc-cillin/vinfo/`

- Dr. Solomon's Anti-Virus: `http://download.mcafee.com/updates/`
  `4xa.asp?as=true&ref=5`

TIP

Many virus packages offer online updating of virus signatures and engines. Often these can operate automatically, downloading updates in the background. You should check the online updating features of your antivirus software and use them to keep your virus software as up-to-date as possible.

23

MAINTAINING
YOUR PROTECTION

Your Internet Security Hardware and Software

If you keep your security patches updated in your operating system, Internet applications, and antivirus software but then fail to keep your Internet security hardware and software updated, then all your efforts might be for naught. After all, personal firewall software or dedicated hardware firewalls are just as susceptible to security bugs and flaws as any other type of software. The inherent reality of any type of computer program (implemented as software or hardware) is that it will contain some number of bugs; bugs in Internet security products can easily create security holes.

> **CAUTION**
>
> Software patches are easy to implement, but if you have a hardware firewall, the process is somewhat more difficult. This is because it involves overwriting the memory of the unit, and if the process fails, it could render your hardware firewall inoperable. Nonetheless, if you need to update your hardware firewall, it is better to do so than not do it because you are afraid of the process not going smoothly. Failures are rare, and if you pay close attention to the updating instructions provided by your vendor, things will go fine.

The following Web sites provide update information for popular software and hardware firewalls:

- BlackICE Defender: `http://www.networkice.com/downloads/index.html`
- McAfee Firewall: `http://download.mcafee.com/updates/fire_update.asp`
- McAfee Internet Guard Dog: `http://download.mcafee.com/updates/igd_update.asp`
- Norton Personal Firewall: `http://www.symantec.com/techsupp/`
- Zone Alarm: `http://www.zonelabs.com/`
- Tiny Personal Firewall: `http://www.tinysoftware.com/pwall.php`
- Sygate Personal Firewall: `http://www.sybergen.com/products/shield_ov.htm`
- NetBarrier (Macintosh): `http://www.intego.com/services/updates.asp`
- IPNetSentry: `http://www.sustworks.com/site/prod_ipns_overview.html`
- D-Link Cable/DSL Internet Gateways: `http://support.dlink.com/`
- EtherFast Cable/DSL Routers: `http://www.linksys.com/download/firmware.asp`
- NetGear Internet Gateway Routers: `http://www.netgear.com/support_main.asp`
- Asante FriendlyNET Cable/DSL Routers: `http://www.asante.com/product/routers/fncable-dsl-firmware.htm`
- Macsense Xrouter Internet Sharing Switches: `http://www.macsense.com/Product/mih130.html`
- Nexland Internet Sharing Boxes: `http://www.nexland.com/download.htm`
- SMC Barricade Broadband Routers: `http://www.smc.com/smc/pages_html/products.html`
- 3Com Home Ethernet Gateways: `http://www.3com.com/products/en_US/detail.jsp?tab=support&sku=3C510&pathtype=purchase`

- SonicWall Internet Security Appliances: `http://63.97.246.80/download/index.asp`
- WatchGuards SOHO Firewalls: `https://www.watchguard.com/support/patches.asp`

TIP

Like antivirus software, some personal firewall software packages offer online background-updating features. Check your firewall software's documentation to see whether it supports online downloading of product updates in the background.

Watch for the Signs

Finally, the most important step you can take to help maintain ongoing security is to watch for signs of your security being breached. There are lots of possible signs that this might have happened:

- Your computer becomes unstable even though you haven't installed any new software.
- You can no longer log in as a particular user.
- The network traffic from your PC suddenly increases. For instance, if you start seeing frequent collision lights on your hub where before there were none, you are seeing a significant increase in network traffic. Even if you just feel that the Internet is noticeably more sluggish than it used to be, you might have an increase in network traffic coming to or from your PC.
- The load on your PC suddenly increases even though you aren't running additional software or services. Your PC might seem more sluggish than normal, or might be totally unusable because it is too slow.
- Your hard disk is in use constantly, even when the system is completely idle. Remember, in some operating systems such as Windows 2000 and Linux, you will see disk activity when the system is idle as background tasks perform their work; however, if disk activity is constant during idle time, this might indicate something non-standard taking place.

If you suspect that a security breach might have occurred on your system because of one of these symptoms or some other strange behavior, then you need to analyze the state of your computer. Three useful techniques for doing this are

- Analyze running processes to find strange or suspicious processes.
- Check user accounts on your system for ones you didn't create or aren't sure about.
- Analyze your logs for signs of security breaches.

23

MAINTAINING YOUR PROTECTION

Checking Running Processes

One purpose of attacking computers on the Internet is so that the attacker can take advantage of another computer's resources. They will use a computer to run programs for cracking passwords or even attacking other computers (this can help hide their trail when they finally attack their intended target). This means a compromised computer might be running applications in the background on behalf of the attacker.

To check this, you need to be reasonably familiar with the software that should be running on your system, and then look at all running software (known as processes) to see whether anything strange or suspicious is running.

The method for checking running processes differs from operating system to operating system. Windows NT and 2000 make it relatively easy to do so using the Task Manager:

- When logged in, press Ctrl+Alt+Del. Windows will display the Windows Security dialog box.
- Click on the Task Manager button. Windows will display the Task Manager window.
- Click on the Processes tab. The Task Manager will display the Processes page as illustrated in Figure 23.1.

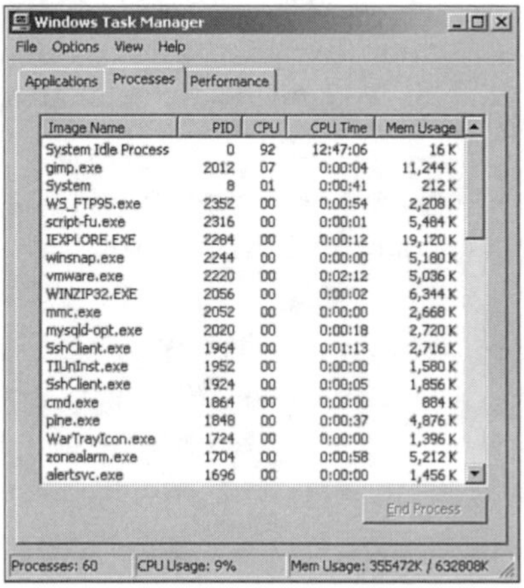

FIGURE 23.1
The Processes tab of the Task Manager.

On the Processes tab you will see a list of all running processes, including the filename of the application and the amount of CPU and memory resources it is using.

Viewing running processes in Windows 98 and Me is not as easy, because there is no equivalent to the Windows NT and 2000 Task Manager. Still, it can be done using third-party software.

One example is Task Info 2000, a low-cost shareware program that will run on Windows 98 or higher. Task Info 2000 is available from `http://www.iarsn.com/`. A typical Task Info 2000 service, illustrated in Figure 23.2, provides information about all running processes, including CPU and memory use.

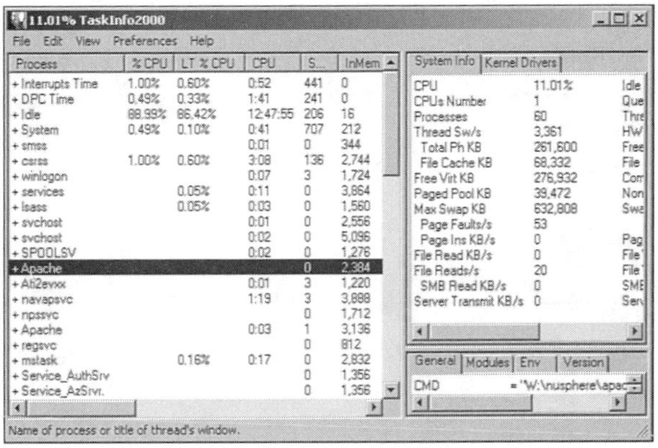

FIGURE 23.2
Viewing running processes with Task Info 2000.

Check User Accounts

On multiuser operating systems, an attacker might create one or more accounts so they can easily log in and use the system. If you are using a multiuser operating system such as Windows NT, 2000 or Linux, you should keep close tabs on the user accounts normally on your system so you can check periodically to see whether there are new accounts that shouldn't be there.

In Windows NT 4, you can check user accounts by selecting Start, Programs, Administrative Tools, User Manager for Domains. In Windows 2000, double-click the Computer Management icon in the Administrative Tools section of the Control Panel. Windows 2000 will open up the Computer Management Tool. Click on Users and Groups in the menu tree at the left side of the window, then double-click on the Users folder in the right side of the window to view a list of all users on the system, as illustrated in Figure 23.3.

If you find users who shouldn't be on your system, you need to take action. The first, and most important step, is to disable the accounts so that the users in question can't log in. In Windows 2000, do this by double-clicking the user's name in the list of users in the Computer Management window. The user's Properties dialog box will be displayed. Make sure the Account Disabled checkbox is selected, then click on the Apply button to apply the changes. You should also change the account's password.

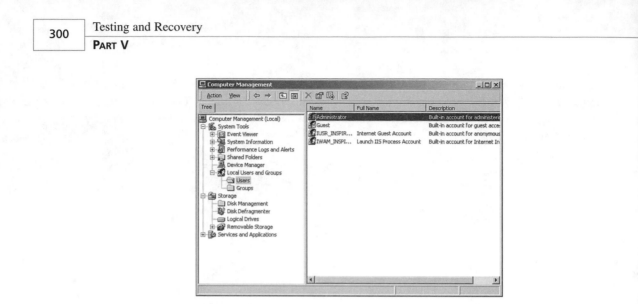

FIGURE 23.3

Viewing a list of users in Windows 2000.

> **NOTE**
>
> You will need to be logged in as an administrator to disable an account or change its password.

> **NOTE**
>
> Windows 98 and Me are not multiuser operating systems, so you can't really check for invalid users the way you can in Windows NT and 2000.

Watch Your Logs

As outlined in Chapter 21, "Managing Your Logs," analyzing log files generated by your system and the software that runs on it is an important security-related task. It can also help you identify whether your security has been breached when you suspect as much.

You will want to check logs generated by some or all the following when you think your security is compromised:

- Operating system authentication and login logs
- Logs generated by any server software you are running (such as Web server software)

- Logs generated by any antivirus software you use
- Logs generated by your personal firewall software or hardware firewall system

Chapter 21 addresses questions of log management in more detail.

Summary

This chapter has provided you with a general overview of how to maintain your level of protection after you have set up your security system. New threats constantly emerge and security software and hardware needs to be updated to address these new threats. You can only ensure ongoing protection by keeping yourself informed and keeping your system up-to-date.

The next chapter deals with a subject that is not directly a security subject, but which is important nonetheless: backup strategies. Although it won't make your system more secure, a sound backup plan can enable you to easily recover from a breach of your security. You can recover your files to a pre-infection state if your system gets infected; or in the case of a serious attack where data is corrupted or files are deleted, you can recover the data. Without a sound backup plan, you are always at considerable risk of losing valuable files and work.

Backup Strategies

IN THIS CHAPTER

In This Chapter

In order to understand how to effectively back up the files on your machine, it is vital that you understand why a backup is required. But it is also important to understand what to back up and how often. This chapter will familiarize you with what a backup is, how to do a thorough backup, and will discuss several backup devices along with Microsoft Backup.

What Is a Backup?

A *backup* is simply a second copy of a file, or all the files, on your machine. The purpose of a backup is to ensure that time and money are not lost when something goes wrong on your machine—and chances are high that at some time something will go wrong. Essentially, a backup is made to prevent the unexpected from ruining your computing experience. With a proper backup strategy, even the worst-case scenario is not all that bad.

> **CAUTION**
>
> Backup files should never be used as working copies. They are simply a second copy of a file, and their only purpose is to provide a safety net in the event that you lose data on your system for whatever reason.

Inside your computer there are many different things going on at any given time, and there are many components that come together to create this magnificent machine. But with something so complex, it is always possible that something can—and will—go wrong. Whether a part fails, you accidentally delete or overwrite a file, there is a power surge, or your computer is stolen; knowing that all the important data stored on your machine is still safe will give you peace of mind.

It is important to understand a few more concepts associated with file backup:

- Archiving: This is the process of copying a file or files onto a storage medium (such as a backup tape) for long-term storage.
- Restoration: This is the process of copying stored files back onto your machine, either because the information was lost, or because you have decided to revert to an older version of a file(s).

What Should You Back Up?

While it is true that the programs you run on your machine are important, they are usually stored on a CD-ROM or disk so they do not require a backup. As long as you don't lose or throw out the installation disks, you can simply re-install any programs you need. However, the data on your machine (all the files you create using the software, such as accounting files or letters) definitely requires backing up. These files are where all your hard work and time are stored. Without them you would probably be lost, or at the very least you would have to spend countless hours trying to replace them.

Files are created on and run within programs, such as a file you create within Microsoft Word. However, this data is stored separately on your machine. As such, you don't have to waste valuable time or resources making backup copies of all the programs or applications on your machine.

CAUTION

It is important that you have a physical copy of all the important software that you run on your machine. If you don't have the original disk or CD-ROM that you first installed the program from, it is a good idea to make a copy of the program and store it in a safe place away from your computer.

Strategies for Backup

Now that you are aware of the necessity of file backup, it is important to discuss backup strategies. This involves having a schedule of how often to back up the files on your computer, and which files should be included in each backup.

There are several strategies for file backup including:

- Full backup: This involves making a backup copy of all the files and directories on your machine. This method is the easiest, because you don't have to worry about missing any files, and it also enables a faster restoration of your machine when required. However, this method is also the most time-consuming for the same reason.

- Incremental backup: This involves making a backup copy of only the files that have been altered since the last backup, regardless of the backup strategy. While this method uses fewer resources (memory and processor power), it is a good idea to make a full backup occasionally—either once a week or every few weeks—in order to make the restoration process easier. Otherwise, a full restoration will require you to restore all partial backups to ensure that all files are properly restored on your system.

- Differential backup: This method is a combination of both the full backup and incremental backup strategies. This method requires two backup devices: one for full backups, and the other for incremental backups. With this strategy, you will always have a recent full backup on one storage medium, and any recent changes on the other storage medium.

> **TIP**
>
> When using an Incremental Backup strategy, it is worthwhile to make a full backup once a week or every few weeks to make the restoration process more efficient and effective.

Remember that regardless of the strategy you choose to employ, making a backup is vital to ensuring that your data is safe—and that is the primary purpose of a backup. The strategy you choose to back up your data with is less important than actually making a backup.

Microsoft Backup Tool

Microsoft Backup is a backup tool included with the Windows 95 and 98 Operating Systems. Microsoft Backup enables you to perform a full or incremental backup of your system. If Microsoft Backup is not installed on your system, it can be installed easily with the Windows 95/98 CD-ROM. This section will describe how to install Microsoft Backup, perform a backup, and restore files to your computer after making a backup.

How to Install Microsoft Backup

Installation of Microsoft Backup is nearly identical for both Windows 95 and 98. To install Microsoft Backup on Windows, follow these steps:

1. Access the Settings sub-menu from the Start menu.
2. Select Control Panel from the Settings sub-menu. The Control Panel window will appear as demonstrated in Figure 24.1.
3. From the Control Panel window, double-click the Add/Remove Programs icon. As illustrated in Figure 24.2, the Add/Remove Programs Properties window will appear.
4. Click the Windows Setup tab from the Add/Remove Programs Properties window, as shown in Figure 24.3.
5. In the Windows Setup tab, click on System Tools (Disk Tools in Windows 95), as demonstrated in Figure 24.4.
6. With System Tools highlighted (Disk Tools in Windows 95), click the Details button and the System Tools window will appear, as shown in Figure 24.5.
7. In the Components window, click the check box next to Backup to install Microsoft Backup Tool.
8. Click the OK button to close the System Tools window, and then click the OK button from the Add/Remove Programs Properties window to proceed with installation.

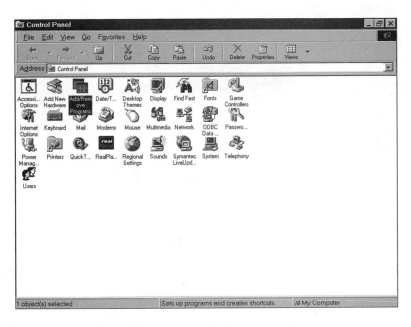

FIGURE 24.1
The Control Panel window.

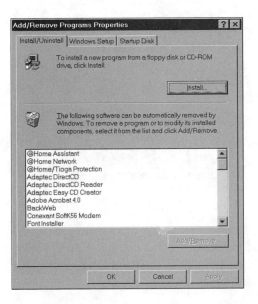

FIGURE 24.2
The Add/Remove Programs Properties window.

24

BACKUP
STRATEGIES

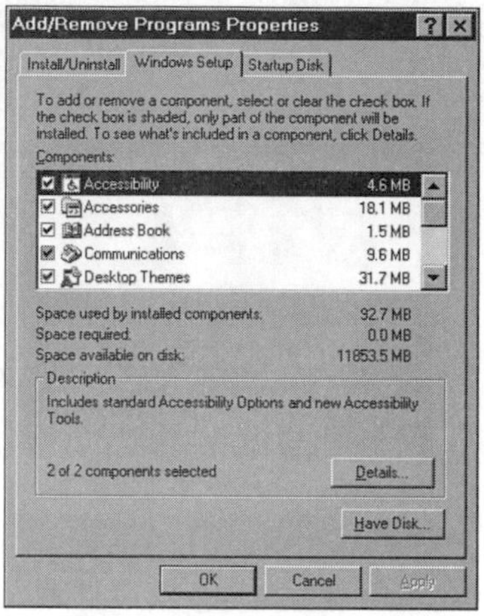

FIGURE 24.3

The Windows Setup tab, accessed in the Add/Remove Programs Properties window.

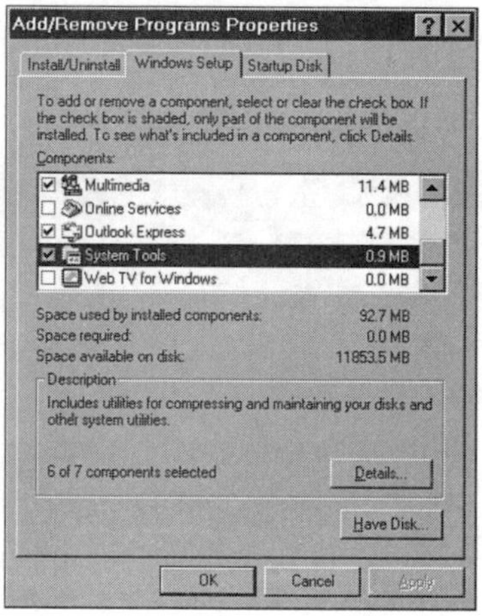

FIGURE 24.4

The System Tools option in the Windows Setup tab.

9. After the installation is complete, you will be prompted to restart your computer from the Systems Settings Change window, as illustrated in Figure 24.6. Click the Yes button to restart your computer immediately.

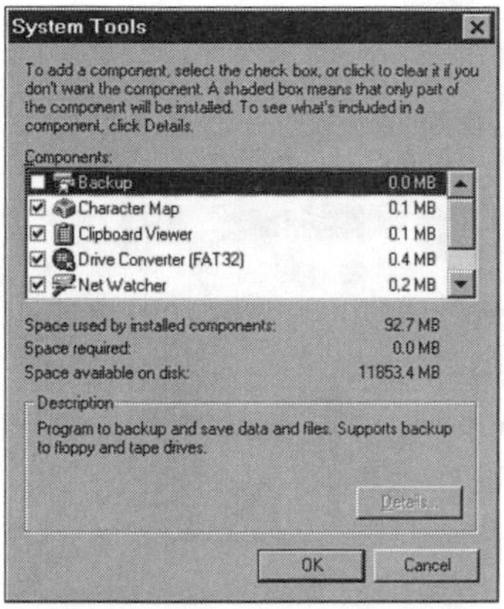

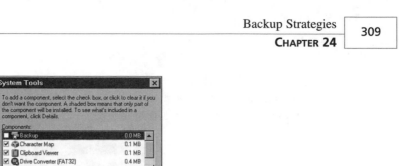

FIGURE 24.5
The System Tools window.

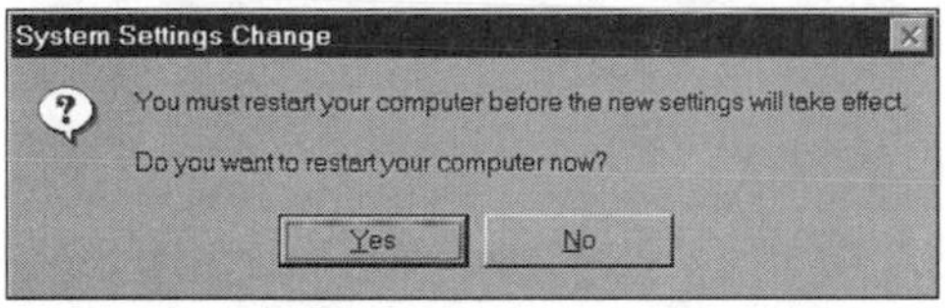

FIGURE 24.6
The System Settings Change window.

> **CAUTION**
>
> You must have the Windows installation disk in the CD-ROM drive in order to install Microsoft Backup.

How to Perform a Backup Using Microsoft Backup

After Microsoft Backup is installed on your system, you can begin using it to perform a backup. To perform a backup, follow these steps:

1. Access the Programs sub-menu from the Start menu.
2. Access the Accessories sub-menu from the Programs sub-menu.
3. From the Accessories sub-menu, select System Tools.
4. Click on Backup from the System Tools sub-menu.

5. Microsoft Backup will now look for a tape backup device. If a tape backup device is not found, you will be prompted as illustrated in Figure 24.7. Click the No button to continue with the backup process.

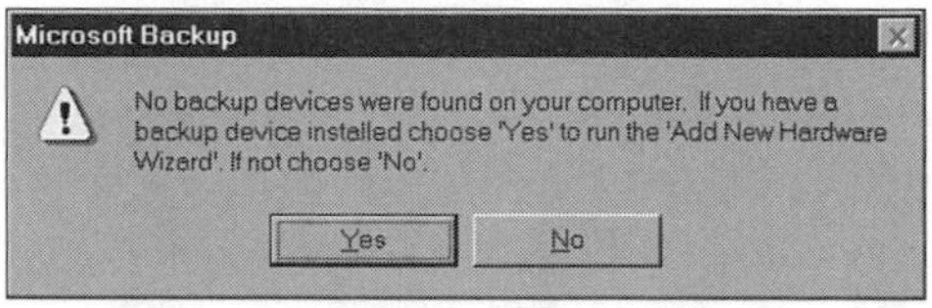

FIGURE 24.7

The Microsoft Backup prompt.

6. From the Microsoft Backup window select Create a new backup job as illustrated in Figure 24.8, and then click the OK button.

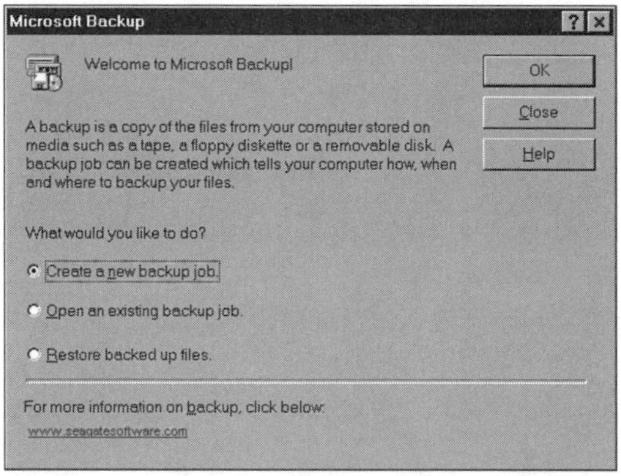

FIGURE 24.8

The Microsoft Backup window.

7. The Backup Wizard window will appear, as illustrated in Figure 24.9. Select the appropriate backup option, and then click the Next button.

8. If you selected the Back up My Computer option in step 7, skip to step 9. If you selected the Back up selected files, folders and drives option in step 7, you will be prompted to select the items you want to back up, as shown in Figure 24.10. Select the appropriate files, folders, or drives and click the Next button to continue.

9. You will be prompted to choose whether to back up All selected files or New and changed files, as demonstrated in Figure 24.11. Click the Next button to continue.

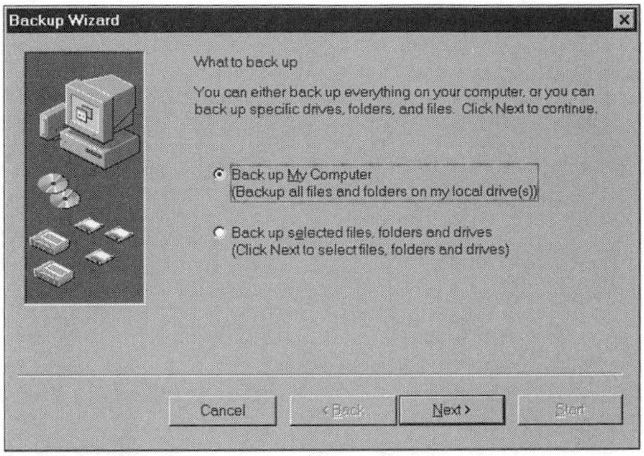

FIGURE 24.9
The Backup Wizard window.

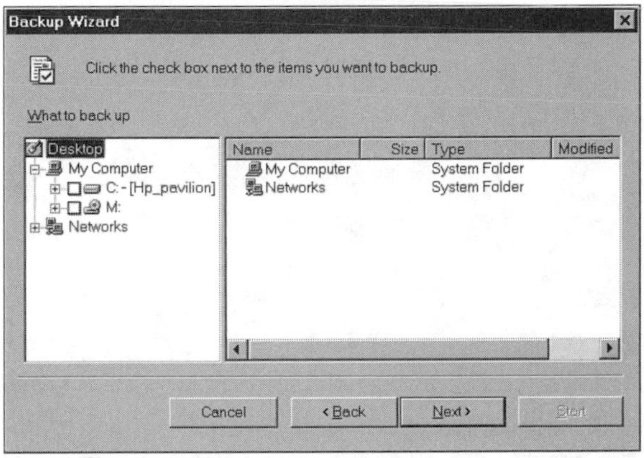

FIGURE 24.10
Back up selected files, folders, and drives option.

10. The following screen asks you to select Where to back up. Click the folder icon to change the filename and location. The default filename and location is `C:\MyBackup.qic`, as shown in Figure 24.12. Click Next to continue.

11. Illustrated in Figure 24.13, the How to back up screen prompts you to choose from the following options:

   • Compare original and backup files to verify data was successfully backed up.

   • Compress the backup data to save space.

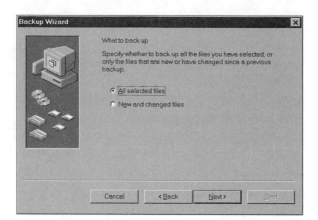

FIGURE 24.11
What to back up.

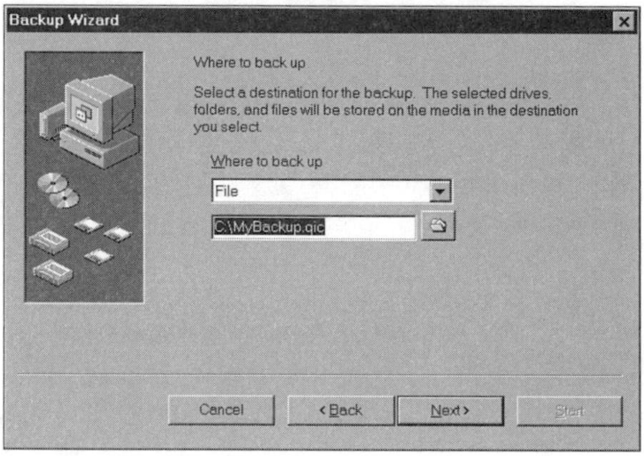

FIGURE 24.12
Where to back up.

12. Click the Next button to continue to the following screen where you are prompted to name the backup job, as illustrated in Figure 24.14.

13. Enter a name for the backup job and click the Start button to begin the backup.

14. After the backup job is complete, a notification window will appear, as shown in Figure 24.15. Click OK to continue.

15. Figure 24.16 illustrates the Backup Progress window. Click OK to continue.

FIGURE 24.13
How to back up.

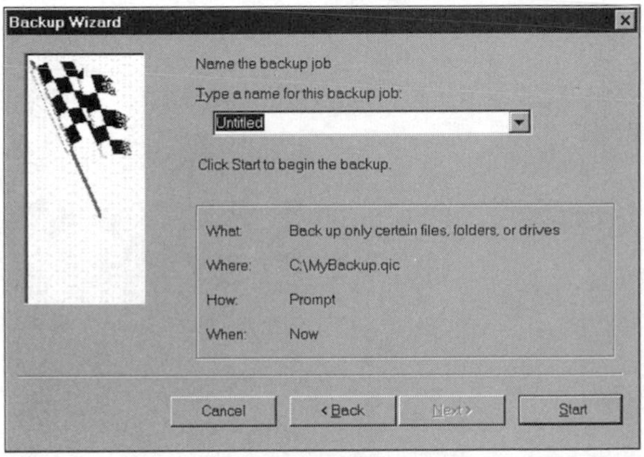

FIGURE 24.14
Name the back up job.

FIGURE 24.15
Operation completed prompt.

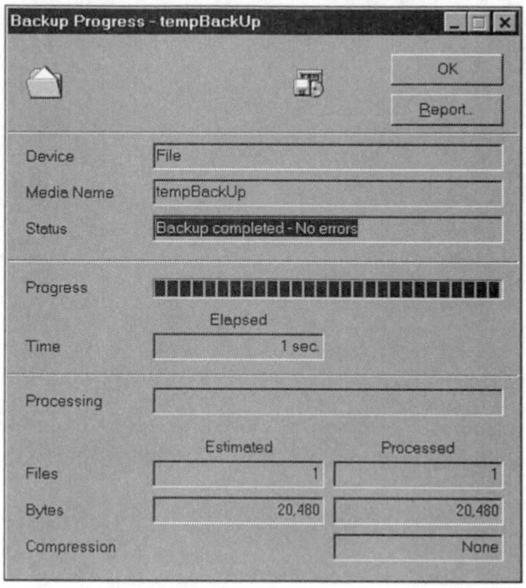

FIGURE 24.16
The Backup Progress window.

16. From the Microsoft Backup window, click the Job menu and select Exit to quit, as shown in Figure 24.17.

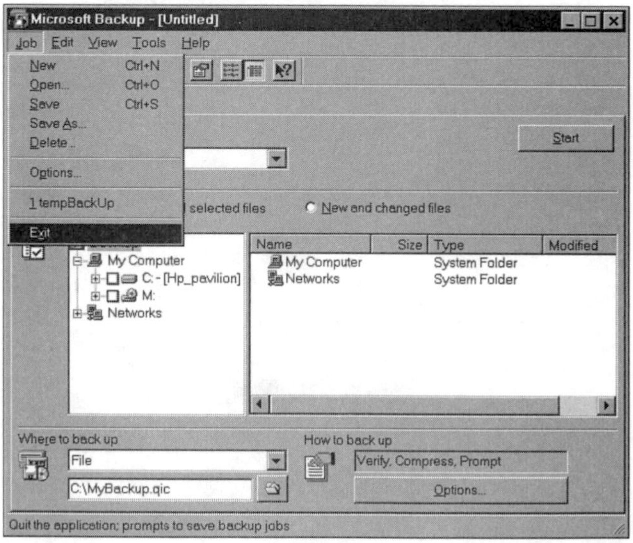

FIGURE 24.17
Quit Microsoft Backup.

How to Restore Files Using Microsoft Backup

After you've performed a backup using Microsoft Backup, you can easily restore the file(s) to your machine.

1. Access the Programs sub-menu from the Start menu.

2. Access the Accessories sub-menu from the Programs sub-menu.

3. From the Accessories sub-menu, select System Tools.

4. Click on Backup from the System Tools sub-menu.

5. From the Microsoft Backup window select Restore backed up files, as illustrated in Figure 24.18, and then click the OK button.

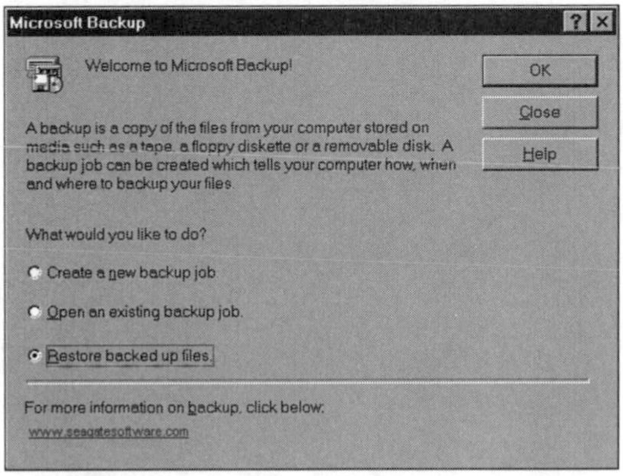

FIGURE 24.18

The Microsoft Backup window.

6. The following screen asks you to select where to Restore from. Click the folder icon to change the filename and location. The default filename and location is `C:\MyBackup.qic`, as shown in Figure 24.19. Click Next to continue.

7. The Select Backup Sets window will appear, as illustrated in Figure 24.20. Click the appropriate backup job, and then click the OK button to continue.

8. As illustrated in Figure 24.21, the Restore Wizard window will appear. Select the appropriate files, folders, or drives to restore and click the Next button to continue.

9. The following screen prompts Where to restore, as demonstrated in Figure 24.22. Select either Original Location and skip to Step 11, or select Alternate Location.

10. If you selected Alternate Location in Step 9, then enter the correct location in the box below it or click the folder icon to open the Browse for Folder window, as shown in Figure 24.23.

24

BACKUP STRATEGIES

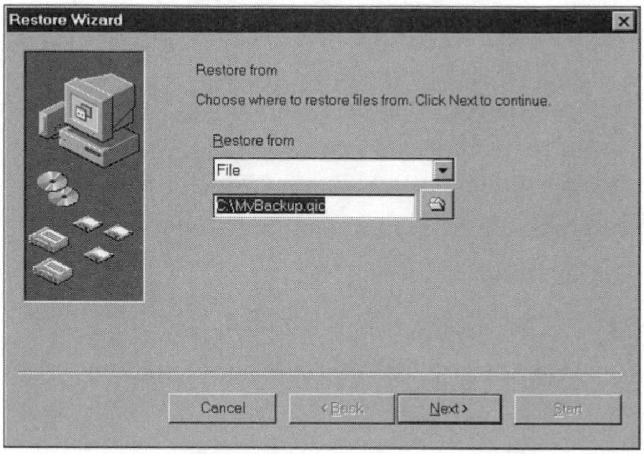

FIGURE 24.19

The Restore Wizard window.

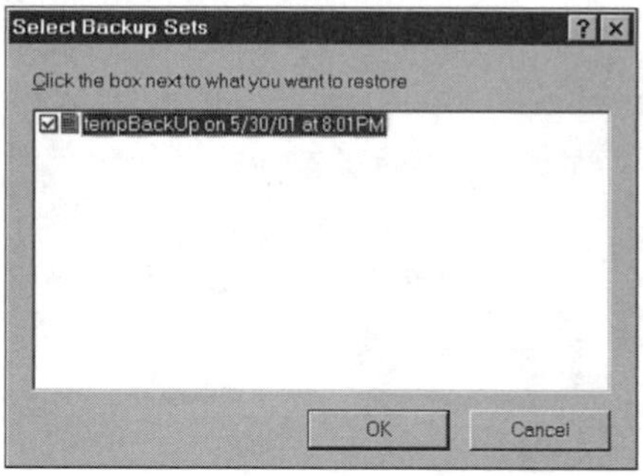

FIGURE 24.20

The Select Backup Sets window.

11. As shown in Figure 24.24, the How to restore option requires you to specify from the following settings. After making your decision, click Start to begin restoring files:

  • Do not replace the file on my computer (recommended).

  • Replace the file on my computer only if the file is older.

  • Always replace the file on my computer.

12. The Media Required window will appear, as illustrated in Figure 24.25. If the required media is available, click the OK button to continue with the restoration process.

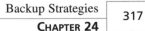

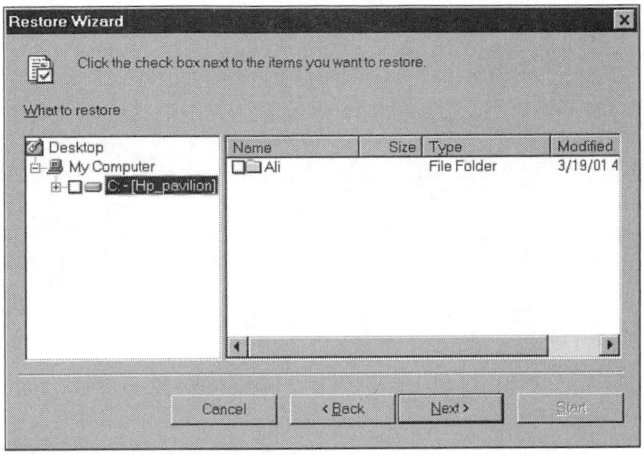

FIGURE 24.21

The Restore Wizard window.

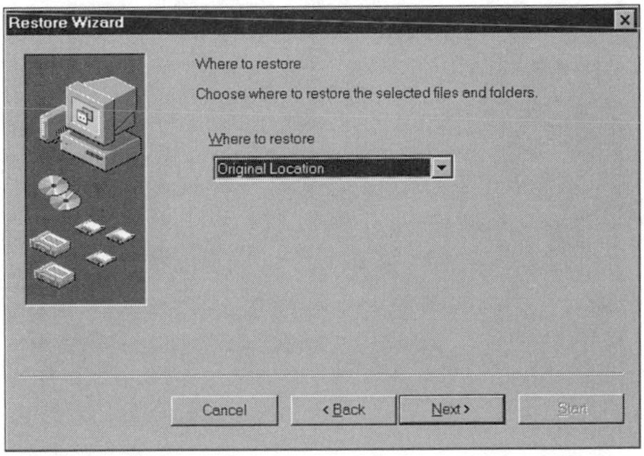

FIGURE 24.22

Where to restore.

13. After the restore job is complete, a notification window will appear. Click OK to continue.

14. Figure 24.26 illustrates the Restore Progress window. Click OK to continue.

15. From the Microsoft Backup (Restore) window click the Job menu and select Exit to quit, as shown in Figure 24.27.

24

**BACKUP
STRATEGIES**

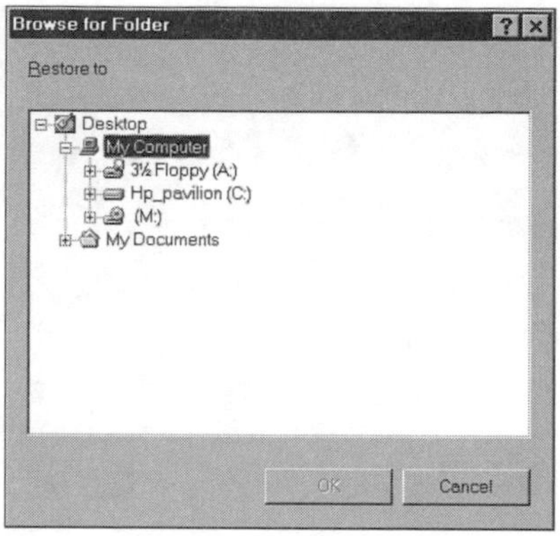

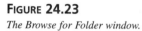

FIGURE 24.23
The Browse for Folder window.

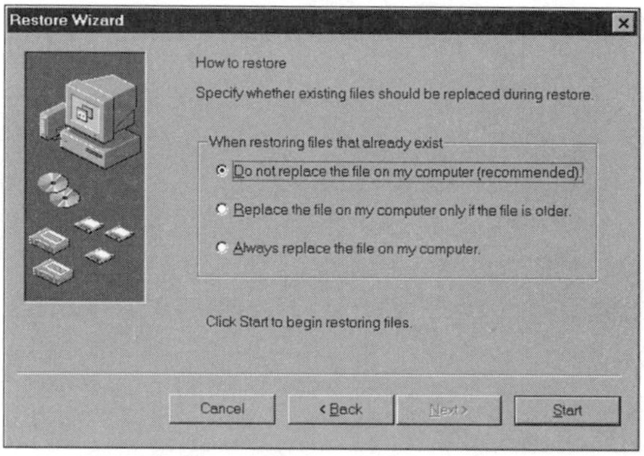

FIGURE 24.24
How to restore.

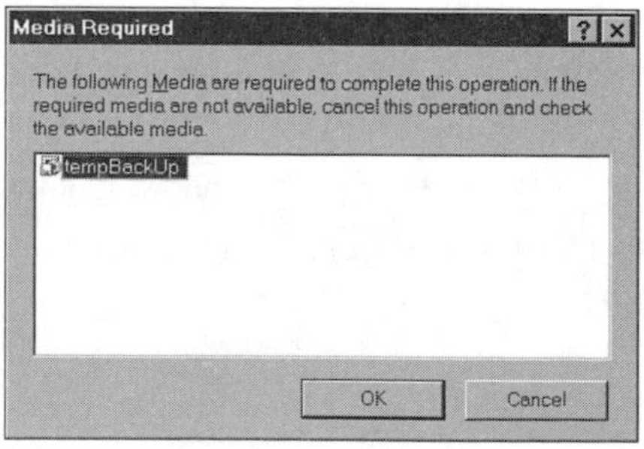

FIGURE 24.25
The Media Required window.

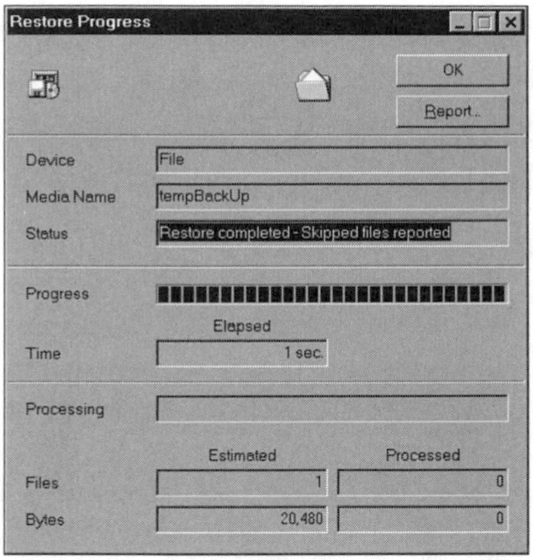

FIGURE 24.26
The Restore Progress window.

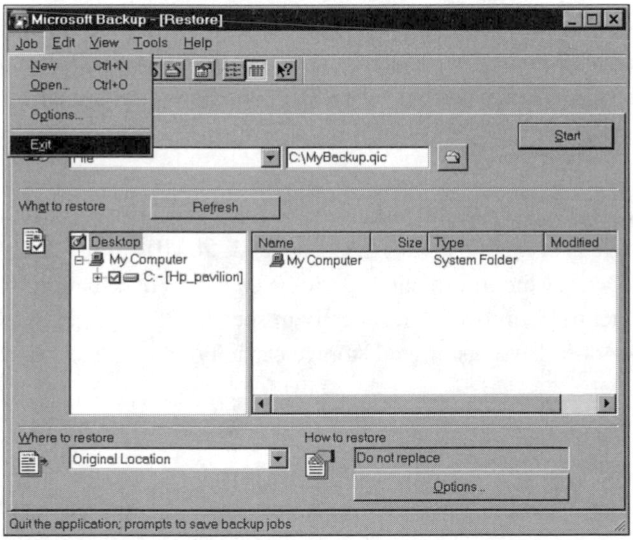

FIGURE 24.27
Quit Microsoft Backup (Restore).

Backup Devices

There are many different devices that can be used to back up the data on your machine. Each device has its benefits and drawbacks, so it is important to determine how important your data is, how much data you have, and how much money you are willing to spend to ensure that your data is safe. In addition, it is useful to consider the possibility of making use of the current hardware installed on your system before going out and buying the latest (and most expensive) backup device. The following is a list of some of the backup devices and memory storage mediums available for data backup:

Zip Drive

The Zip drive, which uses Zip disks, is a dependable and relatively inexpensive backup solution from Iomega Corporation. Currently, both the Zip Drive and its disks come in two sizes: 100MB and 250MB. The 100MB and 250MB Zip drives vary in cost depending on the type of connection (USB, parallel, SCSI) and the model (internal or external). Although the 250MB Zip drive does have a larger storage capacity, it is the same size as the 100MB version. In addition, the 250MB version is backwards compatible with the 100MB disks, meaning you can upgrade the hardware to the 250MB drive, but still use the 100MB disk. While the Zip drive is a safe choice for backing up data, it does have its drawbacks. The Zip drive is not the fastest backup device on the market; it isn't the largest backup medium (considering the massive size of hard drives nowadays); and it isn't recommended for storage of multimedia files; but its affordable price, easy use, and popularity makes it a great tool for doing backups or for transporting large amounts of data. The 100MB Zip drive costs about $100, and the 100MB disks cost about $10. The 250MB Zip drive is about $150, and the disks are about $20.

SuperDisk

This product is exactly that: a super-sized disk. The SuperDisk drive, created by Imation, is a 120MB disk. Its drive is compatible with the standard 1.44 MB floppy disk, but a SuperDisk can hold almost 100 times the information (83 to be exact). While the original version wasn't very fast, this product has improved significantly in speed. Although this product can be used as a standard floppy disk drive, its limited storage capacity among backup devices is a significant drawback.

Jaz

Another product from Iomega Corporation is the Jaz drive. This product is only slightly heavier than the Zip drive, but can hold up to 1GB of data. This product is quicker than the Zip drive, in addition to its significantly larger storage capacity. Because of its fairly large storage capacity, this device is also useful as a secondary hard disk. This product is also better suited for storing multimedia, such as full-motion video. This drive is also highly popular, making it a great tool for backup. The 2GB drive costs about $275. The 2GB disk costs about $100, while the 1GB disk is about $90.

Orb

This product has both a high speed and a large storage capacity. Designed by Castlewoods Systems, the Orb can hold up to 2.2GB of data, including multimedia, and is relatively inexpensive. This product is near the top of the market in all aspects, and can be used as a secondary drive. In addition, the Orb comes in parallel, SCSI, IDE, and USB versions.

CD-RW

The rewritable CD is one of the more recent backup device technologies. While the cost of a rewritable CD is relatively low, the speed of writing is slow, and the size of storage isn't nearly as large as some of the other products, such as the Orb. However, compared to a Zip drive or SuperDisk, the CD-RW's 650MB (or larger) storage capacity is more than adequate, and its ability to play multimedia is also a plus. In addition, the CD-RW drive can be used in place of a traditional CD-ROM, making it even more useful.

Floppy Disk

While the traditional floppy disk is incredibly small and slow, storing a mere 1.44MB of data, it is also easy to use, readily available, and inexpensive. I wouldn't recommend the floppy disk as a backup medium for any advanced users, but if you are only making small backups, this product might be ideal for you. The limitations of the floppy disk are obvious, but why spend hundreds of dollars on a high-end device if you only need to back up a few files or a few MBs of data? In addition, most computers come with a floppy disk drive already installed. However, it is impossible to store any multimedia on a floppy disk because of the large size of most multimedia files, so keep that in mind before you decide.

Peerless

Peerless is the latest backup device from the Iomega Corporation. The Peerless is a high capacity storage and backup device. It comes in two sizes: 10GB and 20GB. Both versions come in a bundle with either a FireWire or USB connection. The 10GB Peerless bundle costs about $360, while the 20GB version is about $400.

Low-end Tape Solutions

There are many different tape drives available for use as a backup device. In this section, only two are discussed: QIC and OnStream's SC drive. The advantages of using tape for backup are its low cost and its storage capacity. Unfortunately, many companies make these types of storage devices and there is no standard, so some products are not compatible. In addition, the biggest limitation of tape drives is that they are sequential access devices. What this means is that the tape drive cannot access a specific file or directory without first reading all the data that precedes it on the tape, much like an audio or videotape.

QIC

QIC stands for Quarter-Inch-Cartridge. QIC is a tape device that looks very much like an audiocassette tape. This medium uses a linear (or longitudinal) recording technique in which data is written onto parallel tracks that run along the length of the tape. Because of the numerous standards for QIC, there are incompatibilities between many models. This device ranges in storage capacity from as little as 80MB (QIC-80) to as much as 20GB (TR-5), depending on the standard and model used.

Echo Drive

OnStream's Echo drive is one of the best in terms of price and storage capacity. This product is suitable for both the home and small business user, and works well for storing and playing multimedia files. The Echo comes in two sizes: the SC 30, which costs about $500 for the drive and $45 per disk; and the SC 50, at $700 for the drive and $55 per disk. The SC 30's storage capacity is 15GB (30GB compressed), whereas the SC 50 has a storage capacity of 25GB (50GB compressed).

Making a Simple Batch File to Back Up Critical Data to a Backup Device

Suppose you want to regularly back up several directories on your hard drive to a backup device, such as a Zip drive. Writing a few simple commands and saving the commands to a batch file (a text file with the file extension .bat) can automate this task, so that it runs with one simple command.

First, let's assume that your directories are stored in the C: drive, and that your Zip drive is G:. Let's assume that the directories on your hard drive are:

```
C:\data
C:\mystuff
C:\keep
```

Create a text file in Notepad (or some other text editor), and save it as c:\bin\backup.bat, containing the following three xcopy commands:

```
xcopy /e /y c:\data g:\data

xcopy /e /y c:\mystuff g:\mystuff

xcopy /e /y c:\keep g:\keep
```

Now, whenever you want to back up these directories, put a Zip disk into the Zip drive and simply enter the following command:

```
C:\bin\backup.bat
```

Or, you can create an icon for this file and place it on your desktop, so that you can double-click the desktop icon to run the backup process.

In addition, Windows NT and Windows 2000 enable you to schedule this task to run automatically at any specified time by adding an additional command. For instance, if you plan to leave your machine on and leave a Zip disk in the Zip drive, you can schedule the command to run at 3:00 a.m. every night with the following command:

```
at 3:00
/every:monday,tuesday,wednesday,thursday,friday,saturday,sunday
c:\bin\backup.bat
```

Note that the names of the directories and the name of the batch file do not have to match the names used in this example; but the names you use should be meaningful, and you should remember to use the commands as written (with the exception of the filenames). However, the file extension for a batch file must be .bat, and the batch file must be placed in the bin directory of your hard drive.

Summary

In this chapter you learned what a backup is, and why it is necessary to have a backup strategy in order to ensure that the data stored on your computer is safe. This chapter discusses the Microsoft Backup tool and how to use it, as well as several backup devices that can be used to store your backups.

24

BACKUP STRATEGIES

Appendices

Glossary

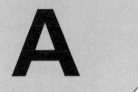

APPENDIX

A

Algorithm   A set of instructions or steps to solve a problem.

Backbone   A main communication channel from which smaller communication lines can be pulled. The Internet is made up of several main backbones from which all other Internet lines connect to the Internet.

Backup   Making a second copy of a file (or all files) on your machine, and storing it on disk or tape in case something happens to your machine or the file.

Boot-Sector   An area of a hard drive where files and programs (executables) are stored to be read and executed by the computer when it is turned on.

Broadband   High-speed Internet services; in the home context, these are normally 128Kbps or faster and include ISDN, Cable, and DSL connections.

Bug   An unintentional flaw in the code that makes up a piece of software; bugs can cause programs to crash, can create security holes, or can simply be annoying by making software behave in unexpected ways.

Cipher text   A message after it has been encrypted.

Cookie   A small text file created and stored on your machine when you first visit a Web site. Intended to store personal preferences and customize a Web site for each user.

Cracker   An individual who breaks into secure systems.

Cryptography   the science of altering messages to make their content secret.

Cryptanalysis   The science of *cracking* or breaking encoded text and determining the correct content of a message that is intended for someone else.

Daemon   A special program (or server) whose job is to answer requests for a specific type of service.

Demilitarized Zone (DMZ)   One or more machines on a pseudo-internal network that allows limited incoming access from the Internet.

Denial of Service Attack   An attempt to deny Internet Service to a Web site, computer or LAN, usually by flooding the server or network with large numbers of requests for service in a short period of time.

Digital Subscriber Line (DSL)   A class of broadband Internet services that use existing copper telephone lines; many homes can receive ADSL (Asymmetric Digital Subscriber Line) service.

Domain name system (DNS)   A network of servers whose job is to translate a hostname into an IP address.

Dynamic Host Configuration Protocol (DHCP)   A protocol that allows new hosts connecting to a network to receive their network configuration including IP address, gateway, and DNS server information from a DHCP server.

Ethernet   A type of network infrastructure that is independent of the physical cabling it runs on but is commonly used in offices and homes.

Encryption   The process of encoding a message in order to make its contents unknown.

File Transfer Protocol (FTP)   A protocol for downloading and uploading files across a network such as the Internet.

Firewall   Software or hardware that protects your private computer (or network) from attacks and intruders by acting as a gateway to your private computer or network, controlling access to it as well as what can travel in and out of it.

Gateway   A host connected to at least two networks that plays the role of gatekeeper and traffic director for packets traveling between the two networks.

Hacker   An individual who illegally gains knowledge of a computer system.

Hub   A device for connecting the reach of a network by splitting a single network line into multiple lines.

Hypertext Markup Language (HTML)   A tag-based language used to specify the structure and layout of Web pages so that a Web browser can render them.

Hypertext Transfer Protocol (HTTP)   The protocol used by Web browsers to request pages from a Web server.

Internet   A system of interconnected networks from around the world, creating a global computer community, also known as the Information superhighway.

Internet service provider (ISP)   A company providing access to the Internet by dial-up or broadband connections.

IP address   the Internet address of a machine. The IP address allows communication between hosts on the Internet.

Internet Protocol Security (IPSec)   A developing standard for virtual private networks. IPsec provides two security services: an Authentication Header (AH) that provides authentication of data, and Encapsulating Security Payload (ESP) that provides both authentication and encryption of data.

Key   Used to create encrypted messages, and to decrypt coded messages. Only the correct key will decode an encrypted message.

A

LAN   A local area network; refers to a closed network of computers communicating over a geographically small area such as a room, a floor of a building, a building, or a self-contained campus.

Log   A record of activity recorded by an application or hardware device for later analysis.

Malicious program   A program designed to attach itself to other programs and replicate with the purpose of doing something bad.

Network   Any situation in which more than one computer is connected in order to communicate. The Internet is a large-scale network.

Network Address Translation (NAT)   A technique for hiding the network addresses of the internal network from the outside world. NAT effectively decreases the opportunities for an intruder to attempt to attack or vandalize a network because he lacks critical knowledge about the network he normally would use in an attack.

Netmask   The Network Mask looks like an IP address, but it is used to tell which part of the IP address identifies the network and which part identifies specific machines on the network.

Packet   The packages of information transmitted on a TCP/IP network such as the Internet.

Patch   An update to the code of an application which can be applied in place without reinstalling a new version of the software. Most fixes for security bugs in operating system software are distributed as patches.

Point-to-Point Tunneling Protocol (PPTP)   A standard proposed by Microsoft and other companies for virtual private networks. This protocol does not specify an encryption scheme for the transportation of data, but leaves this to the implementation.

Port Scan   A technique for looking for vulnerable Internet services on a computer; typically used by attackers looking for systems to attack, port scans can be used to check the integrity of a network's security.

Ports   Numeric identifiers that allow each Internet service to receive connections without conflicting with other Internet services on the same machine.

Pretty Good Privacy (PGP)   A public-key encryption technology that allows the secure exchange of files and messages.

Process   An instance of a software program running on a computer. Computers can have many processes running at the same time.

Protocol   A language used to communicate between machines for a particular purpose, including protocols that allow networking to occur and protocols that allow services to be performed on the network.

Proxy Server   An intermediary between a private network and the Internet.

Router   A host connected to at least two networks that plays the role of gatekeeper and traffic director for packets traveling between the two networks.

Spam   Unsolicited e-mail messages, usually sent as part of bulk e-mail promotion campaigns.

Switch   A device for connecting multiple networks connections efficiently; unlike a router, it does not contain intelligence for the routing of packets but simply sends packets down the appropriate connection as they arrive.

Transmission Control Protocol/Internet Protocol (TCP/IP)   The suite of protocols used by all systems connected to the Internet in order to communicate with other systems on the Internet.

Telecommuting   The concept of working away from the office while connected to corporate computer systems using telecommunications technology such as the Internet.

Trojan horse   Any malicious program that pretends to be one thing but actually does something else, like deleting files on your machine or creating a back door entry point into your computer.

Virtual Private Network (VPN)   A private connection between two networks that encrypts the data sent between the networks and then uses the Internet to transport it, creating a virtual private network similar to a dedicated physical connection.

Virus   A malicious program designed to attach itself to other programs (on your computer) and replicate. They usually spread from computer to computer in a network and over the Internet.

WAN   A wide area network refers to two or more geographically separated LANs that are connected together by some type of long distance connections.

Web browser   A program used to view Web pages or navigate the Internet. Two well-known Web browsers are Netscape Navigator and Microsoft Internet Explorer.

Worm   A specific type of virus that replicates through services running on networks (such as the e-mail). Worms usually cause damage by replicating and plugging up a computer or network's resources.

A

Resources

IN THIS APPENDIX

This appendix provides a quick guide to resources on the Internet you can use in researching, planning, and maintaining your online security. The information includes resources about firewalls, antivirus software, network technology, and operating systems.

Firewall Software and Hardware

The following lists the Web sites for popular firewall software and hardware firewalls (broadband gateways).

BlackICE Defender: `http://www.networkice.com/downloads/index.html`

McAfee Firewall: `http://download.mcafee.com/updates/fire_update.asp`

McAfee Internet Guard Dog: `http://download.mcafee.com/updates/igd_update.asp`

Norton Personal Firewall: `http://www.symantec.com/techsupp/`

Zone Alarm: `http://www.zonelabs.com/`

Tiny Personal Firewall: `http://www.tinysoftware.com/pwall.php`

Sygate Personal Firewall: `http://www.sybergen.com/products/shield_ov.htm`

NetBarrier (Macintosh) : `http://www.intego.com/services/updates.asp`

IPNetSentry: `http://www.sustworks.com/site/prod_ipns_overview.html`

D-Link Cable/DSL Internet Gateways: `http://support.dlink.com/`

EtherFast Cable/DSL Routers: `http://www.linksys.com/download/firmware.asp`

NetGear Internet Gateway Routers: `http://www.netgear.com/support_main.asp`

Asante FriendlyNET Cable/DSL Routers: `http://www.asante.com/product/routers/fncable-dsl-firmware.htm`

Nexland Internet Sharing Boxes: `http://www.nexland.com/download.htm`

SMC Barricade Broadband Routers: `http://www.smc.com/smc/pages_html/products.html`

3Com Home Ethernet Gateways: `http://www.3com.com/products/en_US/detail.jsp?tab=support&sku=3C510&pathtype=purchase`

SonicWall Internet Security Appliances: `http://63.97.246.80/download/index.asp`

WatchGuards SOHO Firewalls: `https://www.watchguard.com/support/patches.asp`

Antivirus Software

There are several main antivirus software packages you can use to keep your system safe from most viruses; these packages are listed in this section.

Norton AntiVirus: `http://www.symantec.com/avcenter/index.html`

McAfee VirusScan: `http://www.avertlabs.com/`

F-Secure Anti-Virus: `http://www.f-secure.com/virus-info/`

PC-cillin: `http://www.trend.com/pc-cillin/vinfo/`

Dr. Solomon's Anti-Virus: `http://download.mcafee.com/updates/4xa.asp?as=true&ref=5`

Antivirus Information

Maintaining virus protection requires keeping informed about the latest virus news. The following sites are good resources for keeping up-to-date on the latest virus threats:

Virus.com: `http://www.virus.com/`

Virus Bulletin: `http://www.virusbtn.com/`

McAfee AntiVirus: `http://www.mcafee.com/anti-virus/default.asp`

Symantec Security Updates: `http://www.symantec.com/avcenter/`

Vmyths.com: `http://www.vmyths.com/`

F-Secure Computer Virus Info Center: `http://www.datafellows.com/v-descs/`

Security Alerts and Information

In order to maintain your online security, you need to be aware of the latest threats, security holes, and software bugs. The following sites offer news and updates about security threats you might face:

Zone Labs Security Resource Center: `http://www.zonelabs.com/CS/security.html`

CERT Coordination Center: `http://www.cert.org/`

Computer Incident Advisory Center: `http://www.ciac.org/ciac/`

Security Portal: `http://www.securityportal.com/`

Computer Security Resource Center: `http://csrc.ncsl.nist.gov/`

ZDNet Bugs, Viruses, and Security Alerts: `http://www.zdnet.com/zdhelp/filters/`
`subfilter/0,7212,6001787,00.html`

Network Technology

In order to maintain good network security, you should be familiar with the technologies you are using to build your network and maintain your privacy and security. The following sites provide information about major home networking technologies, TCP/IP, secure credit card payment technology, and Internet privacy:

Home Phone Networking Alliance: `http://www.homepna.org`

HomeRF: `http://www.homerf.org`

Well-known TCP Ports: `http://www.stengel.net/tcpports.htm`

HTTP Header Specifications: `http://www.cis.ohio-state.edu/htbin/rfc/rfc2109.html`

"The IP Address: Your Internet Identity" by Russ Smith: `http://consumer.net/IPpaper.asp`

American Express Private Payments: `http://www26.americanexpress.com/`
`privatepayments/info_page.jsp`

Discover Card One-Time Transactions:
`https://discoverdeskshop.card2.novusnet.com/discover/service/app_Home.htm`

Mixmaster & Relay Attacks: `http://www.obscura.com/~loki/remailer/`
`remailer-essay.html`

Major Operating Systems

the core of good security is keeping your operating system up-to-date and being sure that you have the latest security fixes and patches. The following is a list of major operating systems and their vendor's Web sites:

MacOS 8, 9, and X: `http://www.apple.com/`

Windows 98, Me, NT, 2000, and XP: `http://www.microsoft.com/`

RedHat Linux 6.2, 7.0, and 7.1: `http://www.redhat.com/`

Caldera eDesktop 2.4: `http://www.caldera.com/`

SuSE Linux 7.1: `http://www.suse.com/`

Common TCP Services and Ports

As you will have noted throughout the book, the key to good firewall security is understanding which ports should be controlled and which you can, or need, to allow traffic to pass through. Table C.1 provides a list of common TCP ports and their associated services. You can use this as a guide for when your personal firewall software alerts you to traffic that you might want to block or when you need to decide how to configure your hardware firewall unit.

TABLE C.1   Selected TCP Ports and Services

Port	Service	Description
20, 21	FTP	The File Transfer Protocol uses two primary ports: Connections are initiated on port 21, but return connections are made on port 20.
23	Telnet	Telnet allows remote interactive login to a command prompt on a remote machine. Typically Windows systems do not offer Telnet services (although Windows 2000 does), but you might need to use Telnet to access remote machines.
25	SMTP	The Simple Mail Transfer Protocol is used to route and deliver mail messages on the Internet. Your system might use SMTP to send outgoing messages or, in some cases, will actually receive messages directly using SMTP.
80	HTTP	The Hypertext Transfer Protocol is used to request Web pages from Web servers.
110	POP3	The Post Office Protocol is used to download mail messages from a POP3 mailbox server.
113	IDENTD	The Internet's identification and authentication service runs on port 113. When you connect to a remote computer to request a service from it (such as POP3 mail), that computer might try to connect to your port 113 asking your system to identify itself and provide information about you.
137, 138, 139	NetBIOS	NetBIOS is used for Windows printer and file sharing. Unless you need to use Windows printer and file sharing on the Internet, these ports are typically blocked in both directions on a strong firewall.
143	IMAP	The Internet Message Access Protocol is used to access mail messages stored on an IMAP server.
443	HTTPS	Secure Web connections are typically made on port 443 using the Secure Socket Layer encrypted form of the Hypertext Transfer Protocol.

Of course, this is just a selected list of ports. Table C.2 shows a more comprehensive list of ports with the services they are associated with. Most of the services won't be running on your home PC, but if you ever see references to them in your logs, you can use this list to find out which service is involved.

TABLE C.2   Ports and Their Services

Port	Service
7	Echo
22	Secure Shell
37	Time
43	Whois
53	DNS
69	TFTP
70	Gopher
79	Finger
109	POP2
115	Secure FTP
119	News
123	Network Time Protocol
161	SNMP
220	IMAP3
389	LDAP
540	UUCP
1812	Radius Authentication
3306	MySQL
993	Secure IMAP
995	Secure POP3
5432	PostgreSQL
6667	IRC

C

COMMON TCP
SERVICES AND
PORTS

INDEX

SYMBOLS

3Com Home Ethernet Gateways Web site, 334
3Com Web site, 37
10 Base-T Ethernet, 36
802.11b protocol. *See also* wireless Ethernet
802.11b standard. *See also* wireless Ethernet

A

accessing
Internet services, IP addresses, 191-192
logs, Norton AntiVirus, 281-282
accounts, users, 299
activating logs
Etherfast, 278-279
ZoneAlarm, 276
Activity Log dialog box, 282
adapters
phoneline networking, 50
wireless networking, 52
Add button, 65
addresses
broadcast, 27
assigning addresses, 27
e-mail, 201
anti-spam e-mail services, 201-202
functions, 231
IP, 10, 24
bytes, 24
dynamic, 158
functions, 230-231
Internet services, 191-192
multiple computers, 24
static, 158

W-Y